THE WONDERFUL
WORLD OF BULBS

THE WONDERFUL WORLD OF

BULBS

by BEBE MILES

with photographs
(except as noted)
by OSCAR C. FREAS

and drawings by
CHARLOTTE PRUDHON MEYERS

D. VAN NOSTRAND COMPANY, INC.
Princeton, New Jersey
Toronto   New York   London

D. VAN NOSTRAND COMPANY, INC.
120 Alexander St., Princeton, New Jersey (*Principal Office*)
257 Fourth Avenue, New York 10, New York

D. VAN NOSTRAND COMPANY, LTD.
358 Kensington High Street, London, W.14, England

D. VAN NOSTRAND COMPANY (Canada) LTD.
25 Hollinger Road, Toronto 16, Canada

Printed in the United States of America

FOR MY HUSBAND
a patient and valiant man

MY THANKS TO THESE

There may be gardeners who jealously guard their secrets and do not help each other, but I have never met one. Gratefully I acknowledge the generous assistance given me by such busy people as Jan de Graaff, Romaine B. Ware, George B. Park, Dr. Cynthia Westcott, Dr. C. J. Gould and Leonie Bell.

Some of the material in this book first appeared in *Flower and Garden* magazine and *Flower Grower, the Home Garden Magazine,* and is used here with the kind permission of the editors. Parts of several additional chapters were originally prepared for *Flower Grower.*

Helen Van Pelt Wilson has been an author's dream as an editor, and the staff of Radnor Memorial Library deserves a vote of thanks, as does Helen Hester for emergency typing. Prompt replies to innumerable questions came from such varied sources as Ronald Vance for the Associated Bulb Growers of Holland, Adnan Ozaktas at the Turkish Information Office, various members of the U.S. Department of Agriculture and of state agencies as well as from the secretaries of plant societies. My thanks too to Gustave Springer of the Associated Bulb Growers who read the manuscript for factual error.

Lastly, I must salute the patience of Oscar Freas and Charlotte Meyers whose talent with camera and pen have done so much for this book. My heartfelt thanks to my husband and daughters who put up with so much while Mother wrote a book!

FOREWORD:
PLANT NAMES AND MY VIEW

All gardeners are optimists at heart whether they are planting marigold seeds for quick summer bloom or beginning the
years of work required to produce a new hybrid daffodil. The
gardener who uses bulbs has every right to be hopeful: nothing
you plant gives surer beauty for less effort.

I know this book emphasizes any bulb's good points more
than it points out any deficiencies. But then, I am a gardener
too. When I plan a planting, my mind dwells on the possibilities
of success. Difficulties are challenges, not dead ends. Failure
will be overcome in next year's attempt, which is bound to be
better! Such fine bulbs are available nowadays from reputable
dealers that even small children can garden triumphantly with
them. The few important rules for growing are simply mastered.

Since my primary purpose is to acquaint you with bulbs to
grow in the garden, the short chapters on indoor growing are
only meant to whet your curiosity if you are enthusiastic about
window gardening. If I have favored hardy plants over those
that must be lifted where winter temperatures fall below freezing, it is because my own gardening has always had to be
sandwiched in between the details of daily living. It is just this
constant necessity to conserve time that makes bulbs such perfect garden subjects.

This book does not try to be definitive. It is rather an attempt
to select from a vast horticultural section those bulbous plants
that are easiest to grow and buy. Writing for the average gardener, I have kept in mind that most of you do not have hired
help and must reckon with a limited budget and time which
must be alloted to family, work, and friends as well as to gar-

dening. Where possible, we will take the simplest way of doing.

Bulb catalogs are your best current guide to this exciting new world. In them you will discover exactly what is available for you to plant during any one season. My book can be compared to a large-scale map of a country: it gives you an overall view of a tremendous area and charts a possible itinerary. To know and love even a small part of the whole means studying an up-to-date detail map and then making the journey yourself. A good catalog keeps abreast of the newest introductions while retaining the best of the older varieties. It settles how much you can purchase at any one time because it is the only possible key to what your budget can cover. Local garden centers also offer bulbs for sale and may have lists for you to study.

You will not find here long lists of named hybrid daffodils, tulips, lilies or other popular bulbs because fashions change in bulbs as in other things. What I have tried to do is to describe the *types* of flowers which a genus contains. A current catalog will then detail what is in stock under the various categories.

About Names

To make it easier for everyone to know just which plant is what, botanists long ago adopted what they call binomial nomenclature. (Zoologists use it too.) Every identified plant is given two names, one signifying its genus and one its species. Both are in Latin, to avoid complications of language barriers around the world. Often the species half of the name gives details of color (*ruber:* red); height (*nanus:* dwarf); growing habit (*palustris:* marsh-loving); leaf (*pubens:* downy) or geography (*Californicus:* of California).

Thus we have *Tulipa kaufmanniana*. When you see *tulipa* you know a plant belongs to a certain genus. The *kaufmanniana* immediately tells you I refer to one particular kind of tulip that is different in specific details from all other tulips. You can remember this if you keep in mind that you go from the general (genus: *Tulipa*) to the specific (species: *kaufmanniana*).

Related genera are grouped into families. Such plants as tulips, colchicums, hyacinths and lilies, to mention only a few, go under the lilies (*Liliaceae*). Many other bulbs belong to the families of amaryllis (*Amaryllidaceae*) or iris (*Iridaceae*). The family classifications are interesting but of little importance to the ordinary gardener except as clues to general habits and treatment.

At the opposite end we have what are called variations, differing plants within a particular species. These are often listed thus: *Tulipa kaufmanniana César Franck* or *Tulipa kaufmanniana var. César Franck*. These tulips are intimately related to the species, *kaufmanniana*, but they vary a little from the tulip which was originally identified as the typical *kaufmanniana*, often in their color. Hybrids, individually named or as varying strains, are the result of breeding between different species or other hybrids and are always capitalized.

How to Find What You Want

What does all this mean to you, a plain-dirt gardener? It ought to make your task of ordering exactly what you want much easier. You will note throughout this book I have listed in parentheses the Latin names of a bulb that many of us have grown up knowing under a familiar name like snowdrop (*Galanthus*) or snowflake (*Leucojum*). A particular bulb gets the full treatment: *Galanthus nivalis*. My reason for doing this is precisely that which drove the scientifically-unnerved botanists to insist that some universal system of names was necessary.

Here's an example of the problem. In one part of the world a pretty spring lily may be known as a dogtooth violet, but in another it is trout lily or adders-tongue. This ambiguity leads to confusion. Only if you and I and the bulb dealer know we are talking about *Erythronium,* can we begin mutually to understand our quest. Then we must decide whether you want a yellow trout lily such as *E. americanum* or a white (*E. albidum*) or a lavender (*E. hendersoni*).

Bulb catalogs grow more scientific each year so that almost all the big ones now list the Latin name at least in parentheses.

The exceptions to this are in the long lists of hybrids. Here the catalogs present the commercial name given a bulb by its originator. Thus, the new daffodil, Mother Catherine Grullemans, has no scientific name. For the gardener the specific hybrid name is quite enough if the catalog lists them by types such as parrot tulips, double early tulips, lily-flowering tulips, etc. There has been a deplorable practice lately, especially among the tulips, to give the same hybrid two different common names. The new Darwin hybrid tulip Gudoshnik is also called Golden Freckles, for instance. It is time bulb retailers stopped this nonsense. The breeders register the names they give new introductions so there is no good reason for confusion.

To aid us even more, certain very varied genera like daffodils and dahlias have been formally classified by agreement between the fanciers and growers. These systems seem complicated at first glance, but study rewards you with a much more precise view of the variation in shapes and sizes available. There can be far more to daffodils than big golden trumpets, as you are soon to see. The more advanced catalogs help you select what you want by using the classifications as guides.

There is one small worm in the botanical paradise of binomial nomenclature: botanists are only human beings. Sometimes they change their minds as to where a flower belongs in their scheme of things. I can easily forgive them that in the interest of scientific harmony, but I find myself increasingly impatient with another change. Traditionally, the first man to identify a plant gets to name it. Suppose a hundred years after everyone has been used to calling a plant by one name, the botanists discover some other plant hunter actually deserves the honor by virtue of prior identification. The name he preferred is then the rightful nomen.

We can only sigh philosophically and tuck into our heads the knowledge that tritoma is now kniphofia (but hardly a favor to any plant, that!) and ipheion is more accepted for tritelia than any of the other labels it has carried. Hardly anyone thinks to erect statues to botanists and plant explorers so I suppose we should not carp overly if they prove jealous of their prerogatives. At least they do not shoot each other, and the binomial system is actually of incomparable value in finding our way through the maze of plants.

Bulb dealers, no less than we, find it hard to know which name to use when there has been botanical disagreement or change. Unlike the botanist who must be absolutely right, the dealer needs to help his clientele find what they want. Some catalogs will use one scientific name, others favor a second; a few list both as an aid, and most also give the common English name if there is one. Where such confusion still exists, I have tried to include both Latin tags for a genus as well as the most common vernacular name.

I must confess that to my secret self many bulbous favorites live under the untechnical but sometimes more descriptive nickname given them by some imaginative gardener. While the botanists quibble over tritoma or kniphofia, I remember the plant affectionately as red-hot-poker! To get exactly the plant you want, however, you must know its botanical name; I have tried to make this as easy as possible for you.

Magic or Miracle?

Every gardener soon realizes he will never know everything about this vast and complex world of growing things; he will also discover that he never stops learning. Truly, you grow with your garden. I envy the reader who finds new friends in these pages. You have such a marvelous treat in store.

The non-gardener appreciates the beauty of the eventual flowers which bulbs provide, but the compensations to the person who plants them range far beyond the blooms themselves. Gardening smacks of more than necromancy to me. I shall never be able to consider the miracle of the acorn's becoming a tree merely in cold scientific objectivity. The seed, the nut and the bulb are to me reassuring signposts of the immortality of life. Not mine personally, but rather that secret ingredient that differentiates the living seed from the inert pebble.

A dormant spring bulb typifies the whole wonderful process. I get satisfaction out of all proportion to the task from tucking several hundred into the warm, autumn earth. Partly this is due to my faith in their productivity. I am not really burying bulbs so much as I am planting flowers. It is an attitude I hope you will share.

BEBE MILES

Wayne, Pennsylvania
March, 1962

Contents

My Thanks to These   vii
Foreword: Plant Names and My View   ix
1. THE WONDER OF BULBS   1
2. GROUND RULES   14
3. LITTLE BULBS FOR A BIG SPRING   42
4. SECOND WAVE OF LITTLE BULBS   57
5. TULIPS HAVE MANY FORMS   77
6. SPECIES TULIPS ARE DIFFERENT   94
7. A HOST OF CAREFREE DAFFODILS   103
8. HYACINTHS: OUTDOORS AND IN   129
9. A REVOLUTION IN LILIES   136
10. SUCCESS WITH LILIES   154
11. HARDY BULBS FOR SUMMER BLOOM   168
12. THE TENDER SUMMER BULBS   179
13. GLADIOLUS CAN BE GRACEFUL   200
14. DAHLIAS FOR LAVISH DISPLAY   207
15. BULBS FOR AUTUMN COLOR   219
16. BULBS MAKE FINE HOUSE PLANTS   228
17. FORCING BULBS FOR AN EARLY SPRING   243
18. HOW TO GROW BULBS FROM SEED   260
19. OTHER METHODS OF BULB PROPAGATION   267
20. BULBS FOR ARRANGEMENTS AND EXHIBITS   273
21. COLORFUL COMPANIONS FOR BULBS   285
22. TO KEEP BULBS HEALTHY   299
23. THE COMMERCIAL STORY   314
    BULBS FOR SPECIAL USES   322
    PLANTING CHART FOR TENDER BULBS OUTDOORS   326
    PLANTING CHART FOR HARDY BULBS   329
    PLANT SOCIETIES   335
    SUPPLIERS OF BULBS   336
    EXTRA READING   339
    INDEX   341

List of Illustrations

IN COLOR

COLOR PLATE   BETWEEN PAGES

I   Crocus Cloth of Gold and C. Cloth of Silver   46–47
II   Narcissus Geranium and red primroses   46–47
III   Winter aconites (Malak of Ottawa)   46–47
IV   *Tulipa kaufmanniana* and *T. biflora alta*   46–47
V   Tulipa tarda (dasystemon)   46–47
VI   Bulbs naturalized on a small lot (Genereux)   46–47
VII   Grape hyacinths, primroses and candytuft   46–47
VIII   Tulip Morocco Beauty and candytuft   46–47
IX   Lily tulips and The Skipper (fringed tulip)   78–79
X   Double tulips (Malak of Ottawa)   78–79
XI   Mid-Century hybrid lilies (Herman v. Wall)   78–79
XII   Canna Eureka (Doris E. Price)   78–79
XIII   Dahlias brighten the summer garden
       (Genereux)   78–79
XIV   Colchicum Waterlily and annual alyssum   78–79
XV   White and lavender single colchicums   78–79
XVI   White autumn crocus   78–79
XVII   Golden Sternbergia lutea   78–79
XVIII Blue autumn crocus   78–79
XIX   Purple autumn crocus   78–79

IN BLACK AND WHITE

ILLUSTRATION
1. Daffodils in the Keukenhof (Malak of Ottawa)   3

2. Spring bulbs around a rocky outcrop
   (Malak of Ottawa)   17
3. Bulbs complement each other (Roche)   35
4. Red and white trilliums (Roche)   66
5. Camassia   67
6. An allium for partial shade   69
7. Dutch iris (Roche)   72
8. Ranunculus (Courtesy Brown Bulb Ranch)   75
9. Bouquet tulips (Courtesy George W. Park Seed Co.)   84
10. Early tulips in the Keukenhof (Malak of Ottawa)   90
11. Narcissus and plumy bleedingheart   108
12. Orchid daffodils (Courtesy George W. Park Seed Co.)   127
13. Hybrid lily with ferns (Herman v. Wall)   145
14. *Lycoris squamigera* (Roche)   171
15. Eremurus (Genereux)   174
16. Acidanthera (Genereux)   184
17. Tuberous begonias (Courtesy Brown Bulb Ranch)   187
18. Peruvian daffodils (Genereux)   192
19. Tigridia (Roche)   197
20. *Ornithogalum thrysoides* and its hardy relative   234
21. Paper-whites in an arrangement (Roche)   246
22. Tritelia with candytuft and *Dianthus*   287
23. Wall garden with tulips (Roche)   292
24. Lilies and phlox (Genereux)   294

IN LINE

FIGURE

1. Different kinds of bulbs and how they grow   6–7
2. Bulbs in the sunny garden   11
3. Bulbs in the shady garden   20
4. Bulbs for a sunny corner   25

5. How to plant a bulb 29
6. A doorstep garden 43
7. A tulip is many things 79
8. The parts of a daffodil 113
9. What is a daffodil? 117
10. Milk carton flats for early planting 181
11. Dahlias come in many shapes and sizes 209
12. An autumn bulb garden 220
13. Planting bulbs in pots 230

CHAPTER 1

The Wonder of Bulbs

Bathed in the dew of heaven each morn
Fresh is the fair Narcissus born,
Of these great powers the crown of old:
The Crocus glitters robed in gold.[1]

More than 2,000 years have passed since those lines were written by a great Greek dramatist, but gardeners still echo his views. I have just been investigating in the snow where the green shoots of early daffodils and crocus await a few more days of sunshine before pushing their hidden buds up to the daylight. In a week, perhaps two, the first brave flower will open, and I shall know that winter is truly leaving. No wonder these bulbs have been beloved so long. Small wonder that each fall American gardeners tuck millions of them into a protecting blanket of soil with sure knowledge they will awaken to welcome spring with a magnificence transcending any man-made symbol.

What miracles are concealed beneath the dry, brown wrappings of all the plants we call bulbs! What glories wait only for planting and the right season. From one end of the growing year to the other they bring beauty to formal borders or light up little nooks, nod welcome beside walks and steps or stand elegantly in front of shrubs and evergreens.

[1] Sophocles, "The Beauties of Colonos," trans. Robert Potter, *The Greek Poets*, ed. Nathan H. Dole (New York: Crowell, 1904), p. 224.

1

Tall or short, dazzling or quietly lovely, they come from all over the world. Dahlias and tigridias from neighboring Mexico or tulips from Persia and Turkestan join lilies from remote Asian mountains. The daffodils and crocus from the Mediterranean grow in harmony here with camassias and trout lilies of the American woods. In my garden just north of Philadelphia, I treasure them all—from the first bright gold of the winter aconites in February to the last rosy, frost-bitten cyclamen in December.

Now More than Ever

In these times of uneasy peace a gardener wishes all men were raising crocus instead of making 100-megaton bombs. I am planting more new bulbs in any case. If mankind goes mad, the survivors will need the assurance of eternal spring that those bulbs will bring. The world today needs the sanity of optimistic gardeners like Don Rose, who wrote recently in a Philadelphia paper:

> It was announced last week that ten million tulip, daffodil and hyacinth bulbs have been planted in a park known as the Keukenhof, in Amsterdam (Holland), which are due to bloom next spring. Simultaneously it was reported that 50 courageous families in Long Island, N.Y., are leaving town to live in Chico, Cal., a community considered safe from the deadly effects of atomic fallout, but not particularly favorable to the growing of tulips and daffodils. . . .
> "It might be better in the long run to stay home and plant a tulip in faith, hope and charity. . . . Much of our day's work and planning is based on the more cheerful assumption that the world will survive the atomic crisis as it has lived through many others. . . . I plan to plant a few daffodils against the new garden wall this weekend."[2]

Why Bulbs for Your Garden?

If you are new to the magic world of growing things, by all means start your gardening with bulbs. For ease of planting

[2] *Philadelphia Evening Bulletin,* September 19, 1961. Used by permission.

1. Daffodils naturalized in the Keukenhof gardens, Holland. Grouped at the base of trees, narcissus may be conveniently left until their foliage matures and grass cutting can proceed (Malak of Ottawa).

and care, low initial cost and sure results, these flowers win all horticultural races hands down. The experienced gardener already knows that they are as appropriate in the postage-stamp courtyard as in the vistas of an estate. Bulbs can star as the central planting of a garden, but they are also an interesting foil for other plants. There are bulbs for every climate, for sun and shade, for dry spots and even a few for moist areas. This book will introduce you to all these; it will help you integrate any that are strangers into existing beds. Some bulbs are easy to grow, others test your ingenuity and thrill you when you succeed. There is something for everyone in this delightful, varied tribe.

More than anything else, however, this great division of plants is recommended for its beauty—whether you desire the delicate loveliness of nodding springtime scillas and anemones or the striking flamboyancy of summer cannas. The tiny species daffodils or the "little bulbs" may be only at home in an intimate setting, but there are also exclamation points like foxtail lilies (*Eremurus*) or crown imperials for a large garden.

The bulbs of springtime are especially dear. They bloom when the world is eager for color. In spring, too, there is so little weeding to do! These first bulbs flower without the least effort on my part, and they are doubly beloved for this bonus.

There are bulbous plants to continue this colorful display right through the hottest part of the year and on into autumn. The worst heat does not bother the cannas or the caladiums, and the fall crocus laugh at autumn weather. Some bulbs will even blossom on a winter windowsill indoors.

Corms, Tubers and Rhizomes

Botanically speaking, many flowers you will meet in these pages are not bulbs. A crocus springs from a corm, a dahlia from a tuberous root, and the dazzling alstroemerias from a long rhizome; but all are plants with a well-defined fleshy root or bulbous stem growth at the business end in the ground. All have at least a semi-dormant period when they can be safely shipped without soil. A botanist might rightly be horrified at such an inexact classification, but plain dirt gardeners will immediately understand.

Generally speaking, there is more uniformity among bulbous plants than in many other garden subjects. This is due to the fact that most bulbs (don't forget to substitute corms, tubers and rhizomes when we talk in general terms like this) are reproduced asexually by commercial growers. They have only one parent (often called a clone) which was selected for some outstanding characteristic, and its progeny are vegetatively produced by processes like division and offsets. Each plant is thus in a sense a part of the original, and this fact makes it easy to purchase bulbs by separate colors. Clumps of one shade and type are a simple matter to arrange, and you can create lovely garden pictures with little effort.

Carefree and Certain

Once planted, many hardy bulbs need no further attention for years at a stretch. I have early yellow crocus which have multiplied unbelievably and bloomed heavier each year since being planted seven falls ago. A clump of King Alfred daffodils around the birdbath has not been touched for six years, yet it provided extensive emergency replacements for decorating a church social last spring and still had enough flowers left for a golden splash under the dogwoods. I put less than two dozen bulbs there originally. I suppose I should thin them soon!

If you buy quality bulbs from a reputable dealer, you will have certain bloom the following season provided you plant

Different Kinds of BULBS

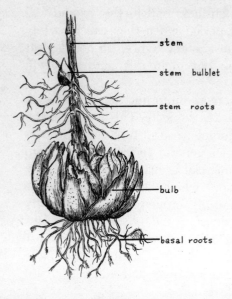

stem

stem bulblet

stem roots

bulb

basal roots

LILY (bulb)

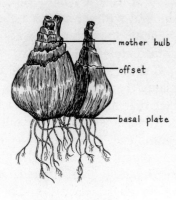

mother bulb

offset

basal plate

DAFFODIL (bulb)

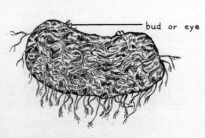

bud or eye

BEGONIA (tuber)

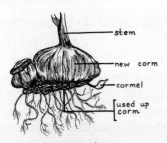

stem

new corm

cormel

used up corm

GLADIOLUS (corm)

and How They Grow 🎔 🎔

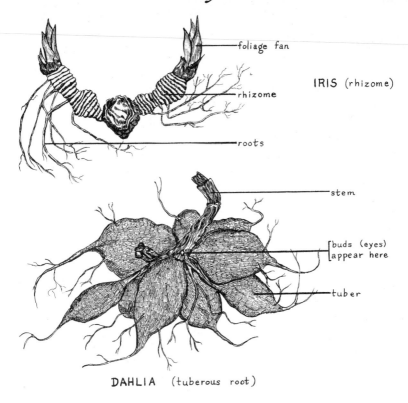

foliage fan

IRIS (rhizome)

rhizome

roots

stem

buds (eyes)
appear here

tuber

DAHLIA (tuberous root)

FIG. 1. The general term, bulbs, includes various types. Lilies and daffodils are true bulbs with different kinds of scales; most propagate by division within the mother bulbs, but some lilies produce bulblets on the stems. Gladiolus and crocus grow from starchy corms; note that the old, shriveled corm has been replaced by new corms of varying sizes and tiny cormels. Dahlias form tuberous roots; when separated, each must have a growing eye, to be found on the stem-end of the tuber. Belamcanda and many iris grow from rhizomes. The begonia tuber bears its growing buds in the hollow top and is propagated by being cut into pieces, each with an eye.

properly, because the mature bulb has stored up all the food necessary for a first flowering. (Sometimes the flower itself is already present in embryo stage when you plant the bulbs.) Nor do hardy types require pampering. The grower has already done the nursing. As the years pass many bulbs multiply, and you increase certain stocks like daffodils with no more effort on your part than to gather in the dividends.

Companions for Bulbs

If there is any drawback to bulbs, it may be that they almost demand companionship. I will say more about this later, but now I only warn you that your order for the first dozen daffodils may be habit-forming. Before you quite know what has happened, your bulbs may lead you to groundcovers, to perennials to space out the flowering season, even to trees and shrubs to round out your plantings.

This ability to merge into the total garden picture is one of the greatest charms and benefits of bulbs. They do wonders in the foreground of shrubbery, blend in beautifully with a woodland scene, liven up any border, and some can even compete with turf if their foliage is always allowed to ripen before the grass is mowed.

Pleasant Planting Times

I look forward to bulb planting times because they never mean a race with wind and weather such as in spring and early fall when I am transplanting and dividing herbaceous perennials. How often has the weather turned unexpectedly hot and dry the day after I have set out little plants? How many hours of soft spraying have I put in during those hectic weeks to get seedling plants to "take" after transplanting?

In contrast, most bulbs can be planted on sunny days. No need risking pneumonia to complete such tasks in a bone-chilling mist. Once they are in the ground, your main responsibility is to see they are left undisturbed until bloom time. Happily, the pests and diseases of bulb plants are negligible in comparison with the unholy legion which may feast upon other sections of the garden.

Where to Start?

Common sense suggests the beginner plant first those bulbs easiest to grow. Heading such a list are the spring-flowering daffodils, hyacinths, tulips and all of the undemanding inhabitants of Chapter 3. Logically, these are the bulbs which are featured most prominently in any bulb catalog, and usually their prices are also the most reasonable. After that, you will be anxious to try the hardy bulbs of summer like *Lycoris squamigera* or the autumn crocus and colchicums.

Once familiar with this type of plant and with the demands and conditions of your own garden, you can investigate rarer kinds. Being more knowledgeable by then, you will be more adroit at figuring out how to reproduce any required situation in your garden.

Most catalogs are explicit about the needs of lesser-known bulbs. To be successful with them, read the fine print and act accordingly. You can experiment too. A plant not reliably hardy north of Washington, D.C., might not survive a winter outside here at Philadelphia; yet I have tried some like alstroemeria, poppy anemones and montbretias just for my own satisfaction, and sometimes I have succeeded. Trials are fun! In the beginning, however, concentrate on the really hardy ones. Limit yourself, too, when ordering tender bulbs that must be lifted every fall and replanted every spring. You want your garden to remain a pleasure.

Attention to heights, colors, flowers or habits of a plant will make for a better garden. Daffodil foliage, for example, grows unsightly before it disappears and so is better maturing behind a plant that will screen it during this period, but the glossy green, strap-like leaves of Peruvian daffodil (ismene) can be used for a cool accent in the summer garden.

Favorable Supplies

This day and age is a particularly good time to be planting bulbs. The years of peace have made possible intensive hybridizing both in this country and abroad. Fine new varieties are being introduced while supplies of old favorites are plentiful and prices reasonable. Trade barriers are lower and quarantine restrictions have been relaxed.

Your garden can have daffodils, tulips and lilies that did not even exist a generation ago, fine hybrids which are healthier and more colorful than anything your parents knew. The demand of thousands of new homeowners with more education and knowledge (plus the leisure to use it) has created a market which has encouraged breeders to propagate extensive stocks of all bulbs, thus lowering prices. And the increasing interest in gardening has stimulated them to carry bulbs which a few years ago could be obtained only by fanciers after much searching. There was never a better time to garden with bulbs.

Certain dealers keep their lists to a minimum; they offer only the most popular bulbs, an unimaginative restriction I think. Thankfully, we find growers who are willing to extend themselves, and as you begin to know your way, you will graduate from the freshman catalogs to the more gratifying reading of upperclassmen. The more complete catalogs are marked with

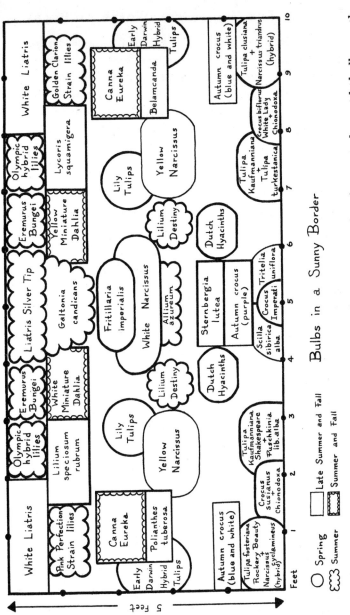

Fig. 2. There are many bulbs for sunny locations. This is a plan for a garden with bulbs as the major planting. Fill in the back sections with tall perennials like hardy asters, phlox, pyrethrum, chrysanthemums and Shasta daisies, or with annuals like larkspur, marigolds, zinnias or bachelor buttons. Amsonia, veronica and flax are good medium-tall perennials. The foreground can include evergreen ground-covers like iberis, arabis, dianthus or thyme to conceal maturing bulb foliage. Alyssum, dwarf marigolds and petunias are fine annuals for the same purpose.

an asterisk under Suppliers listed at the end of this book. Order
a few new ones each year until you discover those that include
what you want. Do not be afraid to write commercial growers
with queries if you cannot locate a particular plant. The
national societies concerned will also help with sources for
specific groups of bulbs.

Older than History

High adventure made these bulbs available for our gardens.
Explorers in the eighteenth century (and still today) braved
steaming jungles and mountain trails to bring them back from
often almost inaccessible habitats—the South American Andes,
the valleys of the Himalayas or the slopes of the Caucasus or
Kurdistan. Usually there were no roads, maps were sketchy
and bandits not unknown. We owe these early botanists a great
debt.

The archaeologists have also contributed to our bulb story.
They cannot tell us much about tulips, but the crocus, lily,
daffodil, anemone and gladiolus apparently have delighted man
for millenniums, particularly in old Mediterranean lands.
Tigridias and dahlias were cultivated by the Mexican Indian
long before Columbus.

The word "crocus" came from ancient Mesopotamia, where
the oldest forms of writing have been found, and the flower
adorns jewelry, vases and frescoes found in pre-historic Crete.
Saffron crocus may have been known in Egypt as early as
2650 B.C. Lilies have a venerable history too. Even before
Homer, descriptions of crocus, anemones and narcissus occur
constantly in Greek literature. No one who dips even slightly
into this early poetry can help feeling kinship with the often-
expressed love for the flowers of spring, many of which are
the bulbs that we also treasure.

Man's love for a garden is a very long tradition, indeed. Sargon of Agade (c. 2380 B.C.) wrote, "I was his gardener," among boasts of conquests on his monument, and there are designs of flowers on fragments of pottery and jewelry found on sites that date before written history.

If at first men's gardens were used solely for food, the archaic peoples would still have seen wild flowers in the fields and on the hills. Who can say when a child was first attracted by a crocus springing magically from the barren earth? Surely, he would have found the flower more interesting than a shoot of barley. Some historians seem prone to deny ancient man any desire for beauty for its own sake. Always a most practical reason must be suggested, a somewhat patronizing attitude for us to take, I think. The few very early records we have are mostly of conquest, of rulers subjecting peoples to the sword, to tortures and deportations, so we cannot say precisely when the crocus or daffodil made its first jump from field to garden.

But the flowers are still with us—a continuing delight as the seasons roll along and evidence that man does aspire. Plant your bulbs hopefully and join the long file of amiable men who have known their wonder and rejoiced.

CHAPTER 2

Ground Rules

Bulbs will endure more neglect than almost anything else you put in your garden, but they will do better if you keep certain needs in mind. The two most important points to remember are that bulbs prefer dryness to moisture most of the time, and that they must have an opportunity to ripen their foliage. There are a few exceptions to the first rule; there are none to the second.

By their very definition, bulbs (and we extend this to mean corms, tubers, and rhizomes) are modified stems which act as storehouses for food during the plant's dormant period. In some cases (tulips for one) you can cut the unplanted bulb in half and find the flower already present in embryo state. You might say bulbs are a kind of instant flower!

LET FOLIAGE RIPEN

The bulb cannot store up this nourishment by itself. It is the leaves which act as the factory, taking carbon dioxide from the air and combining this with water and sunshine to manufacture useful starches and sugars. The chlorophyll in green leaves gives plants this miraculous ability without which no life on earth would be possible. This simple description of one of the greatest of God's wonders is appended here to point up the problem faced by a plant denuded of its foliage immediately after flowering.

Since it is absolutely necessary for the bulb to be restocked with food each season, you must see that the foliage is left to ripen. Only when the leaves begin to brown can they be removed without weakening the bulb.

Cover Plants

True, the foliage in some cases may be unsightly but only for a short while. Right after blooming the gray-green spikes of daffodil and tulip leaves provide a cool contrast for later-flowering plants. The foliage does droop of course eventually, and this is when a little prior planning pays off. When you diagram your garden, place your clumps of daffodils and tulips (two of the biggest such offenders) behind a plant which will begin to grow taller after the bulbs have flowered. The ripening leaves may then be pushed down and nicely hidden until they have fulfilled their purpose.

Some of my tulips, for example, are concealed by the foliage of Shasta daisies which begins to rise just as the tulips wilt. *Amsonia tabernaemontana* is another fine perennial for in front of tulips or even planted among them.

The smaller bulbous plants of spring which belong in the foreground of the garden do not have as blatant foliage, so it is not as important to hide them. Almost any of these plants, however, looks its best when surrounded by or even growing right among one of the groundcover plants. Such procedure not only gives the garden a more finished look, but of course takes care automatically of maturing foliage. Dianthus, perennial candytuft, violas and *Cerastium tomentosum* are some of the plants used for this purpose in many parts of my garden.

Chapter 21 will help you choose other such companions for your bulbs.

Pick the Flower

It is important for the life of the bulb to remove the flowers before they go to seed. This is certainly no hardship at a season when every house cries out for bouquets, but you will want to leave some bloom in the garden for its effect. As soon as the petals fall, make sure you break off the immature seed heads so the bulb will not expend energy forming seed you do not want. Take care not to remove any more leaves than necessary when picking cut flowers.

Summer bloomers are often neglected on this score, perhaps because there is more to do and a myriad of blossoms available for arrangements, but they should not be allowed to form seed either.

Naturalize with Sense

We have all of us held our breath at the beauty of the poet's "host of golden daffodils" making gay beneath trees where they have been naturalized. Such a project is a fine adventure for those who own enough land to be able to leave some of it wild, but it is out of place on the ordinary suburban lot. The foliage of crocus and daffodils, two favorites for naturalizing, does not ripen until late June at least. A suburban lawn with the grass uncut that long is not likely to appeal either to owner or neighbor.

If your heart yearns for the sight of these flowers growing naturally and your house sits on an average-sized plot, you simply have to compromise. Plant the bulbs in clusters close to the trunk of a tree or near an outcropping of rock or perhaps

2. A natural way to plant a rocky outcropping. Daffodils and hyacinths mingle with dwarf junipers. Early multiflora tulips and
puschkinia in right foreground (Malak of Ottawa).

in the corner of the yard. These small sections can be left
unkept until the bulb foliage has browned without making the
whole place look like a jungle. Such a planting is more adapted
to the scale of a minimum lot too.

It may seem as if we have spent a good many words on the
importance of leaving bulb foliage alone, but this is the one
cardinal rule about this branch of gardening which cannot be
broken if you wish to get more than one season from a bulb.
The bloom you cherish the year after you plant is the dividend
given you by wise handling on the part of the bulb grower.
To have such beauty in subsequent years, you yourself must
give your bulbs a chance to replenish their nourishment.

KEEP THEIR FEET DRY

There are a few bulbous plants which thrive with wet feet, but they are decidedly in the minority. Unless this point is stressed about a bulb you meet, you can safely bet it will not stand for undue moisture, particularly during its dormant period.

In the wild, many bulbous plants spring to life with the melting snows and wet weather of late winter. During the hot summer, the soil in which they live may bake all it wishes without harming the bulbs, which are quite content to sit out their dormancy in such safe, dry storage. To you, this means that spring-flowering bulbs are apt to do very well in dry sections and slopes of your garden where other plants cannot thrive. A deep watering after they are planted in fall will stimulate them to set roots, and the spring weather will usually provide enough moisture for their flowering and for the ripening of their foliage.

Bulbs in other situations need good drainage above all to survive. The very nature of their fleshy bulb, corm or tuber makes them subject to rot. The simplest method is to plant bulbs where water does not stand, but you can improve drainage in dubious spots. Excavate at least 2 feet down and place drain tiles so they slant away from the spot if you have a large area to treat. In a smaller spot where natural drainage is not too bad, it is often enough merely to fill the bottom of the hole with stones and gravel. If you are going to all this trouble for bulbs, do it right and make a solid foot of this loose material and try to shape the excavation so it leads water away from the spot.

In other situations you can make a raised bed for your bulbs, using bricks, stones or other materials to fashion a wall to hold in the earth. This is lovely near a terrace or where you may view it from a window.

Frankly, it is a lot easier to confine your bulbs to a spot with natural drainage. Almost any slope is ideal, and here the differences in height make for interest in the final garden. Once in a while even an incline may be underlaid with impervious hardpan. To grow bulbs successfully there, you will have to aid them by excavating an extra foot below planting depth and filling at least the first 8 inches of the hole with coarsely crushed rocks. Then add humus to the soil.

OTHER REQUIREMENTS

Bulbs are a lot less fractious about what kind of soil they inhabit than many other garden denizens. This is one of their virtues. A good garden loam is fine of course. A sandy soil will be improved for all gardening by the addition of humus, and this treatment will also benefit a heavy clay soil. If your soil is too sandy, mineral elements which the plants need are leached out by rain before the plants can use them. Heavy clay soils on the other hand drain poorly and often harden imperviously with the slightest touch of heat. It is asking a lot of a flower stem to insist it tunnel its way to the surface through near-adobe.

Add Humus

Since adequate humus solves both problems, let us look for a moment at how you can add some to your soil.

Humus is made of decayed organic material—leaves, roots, stems, even old wood, as well as the bodies and excrement of countless insects and animals. In the forest these components pile up naturally to make the fertile topsoil we all wish for

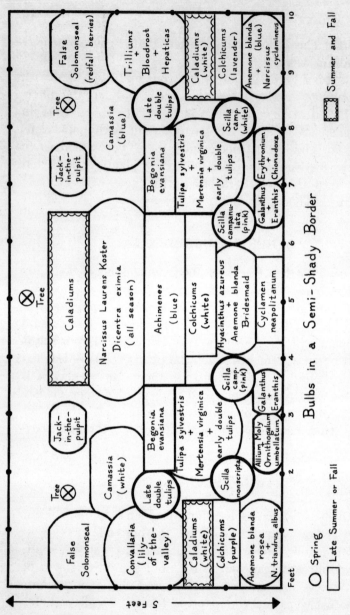

Fig. 3. Under deciduous trees many early spring bulbs will mature their foliage before the leaves cast too much shade. The front of this garden will not be too shaded if it faces somewhat south so perennials like *Phlox divaricata*, pulmonaria and primroses should do well, and violas and forget-me-nots will selfsow freely. Ferns, white eupatorium and snakeroot could fill in toward the shadier back.

our borders. A soil with plenty of humus in it retains water and nutrients better, allows beneficial microbes and bacteria to multiply and breathes more adequately because air can enter through thousands of microscopic openings. Plants grow healthier in such soil since they are better able to garner moisture and food. In addition their roots and stems have an easier time because the physical structure of the soil is ideal.

Topdressing your beds with compost or mulch you have made from old leaves, grass clippings and weeds is one way to help. I actually make a little compost right in the garden itself by piling refuse from weeding and trimming on the soil surface. Time and weather convert this right where it is needed.

Prepare Soil First

Of course if you are adding bulbs to an already existing garden, you need not worry unduly about the soil, except perhaps to check its drainage. Earth that supports other plant material is likely to provide a good home for most bulbs too. You should remember though that even the best garden loam needs constant replenishment of the organic material which made it so ideal in the beginning.

If you are fashioning a new garden, do not make the mistake of digging a few holes here and there with the thought that you will connect them eventually into a continuous garden. I have a neighbor who has done this, and she has found her garden is never free of weeds. The grass roots from her undeveloped sections immediately reconquer spaces so laboriously cleared. Should she ever decide to rehabilitate this section, much of what is already planted will be sacrificed in the digging.

Suppose you visualize a garden but realize you cannot

fashion it in one fell swoop. Then you should clear one section completely of weeds and sod and improve the soil of this small area if it is necessary. When you plant, you can always keep the ultimate garden in mind and plan your work so that all sections will mesh or balance when you are finished. Good records of what you have planted will make that task simpler.

The easiest way to improve the soil where you intend to establish a garden is to order several loads of topsoil. It is also the most expensive! We used this method when we first moved to a development lot where the topsoil was hidden by hardpan compacted by the bulldozers. We justified this shortcut by telling ourselves that it would take several seasons to make enough compost to improve the soil. This envisioned garden occupied a low spot, so before ordering the topsoil, we filled the lowest portions with the inevitable rubble and stones collected from areas where we were sowing grass. This guaranteed good drainage as well as saving topsoil.

In other portions of the property the grade did not need changing, but the surface soil was horrible. We were lucky to hit the topsoil layer in several places a foot or two below the surface. In every case we first turned over the soil with pick and fork. Where necessary we removed perhaps a full foot of clay, saving this excavated subsoil (which the builder had thoughtfully spread atop the good ground) in a pile near where we were making compost. Then we refilled the garden site with our own compost and extraordinary amounts of peatmoss. This was mixed with the remaining earth to a depth of nearly 2 feet. Pockets of sand that turned up along the way were also mixed with the original clay. Each year we tackled a new section of what we intended to be garden and gave it this same treatment. Such beds are easy to weed and to plant, and bulbs and their companions grow happily.

Continue Improvement

Meanwhile, back at the compost heap, the rejected hardpan was slowly mixed in with decomposing green rubbish until in a year it was black and rich and ready to go to work somewhere else. Every garden benefits from such a constant cycle of improvement.

We rake a light covering of fallen leaves onto the gardens every fall. By spring some of this has decomposed of itself. I clear all the beds by hand of course to guard against damaging any emerging shoots, and it is my personal delight on a warm spring day to make myself a little leaf mulch as I go along. Where the leaves are dry, it is but a few moments' work to rub them into a soft meal between my palms, and this residue falls gently to the surface where it eventually is mixed into the top of the soil. A mechanical shredder is an expensive but wonderful aid for doing this on a large scale.

I am admittedly a fanatic about the need to enrich the soil constantly as repayment for what my plants remove from it in their growing. Considering the rape of once-fertile acres by careless farmers and get-rich-quick-contractors across the breadth of our land, my small efforts may seem almost ludicrous, but at least I shall leave the earth in better shape wherever I have worked it. Your efforts in the same cause will be rewarded by lovelier flowers and a clear conscience.

Mulch If You Wish

Beds where bulbs grow are often mulched, which simply means covering the raw soil with a blanket of some organic material. Mulching in spring and summer is a fine way to make gardens sightly, keep roots and bulbs cool in the heat, conserve moisture and also increase the humus content of the earth since some of the mulch will always mix with the soil. Peatmoss, buckwheat hulls, ground corn cobs and grated tobacco stems are some of the best and sightliest commercial mulches. Spread them evenly about an inch thick, and your weeding troubles decline too. Use them for display spots and rake aside the mulch when planting, so it can be reused. I use weeds and clippings to mulch less noticeable areas.

Do not make the mistake of mulching too deeply with peatmoss. A layer which is too thick can actually rob plants of needed moisture because it absorbs water like a sponge. It can soak up all of a rain and allow none of it to penetrate to the roots beneath. For the same reason a peat mulch must be stirred occasionally to keep it from forming a hard crust. Nor do you want your plants to grow in pure mulch. My own garden gets only a thin peat mulch in summer, which is eventually mixed into the soil during cultivation and planting. This is not as neat as it might be if I gave the beds more, but I have known gardeners who used too much peat with deleterious effects. Buying large quantities of commercial mulch is costly too, and we prefer to use well-crumbled compost.

Except for the very light covering of leaves (and we do not have big trees so there are never too many), we do not do any winter mulching on hardy bulb patches. Nor should you. We have some bulbs, however, which are questionably hardy here just above Philadelphia. Not very many, incidentally, because with such a wealth of hardy material from which to choose, we try to limit the number of temperamental bulbs. All of these prima donnas are planted in one easy-to-care-for area. Here I carefully spread a winter mulch of about 4 inches of salt hay or leaves which is topped by a layer of short branches trimmed from old Christmas trees we collect each year. If a bulb cannot live through our winter thus protected, it is crossed off the list

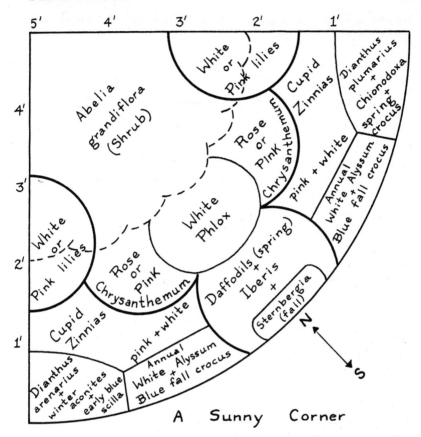

5'   4'   3'   2'   1'

Abelia grandiflora (Shrub)

White or Pink lilies

Rose or Pink Chrysanthemum

Cupid Zinnias

Dianthus plumarius + Chionodoxa spring crocus

pink + white

Annual White Alyssum + Blue fall crocus

White Phlox

Daffodils (spring) + Iberis + Sternbergia (fall)

White or Pink lilies

Rose or Pink Chrysanthemum

Cupid Zinnias

pink + white

Annual White Alyssum Blue fall crocus

Dianthus arenarius + winter aconites + early blue scilla

N

S

A   Sunny   Corner

FIG. 4. Bulbs bring continuous color to this small corner garden from the aconites and puschkinia of spring to the sternbergia and crocus of fall. The abelia bush bears pinkish flowers from summer to frost, and this dictates the colors of the zinnias and chrysanthemums. With a shrub having green leaves or bright, berries in autumn, the mums could be in shades of red, yellow or orange with similarly gay zinnias and marigolds.

or relegated to the tender category which must be lifted each fall.

Fertilize Sparingly

Bulbous plants do not want doses of quick-acting fertilizers. I use bonemeal almost exclusively on the hardy bulb patches, with sometimes a treat of commercially dried manure. Your bulbs will do better with no fertilizing than with too much. Whenever I plant bulbs, I try to work a little bonemeal into the earth below the bulb, and I always mark new bulb patches on the surface with a thin circle of bonemeal too, to remind me of their presence as much as anything.

In subsequent years I try to give old bulb patches some bonemeal in spring after the shoots have emerged. A good rule of thumb is a tablespoon for a big bulb or half a cup for a dozen. Give smaller bulbs less. Work it into the soil rather than just dumping it on the surface. The nitrogen in the bonemeal will be available as the soil warms up, and the phosphorus will be slowly released. Wood ashes are fine for bulbs too; apply in late winter. Never do any cultivating until the shoots have made good top growth, to avoid damaging emerging plants. A good general fertilizer is all right for bulbs in small amounts, but never use one with a high percentage of nitrogen.

Mark Your Plantings

This problem of keeping track of bulb plantings is a small but important point. If you have ever dug a hole in your garden and sliced right through a prize bulb, you will agree with me the only sure safeguard is to put a marker in the middle of every clump you plant. Such a signal also prevents your planting new orange tulips next to established rose hyacinths!

There are fine all-weather markers for this purpose. Mine have always been picked up as trophies by wandering children. In places where I do not have to write down any name to jog my memory, I often sink a clothespin into the earth so that hardly an inch is showing. This goes unnoticed by all except me.

Even better are old popsicle sticks and tongue depressors, which may be bought new from most drug stores. On these, in indelible ink or pencil, I note the genus and the variety name too if it is important to remember. These can be sunk until only a few inches show. Some bulb patches are marked in my garden by a planting of some other flower. Thus I know that two big spreads of *Dianthus arenarius,* for example, are also the home of my autumn crocus. The evergreen foliage protects the bulbs from inadvertent disturbance and acts as a lovely light green background when the naked flowers of the crocus appear in early fall.

Consider Sun and Shade

With spring-flowering bulbs, sun and shade do not make as much difference as with other plants, since most bulbs will have at least a partial chance to ripen foliage before the trees have full growth. Buildings do not vary thus in the shade they cast so remember that the north side of such a structure is shady all year long.

Lilies and other bulbous plants which make their full growth in the heat of summer are another question. Many like a little protection from the strongest mid-day sun, but they will not thrive in darkness. One recent September I recovered a few bulbs of my beautiful *Lilium speciosum album.* When originally planted, they received plenty of sunshine, but over the years the small dogwoods grew up, and the lilies gradually failed.

Several bulbs just petered out, but I could trace two, one with only two small flowers and another nearer the sun which had eight almost normal blooms. When the bulbs were dug, I discovered the heavily-shaded one had actually shrunk to about a third its original size while the one with more sun had retained its full breadth and put forth several fair-sized baby bulbs too.

Underneath the branches of small deciduous trees like dogwoods, silverbells or crabapples you may safely plant almost any of the spring-flowering bulbs if you make sure they do not have to compete too much with the tree roots. Keep the bulbs from areas where roots show on the surface. Trees like maples with shallow roots are not good company for bulbs. Place bulbs on the east, south or west sides of trees. Save the northern quarter for plants which require deep shade. You can help the bulbs a little by trimming away the lowest branches of the trees so there will be some play of sunlight during the day.

Where big trees like maples, beech or elms make a tight umbrella of branches, keep your bulbs on the southern fringes of the trees. They will do better if you grub up big concentrations of roots or choose places free of roots. There are some bulbs and many woodland plants which thrive under shadier conditions, and these will become your standbys if you own a piece of woodland or a copse of trees. A list at the back of this book mentions some of the best of this group. Use a compass or observe the shade at different times of the day to determine just where you can plant which bulbs.

Plant at the Right Depth

One question that faces every bulb planter is how deep to place each genus. In the back of this book I have included as complete a chart of planting depths as I could. To my knowledge it is the first time that *all* the easily-obtained plants have been so treated in one place. Label each bag of bulbs with the proper planting depth before you go outside to work. In all cases my planting depth is measured from ground level to the shoulder of the bulb or rhizome or tuber, not to its shoot.

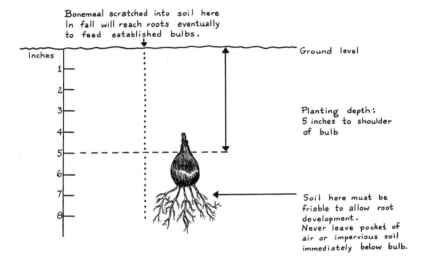

How to Plant a Bulb

FIG. 5. No bulb prospers unless it can develop a good root system so prepare the soil deeper than the bulb is to be planted. Note that planting depth is to the shoulder of the bulb not to the top of the neck, which in many daffodils can be several inches long.

If your soil is very sandy, you might plant a little deeper than my directions. Conversely, in heavy clay lessen the planting depths by an inch. Even better—try to recondition your soil by adding humus, since that will help the bulbs in several different ways.

You will not often have to ponder over which side of a bulb is up. Most have one end slightly more pointed than the other, and the beginning of a shoot may show there too. The opposite end usually has a few root remnants to guide you. An exception is the tubers of various anemones. Often I have turned these over and over, trying to decide how to plant them. Most will have a stem scar or a tiny rootlet left to help you. For all I know the tubers may be able to flip themselves over in soft soil no matter how you plant, but I have planted one on its side to give it a chance when I simply could not figure things out!

Cluster Your Bulbs

No matter how carefully you buy and plant your bulbous garden subjects, the effects will be sketchy unless you group them attractively. Many of us have had to learn this lesson the hard way because the temptation to buy the bargain mixture is always with us in the catalogs. Many times too we want to plant as many different kinds as possible, and so we succumb to the ad which offers an unlabelled potpourri of tulips, daffodils or what have you. (Do not confuse such unknown messes with labelled collections, which are an entirely different and satis-factory proposition.)

Stop for just a moment and you will realize the hazards in bargain mixtures. Planting depths may vary, color and height are bound to be different. Instead of the lovely picture you envisioned, you will have a few blooms now, a few later. A far better procedure is to purchase all your bulbs by the dozen or by the tens, whichever the catalogs offer. Then plant all of one kind and color together. While your budget may decree that this will mean you can only buy a few dozen each year, in time you will have a garden of pure artistry. The effect you gain, dollar for dollar, will be much cheaper in the long run.

In the catalog beside me at this moment a mixture of cottage tulips would cost you $2.50 per twenty-five, but the most expensive cottage tulip on the whole page is only $3.25 for twenty-five, and many individual cottage tulips in this section cost only $2.13 per twenty-five! Since mixtures are apt to be made up of less than top-size bulbs in the first place and never contain many of the more expensive bulbs, no one gets much of a bargain.

Species tulips and daffodils as well as all the so-called little bulbs get overlooked unless planted in clumps. I save time and effort by digging one hole with a small spade. Into the bottom of this I place five or ten bulbs. When they flower, they paint a vivid spot of one color. Even when naturalizing bulbs, it is quicker and more effective to plant several to a hole, and when natural increase makes it imperative they be replanted, it is simpler to dig them up.

With a dozen hybrid hyacinths, tulips or daffodils, it is not quite so easy to dig one hole. In my garden there just is not that much room between other plants. I still try to place my bulbs in groups because they make such a splendid show when clumped. In a big border even the giant bulbs can be beautifully grouped by digging several large holes close together and planting three or four bulbs to a hole.

Last fall I wanted to add a group of the cluster-flowered daffodil, Geranium, to an already-existing garden. The bulbs were mammoth, and all of them were three-nosed (three connected bulbs) so the only possible way to squeeze them in was to dig a hole for each one. All these bulbs were planted in a clump, but the size of the whole thing was about 2 by 3 feet before I finished. Every big bulb in my garden is planted in like fashion—a group of the same color and type in one spot, although there may be other plants sharing the same area, such as my *Dicentra eximia* which grows between bulbs of the creamy white double daffodil, Cheerfulness.

Even in our gardens' first years, when we were more likely to invest our money in necessities for the children than in bulbs, they were admired because almost from the very beginning we bought and planted by name or color. Few who complimented us realized how small had been our investment because of the overall effect given by groups of like flowers.

It is also a fact that repeating the same flower compounds the effectiveness of a garden. With a dozen tulips, all alike, you can create a striking picture, placing two clumps of six fairly close to each other. An equal number of tulips of different colors and heights strung out in a thin line looks like nothing at all.

All of us are intrigued by the new and different, and the world of bulbs right now has an absolutely dazzling array of fringed tulips, bicolored daffodils and other tempting but expensive delights. A dozen bulbs of such recent introductions make a frightening dent in a gardener's pocketbook. In these cases it is often smarter to buy only three bulbs with the hope you can increase your stock yourself. At least that way you can see first whether the variety is really worth adding to your garden.

Plant the three bulbs in one hole for a lovely effect the first spring. If they increase, you will soon have enough to make a big grouping, whereas if each is placed in a different spot, it will be several years before they provide any great garden good. Even an unusual flower, if it stands all alone, may well be overlooked in a garden full of other things.

Perhaps you are wondering how close to plant your bulbs. I have been accused of placing mine too densely, but I like bold splashes of color. Few of my smaller bulbs are put farther apart than 2 inches. Bulbs seem to like their own company, and I would rather have to thin a planting after three or four years (because bloom has fallen off from crowding) than wait three years for a finished look. I will exempt lilies from this statement. Never plant any of them closer than 6 inches, to avoid transplanting as long as possible. The vigorous new hybrids can easily go a foot apart, but I still like to have at least three bulbs of a kind in a group.

The bulbs of the daffodil, Geranium, mentioned previously were planted about 5 inches apart because they were huge and triple. Double-nosed daffodils go two or three to a hole about 4 inches apart. Single daffodils go no more than 3 inches apart, with at least three bulbs per hole. Tulips get the same treatment.

Beware the Bargain

You get what you pay for—in bulbs as in anything else, I suppose. If you are going to put any money at all into bulbs and if you are going to the trouble of digging holes for them, why not invest in good ones? Your bloom will be surer and more beautiful for the same amount of effort and very little more money.

It stands to reason that "bargain" bulbs must have some reason behind the bargain—like being below-size, diseased, not well kept in storage or transit, not properly labelled, not properly matured or perhaps of inferior varieties which other bulbsmen have discarded in favor of better, improved kinds.

All you have to do is buy one poor batch of such bulbs, and you have used up whatever savings you thought you made for the next several years. Buy from reputable dealers, whatever else you do. (See Chapter 23.)

Choose What You Want

Many books on bulbs make a big thing out of lists of recommended named varieties, particularly of daffodils and tulips.

There are, goodness knows, a host of different types, colors, and kinds, and it is not easy to pick your way through such a plenitude of riches. In the pages that follow I will mention various individual hybrids which I have particularly enjoyed in my gardens, but I have steadfastly refrained from specific recommendations except for special purposes.

Only you know how big your garden is, what colors it needs, lacks or cannot integrate. Only you know what bulbs you already have. You alone know what you like. So to create your garden as you want it, you must do the choosing, with a good catalog as a guide, and catalog gardening is at least as much fun as any other kind. I will only add that you will have longer, lovelier bloom if you make a conscious effort to select different types of popular bulbs. Thus, when ordering daffodils you might decide the backbone of your spring garden will feature the big yellow trumpets. For variety you then add a clump of white trumpets, a dozen of some early daffodil species, another dozen of a later-flowering, clustered type and perhaps a few bulbs of one of the exciting new bicolors. And of course you will plant all of them in clumps of one color and type for the grandest impression.

Another item to remember is your vacation schedule. Someone who spends all summer at the seashore will hardly want a garden of summer-flowering lilies, while a gardener who plans trips in spring or fall will plant accordingly so his garden is at its best when he is home to enjoy it.

Size of Bulbs

As concerns the size of bulbs, trust your dealer's integrity and instructions. If he is reputable, he will guarantee his stock's blooming size. Sometimes you will have a choice. In most cases "exhibition" or "extra large" means a premium bulb. If you are

3. Plant spring bulbs to keep each other company. Here snowflakes (*Leucojum*) complement hyacinths and daffodils. Tiny jewel at top is a species narcissus. Violets, violas and primroses finish the picture (Roche).

watching prices, buy "bedding" or "large" bulbs. This is especially true for hyacinths and lilies. Once in a while a dealer will offer clearly-labelled baby bulbs for those who want a bargain, but these will need nursing for at least one season before they bloom and are not recommended for ordinary gardeners. Only the "gyp artists" will foist under-sized bulbs on an unsuspecting beginner. Again I repeat, "Beware the big bargain advertisement."

Order Early

If you want to obtain top bulbs for your garden, order them as soon as the catalogs arrive. Logically, the first orders get the best handling and the choicest bulbs. Most important of all if your order goes in early, your bulbs will be shipped before there is even a chance of their drying out or beginning to sprout, either of which adversely affects a bulb. Those who delay are sometimes disappointed to find a popular variety is sold out.

Bulb orders may be sent to you in more than one mailing since some bulbs, notably lilies, are not available until late. This enables you to plant them one batch at a time. Dealers try to send bulbs at the best time for planting in your locality, but late orders arrive when such houses are in the midst of their rush season, and this may mean you will receive bulbs after the golden autumn days have given way to bitter cold.

Plant on Arrival

Except in the possible case of tulips, do your fall planting as early as you can procure the bulbs. (In dealing with tender bulbs, you must await frost-free spring nights at your latitude.) Because so many bulbs sold in this country are grown commercially in Holland as well as in other countries, there is naturally a time lag between when the bulbs are lifted and when you receive them, but dealers ship and store them under optimum conditions so this does not usually hurt the bulbs. Your own house cannot do as well. Moreover, it is so much pleasanter to plant in the warm sunshine of September and early October than to fight the blasts of winter. I can remember one awful day when I planted late bulbs in a shamefully haphazard way just because I was so cold.

Some of the little bulbs like muscari actually make autumn foliage, and all other bulbs need to get a root system started, so early fall planting is the best for them. If your order went in on time, you are all set even if the weather decides to produce two bad weeks in September. You can afford to delay for a break to do your planting. Later on in the season, you will not dare wait for better weather, and you will find planting even a dozen daffodils can be a disagreeable task if the ground is hard and the wind is knifing through you.

What to do if you were not able to order early or some crisis kept you from completing your task? Plant as soon as you can. Never store these hardy bulbs in the house over the winter. They are better off in the ground, even if you have to break a frost crust to get them in. In some cases they might not bloom in spring after such tardy planting or flowering will be late, but they will be alive and ready for a subsequent season. They are almost sure to lose their viability if stored inside.

Store Carefully

There may be times when it is impossible to plant for a week or two. Open all bags in an order as soon as it arrives to check for dried or rotten bulbs (although from a good bulbs-man you will not find these often). Discard any rotten bulbs immediately and inform the dealer. Dry, shrivelled bulbs require urgent planting and will benefit from a good watering as soon as they are underground.

Leave the bulbs in their labelled bags but with the tops open to allow for air circulation and store them in a dry, cool place. Never subject them to extreme heat or cold or wetness.

There will be times when you may wish to store your own hardy bulbs over the summer. Perhaps you contemplate a move or redoing a border. Or you may have daffodils which are overcrowded. You can dig the bulbs immediately after flowering, making sure that the foliage is not separated from the bulb. Then bundle them and "heel" them in until their foliage is ripened. This means that you dig a shallow trench and place the bulbs in it with a light covering of soil over the bulbs and the foliage out in the air. A lightly shaded place is best, and they will need some artificial watering. Make sure all seed heads are removed first and that proper labels are attached to each variety.

When the foliage has browned, these bulbs should be cleaned and sorted for size. The smallest can be planted in nursery rows for a year or two or thrown away if you do not need them. The larger ones can be kept in a dry, cool place where there is plenty of air circulation, such as a shaded garage, until planting time in early fall. Never pile them into a basket or store in a closed bag. Trays or flats are good for this purpose. I often use the discarded string bags from oranges for storage, and one ingenious method is to hang such bulbs up in bags made from old nylon stockings. And make sure mice cannot get at your stored bulbs.

Transplanting

There are several shortcuts to this procedure. You can transplant the bulbs after flowering, always working so the foliage is not loosened from the bulb and the roots are not overly disturbed. By placing them where you want them to grow the following season, you avoid any storage or heeling in. Even when overcrowding is the reason for transplanting, you can separate big clumps of bulbs carefully and follow this technique, but it works best only with those which are not too deeply planted. The foliage will then ripen at the new spot. Water these new plantings well to lessen the shock.

Most gardeners wait until the foliage is fully ripe at the first location and then dig up the bulbs for planting or summer storage, but you must keep close tabs on the bulbs if you plan to do this. Once the stem is dry enough to break, it may be impossible to find the bulbs or to dig them without damage. You can replant these bulbs immediately if you wish or you can store them for fall planting.

In general my advice to the average gardener who wonders whether to lift his hardy bulbs after flowering is "don't." Why make work if it is not necessary? Interplanting of perennials or annuals to hide the maturing bulb foliage is easier and more rewarding. The only time such transplanting becomes essential is when bulbs have increased to a point where you are no longer getting worthwhile bloom from them.

The handling of tender bulbs and tubers which must be dug before winter and stored in a frost-free location is covered in Chapter 12.

Keep Tools Simple

There are only two tools needed when I am planting bulbs. One is a long, narrow trowel and the other a woman-sized, shovel-spade. (I use that double word because it is hard to tell which it is, and I use it for everything. It was given me by a loving husband who advised me that with it I would never again lift a shovelful of dirt heavy enough to hurt my back. His advice has been heeded with good results!) Both these tools were expensive, but they have been used constantly for years and years without the blades bending, and the shafts are still true and sturdy. Cheap tools are no saving.

The shovel handle is long enough for me to stand upright and use my foot as a pushing aid, but its width is less than 6 inches, and it is ideal for digging holes for a clump of bulbs. It resembles a potting shovel. My narrow trowel is a useful adjunct to this and fine for digging out even a deep hole for a single bulb. If necessary, it can make a very small opening, and it does not require quite as much strength to push through hard soil as a wider one.

A tool called a dibber is sometimes sold for bulb planting, but I do not like it. No one can make nice soft holes with a dibber, and I like my bulbs to lie in a comfortable berth. Moreover, the dibber often leaves a narrow pointed empty space below the bulb. I want loose soil at the bottom so the bulb's roots can do their job easily (Figure 5).

Several other clever tools which act as a kind of hole-digger are also on the market. The trouble is that I usually find a stone exactly an inch from the projected bottom of the holes! My narrow trowel then comes into play anyway so I have simplified matters by eliminating everything but essentials. A pail half full of peatmoss to mix in where needed in our clay soil will also accommodate a package of bonemeal, my trowel and several bags of bulbs, so I can carry everything I need in one trip if I take pail in one hand and shovel in the other.

A pair of sturdy work gloves, preferably leather or plastic for facility, and you are all set to plant all the bulbs you have. Occasionally when I have dozens of big bulbs, each needing a separate hole of its own, I have made myself a cushion to protect the palm of my right hand under the glove. A good wad of disposable tissue and a strip of adhesive do very nicely. Because many bulbs contain irritative alkaloids, I use gloves or protective cream for prolonged handling.

Advantages of Different Exposures

After you have been growing hardy bulbs for a while in your garden, you might enjoy my game of tampering with bloom times to extend the flowering season. Simply by planting them in a sheltered place with a southern exposure, most hardy spring bulbs will bloom as much as two weeks earlier than the expected norm for your locality. The same bulbs in a northern or eastern exposure will bloom several weeks later so that your season can be stretched considerably by judicious choice of differing sites.

To insure success with this technique I load things in my favor by choosing the very earliest species crocus and tulips and daffodils for sheltered nooks facing south. Conversely, some of the later-blossoming daffodils like Cheerfulness and Laurens Koster grow to the north of my spring garden and usually bloom weeks after the big yellow trumpets are completely gone. A splash of late tulips in an exposed position delights me by appearing long after everyone else's tulips are shattered memories.

This kind of finagling is what makes gardening so much fun. There is always a new goal to aim at.

CHAPTER 3

Little Bulbs for a Big Spring

Spring in the garden where bulbs have been knowingly selected can begin long before the first daffodils show color, for a host of dependable early flowers are yours for the planting. Catalogs increasingly feature the glories of the so-called "little bulbs," and high time it is, too. The ones you will meet in this chapter are as hardy and lasting as anything you can plant in your garden.

Practical gardeners prize them for their carefree habits and because they take up so little space. In my own garden many are overplanted with evergreen groundcovers like dianthus, cerastium and hardy candytuft (iberis) which produce their own show later in the season so in a sense the bulbs require no space whatsoever!

And nothing is easier to plant. Because these bulbs are small and do not need deep planting, they can be put in by the dozens with little effort. They increase just as rapidly for commercial growers as in your garden so your initial investment for a start of any of them is modest.

Early and Hardy

If in winter you often dream, as I do, of the spring to come, these first flowers will be equally important to you for the color they bring to a gray world. The farther north you live, the more you should emphasize them on this count. Until a few years ago I regarded them as scarcely more than gay harbingers of glories to come, but when one March brought unusually miserable weeks, I really appreciated what they mean to those whose winters are much worse than ours in southern Pennsylvania.

Here we have come to expect a crocus in February, Emperor

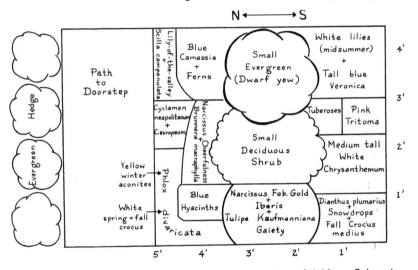

An Intimate Doorstep Garden Needs All-Year Interest

FIG. 6. This little dooryard garden contains several fragrant bulbous plants to welcome the guest and enchant the family passing back and forth. The bush to the south of the cyclamen gives protection from hot sun, but the hyacinths and Narcissus Cheerfulness get enough light to mature their foliage before the shrub leafs out completely. Choose smaller shrubs like deutzias, hypericums or caryopteris. The evergreen hedge protects from the north wind so as to gain the earliest spring and latest fall flowers. Perennials are interplanted with bulbs to get double use from space. Even in winter foliage of phlox, cyclamen, iberis and dianthus is decorative.

tulips with the last snow and daffodils often by mid-March. Sometimes spring arrives almost too soon and lingers only a short while before real heat. In those years our early bulbs come and go so quickly their effect is almost overshadowed by burgeoning perennials. Once in a while even our comparatively gentle climate dishes up an old-fashioned winter. Then we realize why the nodding snowdrops were so beloved of our New England grandmothers.

You will garner the earliest flowers by planting these small bulbs in a sunny, sheltered spot facing south. Evergreens, a slope, a wall or the house itself to the north provide protection and advance their season several weeks. They will bloom just as well but somewhat later in more open situations.

How long these bulbs perform during any one spring depends on how long cool weather lingers. None of them thrives in protracted heat. In years when March and April have continued cool, I have had *Anemone blanda atrocaerulea* in bloom for nearly eight weeks. Snowdrops and winter aconites often stretch their season to six, and one year *Crocus susianus* was in its sixth week and still in fine shape when a hungry rabbit ended its career overnight. On the other hand we had two unexpectedly hot days early one March, and the aconites set seed after less than two weeks of bloom.

Color Range

The majority of these bulbs come in blues and whites, especially those which flower earliest. It is almost as if Providence felt we were not yet ready for brilliant colors after the drab winter, but my eyes long for the golden yellows to reflect the sunshine. Several fine crocus provide this hue as do the aconites. There are varieties of *Anemone blanda*, chionodoxa and wood hyacinths which yield pink blooms. While of slightly anemic hue, they are valuable for this color rare in early spring. Numerous crocus add gorgeous purples to the season's spectrum.

For all their hardiness these flowers appear fragile and many have short stems so they require a foreground spot in the garden if they are to be seen close up. They do well in the rock garden too. By all means plant them where they may be seen easily from your windows. Few cheerier sights are possible on a gray day, so we malign these treasures when we classify them as "minor bulbs." You may not want to plant all of them, but I do not see how you can pull through March and early April without some of them.

IN ORDER OF APPEARANCE

WINTER ACONITES (*Eranthis,* Color Plate III) are aptly named. The Greek translates as "flower of spring," and these are the first bulbs to flower every year in my garden. Four inches high and slightly more than an inch in diameter, they look like buttercups, and indeed belong to the same family. Each pure yellow blossom has a ruff of green stem leaves, but the other foliage is palmlike. It disappears by mid-May when the seeds ripen, so mark and mulch well to avoid summer disturbance.

¶ Plant winter aconites as early in the fall as you can obtain them, about 2 inches deep and the same distance apart.

Eranthis naturalizes gaily on southern banks where deciduous trees provide summer shadow, and it thrives in soil rich in humus. If tubers appear dried or wizened when they arrive, soak them overnight in a saucer of water and then plant at once. We give ours a sheltered southern exposure to get the earliest possible flowers and in mild winters have enjoyed their golden cheer as early as the first week of February. They

weather snow and sleet well, and only unseasonal heat will cut
short their flowering.

Recommended: *Eranthis hyemalis,* still the earliest and best
for naturalizing; *E. cilicica,* blooms a little later, foliage bronzy;
E. tubergeni, a new hybrid with longer-lasting, sterile flowers.

SNOWDROPS (*Galanthus*) are proverbially early. They
open a few days after the aconites and look their best if given
an evergreen groundcover. I have some which shoot straight
out of blue-gray dianthus leaves. These keep the green-tipped
snowdrops spotless through all kinds of weather.

¶ Plant snowdrops 3 inches deep and 2 inches apart in large
patches and leave undisturbed for years.

We once shoveled 5 feet of snow onto some snowdrops. The
first day they saw light afterwards, their stems were almost
parallel to the ground, but with freedom from their icy prison,
they straightened up and remained in good shape for another
three weeks. Delightfully tolerant, snowdrops grow almost as
well in clay as in woods' soil, but they do best with some sun
until mid-May when the foliage matures. Therefore, they thrive
in deciduous woodland, and I have grown them in both moist
and dry situations.

Easy to find: *Galanthus nivalis,* the single white snowdrop, a
favorite for generations; *G. nivalis flore pleno,* a double form
and just as dependable; *G. elwesi,* larger-flowering species and
very early.

CROCUS leads all the other early spring bulbs in range of
color and blooming periods. (The autumn-flowering species
are in Chapter 15.) Every tint of white, cream, yellow, orange,
or purple is represented by a member of this hardy tribe. If you
add some of the winter-flowering species to a garden where the
better-known Dutch crocus is already established, you can

I. Need we wonder why *Crocus susianus* is called Cloth of Gold? *Crocus versicolor picturatus* (Cloth of Silver) has been introduced for contrast. The first milky puschkinias are just opening. Author's garden.

II. Gay companions for the April garden are Narcissus Geranium, red primroses and *Brunnera macrophylla*. Author's garden.

III. Tiny winter aconites bring early yellow color (Malak of Ottawa).

IV. Species tulips are small but bright. Miniature *T. biflora alta* contrasts with *T. kaufmanniana* in the March rock garden.

V. No rock garden is complete without the starry *T. tarda*. Author's garden.

VI. You can naturalize bulbs on a small lot by taking advantage of the terrain. Everything here has been planted in groups and allowed to increase to form generous splashes of color (Genereux).

VII.   Grape hyacinths bring vivid blue to contrast with primroses and perennial candytuft. Author's garden.

VIII.   Two weeks later in the same spot a clump of light blue *Amsonia tabernaemontana* has appeared which will effectively screen the ripening foliage of the late mahogany tulip, Morocco Beauty.

have bloom as early as the end of December and as late as
April, depending of course on where you live.

¶ Plant crocus 2 to 3 inches deep and 4 to 6 inches apart
so they can form huge clumps before you need to thin them.

I hope some day to see the crocuses that color the hills of
Greece and other Mediterranean lands where they are native
and have brought beauty to gardens for untold years. Identi-
fiable crocuses may still be seen on fragments of frescoes
almost 4,000 years old from the Palace of Knossos on Crete,
and it is not unreasonable to assume that they have been
cultivated by man as long as any other decorative plant.

Some authorities stress the value of the anthers of the
autumn saffron crocus in medicine, flavoring, dye and per-
fumery to explain the frequent appearance of the crocus in
archaic Cretan art. But also pictured are iris, lilies and anemones, on pottery, murals and jewelry. I believe the ancients
loved flowers as much for their beauty as for their use. Few
flowers are more often described by the early Greek poets
writing of spring than crocus.

Given a place with plenty of early spring sun and no summer
disturbance, crocus corms will multiply rapidly in this temperate climate. They are perfect for a rockery facing south, but I
have several species which have formed spectacular groups in
the foreground of gardens which are dryish and partially
shaded all summer. The foliage persists well into June so plan
to conceal it if necessary.

I like crocuses much better in the garden than in the lawn
and in groups of just one color adjacent to a contrasting shade.
Truly it is a shame to sentence them to a half-life competing
with grass. Give them instead a nook of their own in the garden
and prepare for a surprise if you have never seen them luxuriat-
ing this way.

After some years the corms in a mature clump may be visible

at the surface of the soil due to natural increase. When I see this, I scrape away the soil carefully and remove only the top-most corms so a planting remains thrifty but full and beautiful for years and years. Thinning is best done after the foliage has browned off in June.

There are a tremendous number of good crocuses. One catalog lists seventeen different named Dutch varieties and forty-five winter-flowering species. In general the Dutch crocus, which are really Mediterraneans too but have been hybridized, bear later, larger blooms than the species. They have brilliant orange or yellow stigmata in the center for contrast.

Four recommended ones: Snowstorm, white; Remembrance, purple; Striped Beauty, white with lilac; and Large Yellow Mammoth, the earliest Dutch type. Buy and plant by name or color for loveliest effect.

My preference is for the winter-flowering sorts. I would heartily endorse any, and I only hope to live long enough to grow them all. The earliest in my garden is *Crocus ancyrensis,* a small, starry, orange-yellow which opens in February and March, but many report the lilac *C. imperati* even earlier, par-ticularly in the South. Another very early one is *C. sieberi* in purple shades. One of the largest in this group, *C. versicolor picturatus* (Cloth of Silver) bears striking white and lilac-striped blooms with orange stigmata. Other fine purples are found among the hybrids of the famous Tommy crocus (*C. tomasinianus*). A whole new series of *Crocus chrysanthus* hy-brids is now available in shades of blue, cream and yellow, and each seems more beautiful than the other.

Year in, year out, my favorite remains *Crocus susianus,* a venerable species reputed to have been cultivated by the ancient Persians. Louise Beebe Wilder gives 1587 as the date for its introduction to Europe from Constantinople. Almost as early as *C. ancyrensis* here, it lasts for weeks, no matter what the weather, multiplies prolifically and each corm yields a succession of golden flowers that literally glow in the sun (Color Plate I). Mine get half shade after the dogwood leafs out, and they grow in rich but fairly dry soil, which must be what they want because the planting in the photograph originally held only twelve bulbs!

GRECIAN WINDFLOWERS (*Anemone blanda*) in shades of blue, white, and pink are reliably hardy north of Washington, D.C. We have grown them without any protection just above Philadelphia and found them dependable through the worst winter we have yet experienced.

¶ Set *A. blanda* 2 to 3 inches deep and 4 inches apart in soil with humus added.

Planted in a sheltered spot, they begin to flower a few days after the first crocus. They have a unique charm, due partly to the graceful, ferny foliage, but the daisylike flowers (2 inches wide and 4 to 6 inches high) also went straight to my heart the moment they first opened in my garden to show their golden stamens. Somehow these are the most joyous of the spring bulbs—a herald of warm weather with its host of bright field daisies.

The anemones open when winter is still likely to deal us much unpleasantness, and like the crocus and other spring bulbs, they fold up their petals when there is no sun or at a drop in temperature. Thus they are able to withstand any onslaught of March wind, ice, and snow. When the sun shines again, the many-rayed anemones reopen, and if the weather stays cool, they continue to produce color for six weeks. By planting them in various exposures, I have stretched their flowering period to two full months.

The delicate foliage forms a mound seldom higher than 4 inches and lasts well into late June. This anemone requires some shade in summer heat. Both blossoms and the graceful leaves combine well with other small early bulbs. Presoak the odd gray tubers if they look dry and plant early just like the aconites, to which they are related. Usually a few rootlets remain as a clue to which side is down, but I have successfully planted them sideways when in doubt.

The best of a fine selection: *Anemone blanda atrocaerulea,* electric blue petals with many prominent yellow stamens; several named forms exist (Blue Star, Blue Beauty), similar is *A. apennina;* Bridesmaid, a white daisy in March! outside petals are tinted pink so when folded up on cloudy days, Bridesmaid has a quite different appearance; Charmer, the best of the pinks.

RUE ANEMONE (*Anemonella thalictroides*) is a dainty but hardy American wildflower, closely related to the anemones, with clusters of small white flowers in spring. It likes semi-shade and humus-rich soil. Rare rose and double forms exist.

¶ Plant the tri-lobed tubers, about 1 inch deep, in colonies.

HYACINTHUS AZUREUS properly belongs in Chapter 8 since it is a true hyacinth, although often listed under Muscari. Buds show color from the moment they emerge from the soil, often in early February, and it is a magic hue, the vivid blue of a summer sky.

¶ Each bulb yields several flower stems, so plant *H. azureus* 4 to 5 inches apart and 3 inches deep.

This hyacinth's charm is intensified by the placement of the flowers, which resemble tiny bells tightly bunched on the stem like a grape hyacinth but with the open side facing outward. Bells at the bottom of the tiny truss unfold first, and the stem lengthens to 5 or 6 inches as the flower matures, a process which is satisfying long. In a cool spring I have had color from a clump for more than two months. Increase is good, both by offsets and seed. The foliage remains neat and unobtrusive until June and reappears in fall. A white form is sometimes offered, but the blue is preferred for its perfect color. Taller stems differentiate the similar *H. ciliatus.*

Much later (May) the related H. AMETHYSTINUS bears loose heads of light blue bells. It is a darling for half shade, but should be planted by itself in clumps since it is too delicate to compete with the big perennials of spring.

GLORY OF THE SNOW (*Chionodoxa*) quite literally lives up to this translation from the Greek. In various climates I have seen its flowers emerge unscathed from a blanket of March ice and snow. Needing no protection, it naturalizes well, and the unobtrusive foliage disappears quickly so it is fine for the front of the garden. If not disturbed by cultivation, it will seed itself and eventually make sheets of vivid blue, white or pink.

¶ Plant chionodoxa 3 inches deep and only 2 inches apart.

Because the white-throated flowers face skyward in a cluster, I prefer chionodoxa to the less floriferous, pendant, true-blue squills, which bloom about the same time; but except for the gentian-hued *C. sardensis,* the most popular chionodoxa come in lavender shades. Two good ones are *C. luciliae* and *C. grandiflora,* a larger form. The pure white stars of *C. luciliae alba* make a lovely picture, while Pink Giant is well worth its price. It is a bit taller than the 4 to 5 inches of the others. Chionodoxas need a dainty low groundcover like arabis, or sow a dwarf annual like sweet alyssum over them. Always plant chionodoxa separately in clumps of one color or in association with some other spring bulb.

LEBANON SQUILL (*Puschkinia,* Color Plate I) has delicate flowers of milky-white pendant bells in loose clusters on stems about 6 inches high. Each petal is striped with a thin blue line. Related to the scillas, it withstands any weather except protracted hail. The buds show color as they emerge from the soil in early March, and the foliage matures quickly, so this is another good bulb for the foreground. Protected from disturbance by mulch or a groundcover, it increases rapidly by multiplication and by seeding.

¶ Plant Lebanon squills 2 to 3 inches deep and 4 to 5 inches apart.

Why this bulb is not used more, I cannot understand. We have flowered it successfully for years under a variety of conditions and with no protection other than that afforded by neighboring plants. There is a white form, (*P. libanotica alba*) which is about the most exquisite early spring bulb you can have in your garden. Both types have a faint fragrance and last well in bouquets.

BLUE SQUILL (*Scilla*) is the bluest of all the hardy, early things, and the color is lovely with daffodils, early tulips and many of the other little bulbs. Several nodding starbells are borne on each 4-inch stem and foliage is unobtrusive.

¶ Scillas naturalize well and go 2 inches deep and 3 to 4 inches apart.

The best two are *S. sibirica* and its larger form, Spring Beauty. A comparatively recent introduction, *S. tubergeniana,* is a softer blue. The white form (*S. sibirica alba*) is charming especially when clumps are interspersed within plantings of blue squills. Earliest of the family, *S. bifolia* shows considerable variation in color, detracting from its effectiveness; it multiplies madly, looks best with a groundcover, and has blue, pink, and white forms.

GRAPE HYACINTHS (*Muscari*) total nearly fifty different species, many quite unlike the well-known blue globular form.

Some interest only the botanist, but others have real garden merit. By choosing several you can stretch bloom from March to June.

¶ In height muscari seldom exceed 8 inches; they need no protection and are all planted 3 inches deep and 4 to 5 inches apart.

Many increase prodigiously both by multiplication and seed, particularly *Muscari armeniacum*. So undemanding is this species that I have transplanted clumps in bloom without incident. Because foliage is blowsy and in evidence much of the year (new shoots appear in August) and also because of its sturdiness, *M. armeniacum* is best grown in rougher parts of the garden where it will not overrun less rugged plants. It withstands considerable moisture and shade (Color Plate VII).

In my garden *M. botryoides album* is the first to flower, often in March. Except for its pure whiteness, it is identical with the common grape hyacinths. Heavenly Blue, is one of the best blues. Also good are Early Giant and *M. tubergenianum*, with spikes from bright blue at the top to deep Oxford-blue below. All three are April-flowering.

Among later-blooming muscari, the feathered hyacinth (*M. plumosum*) has interesting violet spikes of twisted and elongated petals which do resemble feathers. In a cool spring it blooms well into June here.

The tassel hyacinth (*M. comosum*) looks strange in May with a loose raceme of olive-green flowers, topped with a purple tuft. It has to be seen to be believed and varies from 8 to 18 inches high. The starch hyacinth (*M. paradoxum*) has dull navy blossoms, and *M. massyanum* starts out carmine, turns dark and ends up pinkish-yellow over a long period in May.

SNOWFLAKES (*Leucojum*, Illustration 3) belong to the amaryllis family like their close cousins, the snowdrops, but the snowflakes are bell-shaped—white, tipped green. They tolerate some shade but do best in sun, where they are a long-lived addition to any garden.

¶ Plant snowflakes 3 inches deep and 3 to 4 inches apart.

Flowering in February and March, *L. vernum*, often called the spring snowflake, bears a single flower on a 5-inch stem. I prefer the summer snowflake (*L. aestivum*) because it flowers in April and May after most other spring bulbs are finished. It tends to produce more than one bloom per stem, but its 12- to 18-inch foliage is nearly as prominent as many daffodils, so it cannot be planted in the foreground. Foliage disappears by the end of June. This later-blooming snowflake with its tiny bells and narrow foliage is a delightful contrast to tulips.

LILY-OF-THE-VALLEY (*Convallaria majalis*), a perennial often classed with bulbs, is by far the most fragrant of the early spring flowers. The spotless white bells are daintily scalloped, and the fresh green leaves carpet any shady spot where soil is moist and contains humus. It will flower even in clay hardpan if some peat is mixed in it.

¶ The creeping rootstock of lily-of-the-valley is planted horizontally about 1 inch deep with the pips just showing. To encourage flowering, sprinkle dried cow manure generously over the site in late winter. After some years you may have to thin the bed, since flowering is better if plants are not crowded. Do this in late summer and water new plantings well. There is a so-called pink form which is often magenta, lacks fragrance and is hardly worth growing.

WOOD HYACINTHS (*Scilla nonscripta* and *S. campanulata*) resemble lily-of-the-valley and flower just afterwards.

They are often a foot high, unlike their earlier, smaller relatives, the squills. Although blooming splendidly in sun, they are usually planted in partially shaded spots, since they are one of the few bulbs which flower satisfactorily there.

¶ Plant wood hyacinths 3 inches deep and 6 inches apart.

In the catalogs you may find them listed as SPANISH BLUE-BELLS (S. *hispanica* or S. *campanulata*) or ENGLISH BLUE-BELLS (S. *nutans* or S. *nonscripta*). They are similar. Only blue and white forms of the English type are usually listed. Much hybridizing has been done on the campanulata types which feature good whites, many blues and several pinks. A new giant strain of named S. *campanulata* is very fine. All look best planted in groups of one color and are lovely to edge a path in open woodland. These may also be catalogued as ENDYMION.

STAR-OF-BETHLEHEM (*Ornithogalum umbellatum*, Illustration 20) is so rugged and multiplies so quickly, it is considered a pest in some gardens. However, the white blossoms, each with a yellow center of stamens, are a delight in spots where other bulbs may not prosper. I have grown it in dry clay, in partial shade, in very moist situations and on grassy banks where it had to fend for itself. In every case it flowered generously in May.

¶ Plant star-of-Bethlehem 2 inches deep and 4 inches apart and let it alone to form mats.

Numerous blooms are borne on each 6-inch stem. They close in the afternoon to show a green-striped reverse. The grassy foliage appears early but withers soon after flowering. The related *O. nutans* with white and green stars on 20-inch stems is also good for naturalizing and needs slightly deeper planting. Flowers of both types seed prolifically, but you can avoid this in the garden by picking first.

CAPSULE VIEW OF THE LITTLE BULBS

These hardy little bulbs require no coddling. Most are native to Mediterranean regions so their natural preference is for hot, dry summers and cold, wet winters and springs.

Plant early in September in groups of at least a dozen no farther apart than 2 to 3 inches for immediate effect.

Although they increase well, you may leave them undivided for years. With patience and enough space, you can eventually create large colonies by planting them farther apart than 3 inches, and then they look lovely in woodland or among large shrubbery plantings.

For earliest color, plant facing south with protection from north wind.

To encourage increase, provide an overplanting or a mulch; otherwise you may disturb seedlings when weeding or transplanting other things. Gauge your overplanting by the height of both bulb and groundcover. Perennial iberis is fine for rugged muscari but too thick for the delicate chionodoxa.

You can plant the earliest bulbs safely in spots where deciduous trees cast filtered shade since they will mature their foliage before the shade deepens.

CHAPTER 4

Second Wave of Little Bulbs

Some of the bulbs in this chapter are almost as early as the harbingers of spring we have just discussed, and all have something special to offer you. Although you may not consider them indispensable, any one will be an arresting addition to your garden. As a class they are not as hardy or dependable in every climate as those of the preceding chapter. Beauty they have, and many have bloomed heavily for some years for me near Philadelphia, but there are reservations with many of them.

This is not to say that they are not recommended, especially those suitable for your particular geographical area. I could not garden without several of them. A few are so beautiful it is worth several attempts to be able to enjoy them, even temporarily. Others are fun to try if only for your own satisfaction, although I like to experiment with only a few such kinds in small quantities each season. Those which appeal or which fill a specific need in some section of my garden may then be added in whatever amounts I want after I determine their usefulness.

Because these bulbs may not always be dependable under every condition, try them first in some spot where their failure will not leave a glaring open space. Again they have been listed in the order in which they usually flower here near Philadelphia, and I have tried to note better known bulbs or

57

perennials which bloom at the same time to aid you in working them into your garden scheme.

My own opinions naturally color my feelings about all the plants I write about, but I do not apologize for that. Life without a dram of honest conviction would be pallid indeed. These bulbs, like those of the rest of the book, are described as they appear to me, a plain dirt gardener. I can tell you what they added to my gardens, and their limitations are honestly noted for your guidance. Where other authorities have suggested possible horticultural techniques which may aid you in successfully keeping these bulbs in your garden, I have included them for your consideration. This is particularly true for those native to our own West or to alpine regions. It is not easy to make these at home here in the Middle Atlantic states nor in the Northeastern and Central sections either.

IN ORDER OF APPEARANCE

ROCK GARDEN IRIS (*Iris reticulata*) grows from bulbs with a curiously netted appearance and blooms in February or March when its dark purple makes a striking contrast with the earliest daffodils. Since part of its appeal lies in its early blooming, give it a sheltered sunny site facing south wherever you live.

¶ Planted in early fall 4 inches deep and the same distance apart, *I. reticulata* winters at Philadelphia without protection, but further north give it a mulch of several inches of salt hay or oak leaves or a pile of evergreen boughs.

Even with the yellow blotch on its lower petals, this iris does not show up well against most evergreen foliage because of its very dark hue, so try to arrange a light background. I am going to overplant mine with the gray-leaved *Cerastium tomentosum.* Outside, blossoms each last at least ten days but die quickly when brought into warmth. The oft-mentioned violet fragrance is very faint. The flowers are hardly 5 inches high, but the thick foliage reaches a good 18 inches later on, so do not put it in the very foreground of a garden; it disappears in June. It is perfect for rock gardens and protected nooks.

I prefer several reticulata forms with bluer blossoms, notably Cantab, Clarette, Harmony and Joyce. For purple shades try J. S. Dijt, Wentworth and Hercules. Of all the group the related *I. danfordiae,* a bright yellow, is the gayest and often the earliest.

Some authorities suggest these should be dug up after the foliage matures and kept dry and warm all summer, but I do not bother. Mine are planted where the soil remains very dry during the hot months, and they have increased well. If yours die out, it is inexpensive to replace them with new bulbs the following fall. Blooming sturdily through wind and sleet, they are worth planting every year just for their jewel-like presence on one of those days when it seems winter will never leave.

SPRING MEADOW-SAFFRON (*Bulbocodium vernum*) is a shy spring rarity which pops crocus-like, pinky-lavender flowers out, quite naked of any foliage, in company with the earliest flowers of spring. The foliage is never obtrusive and does not last too long.

¶ Plant bulbocodium 3 inches deep and a few inches apart somewhere in the foreground of a sunny garden.

Each bulb yields several practically stemless blossoms with curly petals. They last for weeks, but are at best unspectacular, being most useful for their color, which is hard to find so early. They look best in the rock garden with the foliage of some groundcover to soften their appearance.

CORYDALIS HALLERI (*C. solida*) blooms just a little earlier than the plumy bleedingheart to which it is related. The delicate foliage is somewhat similar to the dicentra too, but the lavender flowers remind me more of tiny snapdragons and are sometimes doubletailed, which I suppose explains the name; corydalis is Greek for crested lark. Neither leaves nor flower attain much more than 3 inches. Buds usually show on the corky tubers to indicate the tops.

¶ Plant corydalis 3 inches deep and 4 inches apart in humus-rich soil and partial shade.

While this is rather an insignificant plant whose foliage rapidly disappears after flowering, it is a pretty little thing for the foreground of a garden with early cream primroses to bloom with it and also lovely with *Muscari botryoides album*. If cutworms attack your corydalis, protect the emerging stems with paper collars.

The related *C. lutea* is usually regarded as a perennial and bears yellow flowers on longer stems during the summer. It is useful for the shady rock garden. Few nurseries carry plants, but seed is available.

CROWN IMPERIALS (*Fritillaria imperialis*) will never be termed insignificant! The big brick-red or orange bells hang downward on sturdy 3-foot stems and give off a perceptible skunky odor. To complete the picture a tuft of green foliage surmounts the blossoms. The big bulbs are scaled like a true lily and smell dreadful too so there may be something to the report that a garden where they are planted is never troubled by rodents.

¶ Plant crown imperials as early in fall as you can obtain them 5 to 6 inches deep and at least 8 inches apart.

Some compost should be added to clay soils, and the plants benefit from an annual feeding of dried cow manure and a

pinch of lime at flowering time, when they also need deep
watering if spring is dry. Never move them if they are doing
well. The foliage dries up quickly so they may be used for a
sunny focal point where some later plant such as a peony will
soon be holding forth. In my garden white trumpet daffodils
make a striking contrast with the imperials.

Since they bloom in early April here, the flowers in sites
which are struck by the first rays of the morning sun are some-
time spoiled by a late frost. Those in more sheltered places
where the frost melts before the sun hits them have never
shown damage. The cold does not seem to harm the foliage.
Some catalogs list crown imperials by selected colors—yellow,
orange or red.

GUINEA HEN FLOWERS (*Fritillaria meleagris*) are also
known as snakeshead or checkered lilies, and it is hard to
believe they are closely related to the crown imperials. One or
two dainty, purplish, checkered, campanulate flowers nod from
foot-long stems, and the graceful lily-like foliage is unobtrusive
and short-lived.

¶ Plant these fritillaries 3 inches deep and 3 inches apart in
light, moist soil which is well-drained and partially shaded.

The pure white form is much to be preferred and charming
anywhere, but the purple sorts need a light background to
show. These April flowers should also have a sheltered spot
not facing east, for mine have been caught by frost. North of
Philadelphia give winter mulch and a southern exposure where
there will be shade later on; even then they may prove short-
lived. Some lime may help. Dutch growers sell named hybrids.

Our own West contains several lovelier cousins which drive
Eastern gardeners wild with their eccentricities. They are hard
to find, difficult to establish and indescribably lovely when you
succeed. Tallest is *F. recurva* (mission bells) with 24-inch

orange-red flowers and a love for partial shade and rich, loose soil. The best of the others are most suitable for sunny rock gardens: *F. pudica* is yellow; *F. pluriflora* is pinkish-purple. The rare *F. camtschatcensis* from Japan has blackish flowers in

June. It is supposed to be hardy and will appeal to arrangers.

SPRING STAR-FLOWER (*Ipheion uniflorum*—Illustration 22) has had its name changed so often as to be ridiculous, and you probably will find it listed as *Tritelia* or *Milla uniflora*. Nonetheless it is a lovely South American bulb for your garden. Here we grow it beneath a protective covering of *Dianthus arenarius*, whose emerald foliage sets it off beautifully. The single whitish-blue stars are about the size of a quarter and 6 inches high.

¶ Set tritelia in early fall 4 inches apart and 3 inches deep in a sunny place.

North of Philadelphia it probably needs a winter mulch. In kinder climates these bulbs are reputed to increase too rapidly, but mine have multiplied only moderately in six seasons, and I do not expect to disturb them for many years yet. The flowers have a pleasant minty odor, but the bruised foliage is pure onion. The leaves are never bothersome, so plant in the foreground. A large planting will last nearly a month in bloom during April and May and makes a fine accompaniment for late daffodils, early tulips, candytuft and primroses. I prefer the true type, but the variety, *violacea*, is somewhat more bluish.

Sometimes you will find tritelia listed under BRODIAEA to which it is closely related. These latter are sometimes called CALIFORNIA HYACINTHS, and are native to the West but most capricious in other gardens. Usually offered in mixture only, they should be set 4 inches deep and have a chance only in the sunny, well-drained, rock garden. If you get them to survive, you will have an unusual flower which somewhat resembles an allium.

SPRING CYCLAMEN (*C. repandum*) is the despair of many gardeners, but where it will grow it is so beautiful I intend to keep trying until I succeed. If you are lucky, tiny rosy-red flowers, just like the florist's cyclamen in shape, will rise above small, low, silver-marked foliage in April or May.

¶ The corms of hardy cyclamen are planted in early fall with their tops just beneath the surface of the soil in a moist, half-shaded location.

The tubers may lie dormant a whole season and must never be disturbed, since they enlarge and improve with age and live forever if satisfied. So mark the site well and try to be patient. The reward is worth waiting for. Most authorities think a little bonemeal and topdressing of leafmold in fall is beneficial; some suggest lime in the soil. The bigger the tuber the better, but most offered commercially are quite small. Plant them 3 to 6 inches apart anyway in the hope they will eventually prosper.

Other hardy cyclamen which bloom even earlier (February-March) include the *Atkinsi* types which also have marbled foliage and the *Coum* strains with leaves of plain, dark green. Both are similarly treated. Shades of white, red and pink are offered in both strains. Where winters are severe, they need some winter protection and are not reliable in our coldest regions.

HARDY CHINESE ORCHIDS (*Bletilla*) have tuber-like bulbs and yield small, cattleya-like flowers on 10- to 20-inch stems in late spring. Both lavender and white forms are offered, and they form loose clumps in areas where they are hardy. I doubt they will succeed where long, hard freezes are the rule.

¶ Plant bletilla in the fall about 4 inches deep in moist, humus-rich soil and half-shade.

At Philadelphia these unusual terrestrial orchids are hardy enough to spread in a protected location, but mine have been chary of bloom. I suspect they need more sun than I gave them, close to four hours at least a day.

DOGTOOTH VIOLETS (*Erythroniums*) are one of the best native bulbs for moist, partially shaded places, but most produce far more leaves than flowers. In spring they bear dainty, pendant lily-like flowers in shades of white, yellow, pink or lavender on 6- to 12-inch stems. Many have mottled leaves.

¶ Most erythroniums come from the West and are planted as early in fall as possible, 2 to 3 inches deep and about 4 inches apart in woodsy soil.

In the East you are most likely to succeed with them if you have a spot which already supports wild yellow types. The small bulbs do resemble canine teeth. They are also called trout or fawn lilies and once planted should be left undisturbed. Some suggest placing a rock beneath each bulb to discourage wandering; the technique has not helped mine to flower. Catalogs of western bulb dealers are the best sources of the various species. The western types are the most likely to flower well and need less moisture than eastern species. The best bet is a spot which remains damp in summer and has high shade but is never water-logged in winter.

Here the eastern trout lilies grow with SPRING BEAUTIES (*Claytonia*), another native flower which is often classified as a bulb. Both the narrow-leaved variety (*C. virginica*) and the broad-leaved (*C. caroliniana*) bear dainty blush-white flowers in early spring. Their fragrance is so strong you can detect a colony quite far off when walking in the woods. The small tubers are sometimes called "fairy spuds" and reputed to have a chestnut flavor when cooked.

¶ In the wild the tubers are often very deep, but most authorities suggest 2 to 4 inches in moist, humus-rich gardens with lightest shade.

In slightly dryer spots where the soil contains plenty of humus and there is light shade after the deciduous trees leaf, you will be delighted with several other wild flowers which are more or less bulbous. JACK-IN-THE-PULPITS (*Arisaema*) vary from 12 to 48 inches high and produce brilliant red fall berries in addition to the curious hooded spathe of spring. Avoid undue handling of the bulbs and wash skin well afterwards since they contain a powerful irritant. Plant them 5 to 6 inches deep. WAKE ROBINS (*Trilliums*, Illustration 4) have white, pink, or red flowers which may be borne from 2 to 20 inches high. The easiest to introduce into gardens is *T. grandiflorum*, which has large white blooms gradually flushing pink. Plant the tubers about 2 to 4 inches deep with the bud uppermost. SOLOMON-SEAL (*Polygonatum*) with its almost hidden drooping bells and blue fall berries and FALSE SOLOMON-SEAL (*Smilacina*) with its terminal cluster of white flowers and red berries do well in much drier situations, but still prefer leafmold in the soil and semi-shade. Their rootstocks creep and go about 2 inches deep. Both have fine foliage for woodland gardens. Leave all wild flowers undisturbed indefinitely.

INDIAN LILIES (*Camassia*, Illustration 5) are one of my favorite mid-spring flowers. Small blue or white stars begin opening at the bottom of a spire which often reaches nearly 3 feet above lush green mounds of foliage during tulip time. They like a rich, moist soil in partial shade, but will sometimes do well in full sun.

4. Red and white trilliums, violets, ferns and mertensia cluster around a rock in a woodland garden (Roche).

5. In partial shade and deep, moist soil the native American camassia opens ethereal stars of white or blue during May. Author's garden.

¶ Plant camassia 4 to 5 inches deep and at least 10 inches apart.

Often camassia bloom declines after a season or two. Try a good feeding of dried cow manure at flowering time and never let them lack for moisture during and for a while after flowering. We have never mulched them, and I doubt they need it, since most are native to parts of the West where the weather is far from kind. The Indians relished the bulbs as food.

My preference is *C. leichtlini* with light blue flowers. It has a beautiful white form, and a few gardeners report a double white which must be quite out of this world. Others not too hard to find: *C. esculenta*, 1½ feet high, dark blue-purple; *C. cusicki*, 2 to 4 feet, lavender blue. In the wild, much variation between blue and white is common. In my garden the bulbs multiply rapidly, but unless well fed, bloom then falls off.

LILY OF THE ALTAI (*Ixiolirion*) should be in the garden of everyone who loves graceful bouquets of spring flowers. It comes into bloom just after the tulips and is lovely with pinks. The buds emerge very early, so north of Washington, D.C., give a winter mulch of several inches of straw or evergreen branches and a protected location.

¶ Plant ixiolirion 3 inches deep in sun no farther apart than 4 inches since the foliage is slim.

True-blue in sunshine, *I. pallassi* (*tataricum*) has a lavender cast in shade or indoors. Each bulb produces several loose racemes with two to six flowers resembling a hyacinth floret in both size and shape. They are faintly fragrant and nearly 18 inches high, but they are floppy, so front with a sturdier plant to keep them more erect. The variety *I. ledebouri* is lighter in color and earlier.

ALLIUMS get mixed notices from gardeners, partly because there is such diversity among the species. Some such as *A. tuberosum* and *A. racemosum* (*A. odorum*) are too weedy. One (*A. giganteum*) is a monstrous thing 5 to 8 feet tall with a purple umbel, often 9 inches across, that I cannot imagine having a place in any garden. Some of the others are darlings, especially for rock gardens. Flower arrangers are very keen on alliums.

¶ Alliums demand no special soil, and most of them are planted 2 to 3 inches deep and 3 to 4 inches apart.

One of the prettiest (*A. schoenoprasum*) is the least likely to be given garden room because as common chives it was long ago relegated to the kitchen garden. It regularly yields dozens of silvery pink-lavender balls in late May or early June. The foliage is used for salads and soups, but the immature flowers are mildly oniony too and pretty as a garnish. Remove flowers, stems and all, as soon as they begin to get scraggly, and the foliage will be useful until early winter. A few plants are delightful wherever they will not overrun daintier things. As clumps spread, chop out what you do not need, and they will remain healthy for generations.

Several other alliums are fine solely for decorative purposes, and none spreads so rampantly. In half shade *A. moly* (Illustration 6) makes a spot of bright yellow about the time the garden is full of many blues and the pink of dianthus. It bears loose flat umbels several inches wide and about a foot high and has wider foliage than most varieties.

Hardly half that high is *A. ostrowskianum* with similar

6. Most of the varied alliums want sun, but *Allium moly* tolerates a little shade for its golden umbels. Author's garden.

umbels in pink rose. It prefers almost full sun and flowers just before its yellow sister. Early June here at Philadelphia finds A. *azureum* at its peak. The globular 2-inch heads are borne on 12- to 15-inch stems and consist of myriads of starry blue flowers in a loose cluster. The foliage is stringy and needs to be hidden behind some other plant. The broad, flat leaves of A. *karataviense* have a metallic sheen. The lilac, globular heads seldom exceed 10 inches in height.

Although not reliably hardy in the north, A. *neapolitanum* has graceful heads of white flowers about 15 inches high, and I intend to try it here in a sheltered place. If the genus intrigues you, there are many other alliums in the catalogs of specialists.

ST. BERNARD'S LILY (*Anthericum liliago*) is a little-known fibrous-rooted member of the lily family native to the European Alps. We grow it here at Philadelphia without a winter mulch, but in the South it is reputed to have trouble surviving summer heat. So we mulch its root run with peatmoss as we do lilies. It bears a short, erect loose raceme of white star-shaped flowers about 18 inches high.

¶ Plant anthericum in close groups during early fall with the roots growing vertically and the pip just beneath the surface.

Its main use is to fill in during early June when the spring-blooming plants are through and there is a lull in flowers. It is lost, however, unless planted in quantity. Here it flowers in company with the hardy gladiolus with which it is lovely, serving to face them to the ground. A related species (A. *ramosum*) has branched racemes.

ST. BRUNO'S LILY (*Paradisea liliastrum*) is considered even lovelier. It is sometimes listed as A. *liliastrum* and has fragrant white lily-like flowers in 2-foot racemes. It is an alpine which has trouble surviving hot summers.

¶ Try a cool location and mulch the root run.

DUTCH IRIS look more like orchids than iris and come in rich combinations and self-colors ranging from white through yellows and oranges, with some fine blues and purples. Truly handsome, they should be far better known. They last well as cut flowers and grow 2 to 3 feet tall. Give Dutch iris full sun and soil that remains dry through the summer.

¶ Plant in early fall 3 to 4 inches deep and 4 inches apart.

Botanists divide these bulbous iris into several categories, and they are sometimes offered in catalogs as English, Spanish, and Dutch iris, each in a separate section. I feel the Dutch hybrids are the best selection for most American climates, and they come in a wide range of color. Theoretically, there is a slight variation in bloom time between the several types. The Dutch hybrids are the hardiest and sturdiest.

Mine have weathered every kind of winter for years with no protection except accidental garden litter and have slowly increased. They make some fall foliage, so it is easy to find them and to mulch where winters are colder than here.

Sometimes the blossoms are attacked by a small worm, but I liquidate the culprit by hand at the first sign of wilting in the bud. Otherwise he will eat his way down the stalk. Such borers are found on many iris relatives.

These iris are so fine for cutting they are worth growing in a special row if your border is too small to accommodate them. They bloom just after the tall bearded iris and may be planted behind them so the iris fans hide the ripening Dutch iris foliage. Phlox, perennial flax and Shasta daisies are also excellent for screening since their foliage is just high enough at the time the Dutch iris blooms to conceal their somewhat un-

7. Dutch iris last a long time when cut and are available in a range of colors. In the garden plant clumps or drifts of one color for greatest effect (Roche).

tidy stems. As the perennials develop, they hide the maturing iris completely.

HARDY GLADIOLUS really do exist. With a winter mulch of evergreen branches they survived a dreadful Philadelphia winter without trouble. Blooming in early June, they simply electrify garden clubs! They look just like any other gladiolus, but the spikes are shorter, looser and bear smaller flowers which are perfectly grand for arrangements and bouquets.

¶ Plant hardy glads in the fall 3 to 4 inches deep and 4 inches apart in clumps.

In the South the *Nanus* and *Colvillei* varieties do well and are offered in several colors. Here we stay with the hardier sorts: *G. byzantinus rubra,* scarlet; *G. alba,* pure white; *G. segetum,* carmine pink; and *G. communis,* a bright rose with reddish throat markings. The last reaches almost 3 feet; the others are shorter. Mine are overplanted with *Dianthus arenarius,* which makes a thick protective mat in winter and blooms with the gladiolus for a pretty picture.

When ordering, look for the headings "Winter-hardy," "Early-flowering" or "Baby" gladiolus. The so-called "Miniatures" are summer-flowering gladiolus, to be treated exactly as you would the ordinary summer kinds.

BUTTERFLY OR MARIPOSA TULIPS (*Calochortus*) are another group of bulbs from the West which break the hearts of gardeners in other sections. Curiously marked and colored in great variety, they are seldom cataloged except in mixture and are far from dependable, but what a thrill when one does blossom! I had three lavender cups last June, and made more fuss about them than they were worth!

¶ Pick a sunny, well-drained site where they will be able to bake in summer and plant calochortus 3 inches deep and a few inches apart this fall.

Veteran gardeners advised me to mulch them well to prevent winter heaving. Their shoots appeared in February. Eventually the slender, insignificant branching foliage reached higher than 2 feet, so it needs some sturdier plant in front for support.

If you can find a supplier, the related STAR TULIPS or CAT'S EARS are more dependable outside their normal range. These are lower-growing, demand sunny, dry situations, and, like the mariposas, have tiny hairs inside their cups. Pictures of their cousins the FAIRY LANTERNS or GLOBE TULIPS, also native to our West, leave me breathless with their beauty. These are reputed to need a lightly-shaded western slope and a well-drained but rich soil. Some day I shall grow one, and there will be no coming near me if I succeed.

WINDFLOWERS (*Anemones*) we met in the last chapter but those were hardier than those now introduced: *A. coronaria* and *A. fulgens*. North of Washington, D.C., only fall planting in a cold frame is recommended for the first group. My neighbor managed to winter some over in a sheltered spot here at Philadelphia, but they failed to flower. In a sheltered spot and mulched a bit *A. fulgens* will survive even as far north as New York City.

¶ In the frame or in the ground use soil with plenty of humus and plant anemone tubers 2 to 3 inches deep and 7 to 8 inches apart.

They do not like acid soil and sometimes benefit from an occasional light dose of lime.

The various hybrids of *A. coronaria* (St. Brigid and De Caen strains) are often called POPPY ANEMONES and produce both single and semi-double blooms in many brilliant colors as well as white. They do best in the Pacific Northwest, where there is a temperate, moist climate. If you live too far north to winter them over, you can plant them each year in early spring, but I have found bloom sporadic with this treatment, probably because it gets suddenly too hot here. The tubers should be soaked in a shallow saucer of water for forty-eight hours and then planted in humus-rich soil where there is some shade. Storing them each winter is possible, but they must remain absolutely dry.

Known as the scarlet windflower of the Pyrenees, A. *fulgens* has both a single and double form and brilliant red, daisy-like flowers on stems about 8 to 10 inches high.

8. Ranunculus are not reliably hardy in the north, but they are spectacular where the climate is mild, also excellent for cutting. These are the El Rancho Strain (Courtesy Brown Bulb Ranch).

Two hardier anemones will tolerate a good deal of shade, but both are spreaders and should be kept from areas where they might make trouble. White summer flowers distinguish A. *canadensis*, while A. *sylvestris* produces white flowers in spring and may give some repeat bloom. The famous Pasque flower (A. *pulsatilla*) gives big purple chalice-like flowers on 9-inch stems, needs sun for half the day and has proven hardy in most rock gardens since dry soil is to its liking. Its foliage is ferny, and the fluffy seed plumes are decorative on their own.

RANUNCULUS, which resemble overgrown buttercups, are treated like poppy anemones, of which they are the double form. They are not reliable in the North.

CAPSULE VIEW OF THE SECOND WAVE

These bulbs vary considerably in value, color, form, height, manner of growth and flowering time, but all blossom at Philadelphia before the end of June.

They are hardy here with duly noted reservations. Farther north they bloom later and may require more protection both as to winter mulch and protected site.

Make haste slowly in trying these bulbs by planting them in small quantities until you decide which appeal most. Label well until you learn what to look for; I surround very special new bulbs with a circle of small stones to prod my memory until I know how and when they grow.

A great deal of fun awaits you among these bulbs and probably some surprises too. A few will become fast friends the first time you see them flower.

CHAPTER 5

Tulips Have Many Forms

In kindergarten I had one artistic triumph. I could draw a lovely tulip—a fat goblet topped with jagged teeth to represent the petals and bracketed with two wide, pointed leaves. All children and most adults recognized it immediately as a tulip!

More knowledgeable about the genus at this later date, I can assure you that the goblet or egg-shaped tulips exemplified by neat clumps of Darwins, cottage, or breeder types are only the beginning of the story. There are others which look more like lilies, peonies, stars or water lilies. One class gives the appearance of a whole bouquet from a single stem, another has lasciniated or convoluted petals, and there is even a group of weird tulips for those who adore the sick, sick, sick! The greatest differences occur among the species tulips of the next chapter, but variation abounds too among the garden hybrids.

If you are not acquainted with these other tulips, the last part of this chapter summarizes them to help you choose those which will do most for your garden. While many of these "different" tulips are not new, gardeners are just beginning to recognize their wonderful possibilities, and hybridizers have recently been able to cross several types of tulips with exciting results. It is safe to predict even more amazing introductions will be available soon.

These differences in growth habit and flower shape fire the

imagination of the flower arranger and the gardener who tries for something more than mere swathes of color in his garden. In selecting your tulips however, remember they are equally important in a garden for the almost complete spectrum of hues among the various types. The dark purple-reds are nearly black, there are good browns, pure whites and a few which come close to being green. Only a true blue tulip is missing, but there exists every shade of violet, purple and lavender. Spring abounds in other clear blue blossoms which act as marvelous foils for tulip plantings so this absence is no ground for complaint. There is a tulip to add almost any other tint to your spring garden. (Tulips particularly useful for arrangers are listed in Chapter 20.)

The Turks Get Credit

The history of tulips is clouded. Little trace has yet turned up among the treasures of antiquity. There is one small representation on a Cretan vase estimated to be 3,500 to 4,000 years old. No less an authority than the original excavator of ancient Nineveh, Sir Austen Layard, speaks cryptically of bands of tulip designs as typical of Assyrian art, but his books are more than a century old, and the wonders he unearthed are in the British Museum, out of my reach. The bright scarlet tulips of Kurdistan, which he mentions as the earliest flower of spring in that part of the world and which he suggests may have inspired the designs, are undoubtedly one of the species discussed in the next chapter.

Perhaps the little species tulips were too common on the springtime hills to inspire monumental art, but whenever I see a wine goblet, I wonder if the shape was not suggested ages ago by a graceful tulip swaying on some sun-washed slope of Mesopotamia. Botanists believe the tulip originated some-

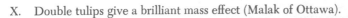

IX. Lily tulips are graceful and come in many colors. Here a yellow combines with a fringed or crystal tulip (The Skipper) in author's garden.

X. Double tulips give a brilliant mass effect (Malak of Ottawa).

XI.   Mid-Century hybrid lilies, derived from crosses between the tiger
      lily and upright-flowering types, do well in any sunny, well-drained
      garden. Shown here: Harmony, orange; Enchantment, orange-red;
      Cinnabar, red; and Prosperity, lemon-yellow (Herman v. Wall).

XII. Canna Eureka's creamy heads are most welcome in summer's heat. They continue until frost, and the clean, green foliage makes a striking accent plant. Author's garden. (Doris E. Price).

XIII. Few bulbs give more color over a longer period than the varied dahlias. Here a corner is lighted by assorted types. Note how unobtrusively stakes are placed. Smaller dahlias need no support (Genereux).

XIV-XIX. Above, left: Waterlily, a double colchicum, with annual alyssum. Right: *Colchicum autumnale minor* and its white form with common thyme. Center, left: *Crocus speciosus albus* with *Dianthus arenarius*. Right: *Sternbergia lutea*. Below, left: *Crocus speciosus globulosus* and hardy dianthus foliage. Right: *Crocus medius*. Author's garden.

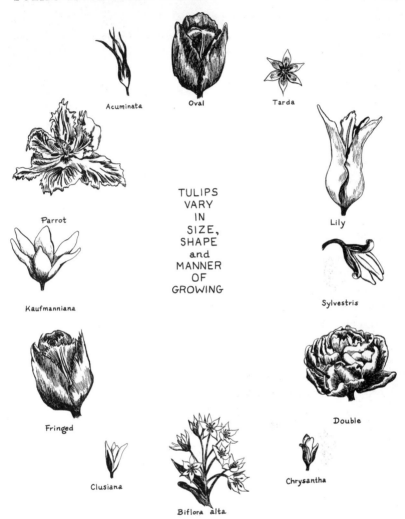

Acuminata

Oval

Tarda

Parrot

TULIPS
VARY
IN
SIZE,
SHAPE
and
MANNER
OF
GROWING

Lily

Kaufmanniana

Sylvestris

Fringed

Double

Clusiana

Chrysantha

Biflora alta

FIG. 7. A tulip bears many kinds of flowers, from the tiny clustered stars of *Tulipa biflora alta* and *T. turkestanica* to the large, oval-shaped Darwins. The species *T. chrysantha,* has the smallest flowers, while the new Darwin hybrids, the doubles, and the lily-flowered tulips are among the largest.

where near the headwaters of the Tigris and the Euphrates rivers, where civilization similar to our own is first recorded.

We are able to credit the immediate ancestors of today's tulips to the Turks, whose sultans doted upon the flowers, organized elaborate tulip festivals, and honored those who grew a new variety. Many of the old palaces in Istanbul were decorated with tulip figures, as are the Eyup Sultan Mosque and the famous Blue Mosque, and tulip tiles have long been a popular art form.

Today the tulip is still venerated in Turkey and the form often appears in designs, especially embroidery. The Turkish painter, Bedri Rahmi Eyuboglu, uses it extensively in his work. In eastern Turkey toward the Russian border the wild tulips bloom in early spring, but in the western area they appear in November and December.

During the eighteenth and nineteenth centuries more than 300 varieties were grown by Turkish gardeners. How long they had been hybridizing is a matter of conjecture, but we do know that Busbecq, an Austrian diplomat, brought back seeds and probably some bulbs too in 1554 when he returned to Vienna from his post in Turkey. Lalé is the Persian and Turkish word for tulip so possibly Busbecq misunderstood his interpreter since the Turkish equivalent of turban (dulban) is the source of his "tulipam." Certainly the flowers do resemble the colorful Turkish headwear.

Tulips became a sensation in Europe. Clusius, a professor of botany at Leyden, Holland, was the first Dutchman to do serious work with the genus although it is reported he charged such outrageous prices for bulbs that thieves finally ruined his garden. By the time of his death in 1609 tulips were firmly established in the land where they are now a national symbol. They reached England about 1578 and were mentioned by

Gerard in his *Herball* (1597). Before Charles I lost his royal head to the Puritans, his gardener is reputed to have grown fifty varieties in his garden.

Madness in Holland

Some measure of the fervor with which Holland adopted the tulip is gained by looking backward at a phenomenon aptly termed tulipomania, a period from about 1634 to 1637 when virtually the entire country gambled on futures in tulips. No doubt the times were ripe for such madness to take hold of a normally intelligent people, but the tulip itself must share some of the blame.

It is a peculiar fact that self-colored garden tulips will "break" into variegated striped, flamed and feathered colors when they are infected with a non-fatal virus known as mosaic. Offsets of a broken bulb will show the same odd markings and colors although seedlings are again self-colored. The seventeenth century burghers were not aware of the existence of any virus. Each tulip which bloomed for the first time after being inadvertantly infected was welcomed as a freak of nature. The more unique the marking, the more sought-after the bulb and its progeny.

America, which has fallen prey to Florida land booms and marginal-buying sprees on Wall Street, should easily understand the craze. Everyone began plunging on bulbs in the hope one of the "bizarres" would appear in his backyard. Normal life was practically suspended during the height of the speculation, and fantastic prices were paid for a single bulb which remained in the hands of a dealer while being traded back and forth. The New York office of the Associated Bulb Growers of Holland quotes the following record of the price of one bulb:

"A load of grain, 4 oxen, 12 sheep, 5 pigs, 2 tubs of butter, 1000 pounds of cheese, 4 barrels of beer, 2 hogsheads of wine, a suit of clothes and a silver drinking cup." I doubt that the owners of a half-submerged marsh on the Florida coast ever did any better!

Eventually, the bubble burst, and the courts of Holland were flooded with suits and countersuits as everyone tried to sell. There is no record of speculators jumping from windows, but the story is told of a Leyden botany professor who so lost his scientific objectivity that he struck with his cane at every tulip he saw. We can be thankful the rest of his countrymen did not take vengeance on a beautiful flower for their own foolishness. The myriad forms of tulips which decorate our gardens are almost all the product of Dutch patience and know-how in growing and hybridizing.

Today's Tulips

Tulips have come a long way since the days of the Sultans. May-flowering DARWINS, the most popular today, are among the more recent introductions. They were first offered for sale at Haarlem in 1889 by Krelage & Son. The mid-season MENDEL and TRIUMPH types date only from after World War I, and the immense, striking DARWIN HYBRIDS resulting from crosses with species tulips did not appear in our catalogs until some years after World War II. The flamboyant Red Emperor, seen from one end of America to the other, won its first award in 1931 but was not in general supply until after the war.

The species hybrids are the tulip stars of the future. Watch your catalogs for new marvels. There is some reason to wonder at the gap of hundreds of years between the first interest in tulips as garden subjects and the collection of new species during the past century in places already combed once by botanists. One might speculate that God had beaten the hybridizers at their own game by recrossing the species with garden escapes! At any rate the breeders are now hard at work in this direction.

The first of the strangely colored and twisted PARROT tulips was introduced before 1690 although modern varieties bear larger flowers on taller stems. All are sports of other tulips which appeared through no one's work but nature's and were immediately seized upon by the breeders as something different. Many new ones have been introduced, but they are best reserved for the flower arrangers, because they do not adapt themselves well to garden use except as an accent plant. For such effects plant them *only* in clumps of one variety; even so, they are quite weird. The prettier FRINGED tulips are a subclass of the parrots and much better for the garden. The so-called GREEN tulips set arrangers agog, but they do not show up well in the garden. All three are short-lived here.

There have been DOUBLE tulips, early and late, for many years although they have never been as widely-used as they deserve. Being sterile like most double flowers, they last longer in bloom, but they must have some protection against heavy rain, which will beat them down due to the weight of the peony-like blossoms. Since the doubles will tolerate some shade, they can be used under the outer fringes of deciduous trees where the sun's rays still penetrate but where branches give some protection. I have deep-planted late white Mt. Tacoma in such a position, and the bulbs have multiplied and continued blooming for years.

For gardens and for picking, my own favorite is the LILY tulip which is now of increasing interest among western

9. Bouquet tulips produce five to eleven flowers on a branched stem from a single bulb (Courtesy George W. Park Seed Co.).

gardeners; the old Turks much preferred its pointed and reflexed petal-shape to the oval type which was the past criterion of hybridizers in Holland and England.

Even more outstanding for providing masses of color in the garden are the BOUQUET tulips. These produce as many as ten flowers on a branching stem from one bulb. The top ones are as large as many Darwins, with the side branches yielding smaller blooms, so each bulb is a complete plant in itself—graceful and needing no facer to tie it intimately to the earth. These bulbs should be planted about 8 inches apart and as deep as you dare in your soil, even to 12 inches, since the bouquet tendency is lost when the bulbs split. The largest bulbs of a planting will regain the bouquet habit if dug and replanted. No other tulip I have ever grown gives as much beauty as these during their first season: a dozen bulbs create a burst of color, looking like living fountains.

This multiflora class of tulips is a good example of how fashions in flowers change. The first of these branching tulips were sports of early Darwins, and the development of them is credited to Nicholaas Dames, a Dutch grower who introduced several varieties at the turn of the century. They appeared in and out of catalogs for many years without ever causing much notice. Then, shortly after World War II, the Dutch bulb firm of J. J. Grullemans & Sons began introducing new varieties. Interest in this class of tulips grew steadily among modern gardeners who like lots of color but have neither time nor money for mass bedding. Yet many large bulb houses had discarded the bouquets years ago as unwanted novelties.

Now multiflora tulips are reappearing in the catalogs, as more and more gardeners become enamored of a tulip which grows in bouquets instead of singly. I have tried a good many of them, and I am convinced the secret of success is deep planting, but none is ever quite so good after the first wonderful year. I have also found the oldest varieties are the most dependable. Wallflower, which is a hybrid developed by Mynheer Dames himself, Monsieur S. Mottet (Ivory Towers), Madame Mottet (Lovely Lady), and Rosemist are the easiest to find. With Georgette (Pink Lemonade) these are also the best of the class to date, and it is regrettable the salesmen should confuse us by changing names.

More than a dozen new named bouquet tulips are in existence, sure sign that our interest has stimulated the growers to experiment with this type. In comparison with older forms mentioned previously, the new ones are somewhat disappointing. I heartily recommend those named above, however, and expect further introductions will be improved.

CULTURAL DETAILS

How Deep to Plant?

Each year I plant my tulips a little deeper, and each year I am happier about how they react. Last fall two identical plantings went in 9 and 11 inches deep in the same bed, and the latter showed shoots first! Only trial can tell you for sure how deep to plant them in your soil. Most veteran gardeners who are planting tulips where they hope to keep them as long as possible settle for 10–12 inches of soil above the bulb in good, well-drained loam. In clay soil a few inches less is probably wise, although my 11-inch planting was in such a mixture.

One gardener tells me of tulips still blooming after 20 years without resetting, although they produce smaller blossoms now. Deeply set tulips tend to retain their form and size much longer, since such treatment retards splitting. Bouquet tulips deeply set have retained their branching habit here for four seasons without transplanting.

In exhibition beds, where you dig up the tulips each season, plant them only about 6 or 7 inches deep. In moist places they will rot if set too deeply, but trial and error will tell you how deep the water level under your garden will allow you to go. Bulbs should never be planted in low-lying spots anyway. For all tulips except the species, always order new bulbs for exhibition purposes to get the very biggest and best flowers. In the case of Red Emperor and large species hybrids where size is of consequence for competition, new bulbs are also mandatory.

Food, Water and Planting

All tulips look their best when planted in clumps of one type and color. Such treatment yields much more for less if your budget is strained. Two groups, each with six bulbs of the same tulip, will often paint a more effective garden picture than dozens of mixed tulips. By choosing representatives from several seasonal groups (in colors that go with your personality and garden), you will be enjoying them over a much longer length of time than you ever dreamed possible if you have up to now grown only Darwins. The first species tulip here opened in March last year, and the last Darwin was still lovely at the end of May!

Usually bulbs planted the preceding fall will blossom a bit later their first spring than in subsequent years, so by adding a new group each year you can stretch the bloom period even more. Tulips may be planted quite late in the fall without harm (with the exception of the species which need early setting), even into December if the ground is not frozen. This is handy for busy gardeners who use early autumn for planting little bulbs and daffodils which demand such treatment. Never plant tulips early if fall is likely to be warm in your climate; southern gardeners can buy pre-cooled bulbs or place opened packages of tulips in the bottom of the home refrigerator for a month before planting. For best results, treat tulips as annuals in warm climates and choose from the later-blooming groups.

A teaspoon of bonemeal mixed into the soil below the bulb (not directly around it) is a good idea. The same amount per bulb is a good tonic to mix lightly into the soil above tulip shoots before they blossom. It will work its way down to feed the bulb in future seasons.

In winter and early spring tulips usually get enough moisture naturally, but to flower their best they need additional watering after the buds show if the weather is dry. If the same drought conditions persist, give them more water while the foliage is maturing. Many gardeners neglect them during this period. During their dormant summer period they thrive on being kept as dry as possible, but with the return of cold weather, they again need an occasional drink to stimulate root production if the season is too dry.

Broken Tulips and Aphids

"Never plant new ones where tulips have been growing any time during the past three years," was an old garden maxim. It is still good advice, for such precaution means tulips will not go into soil depleted of the nutrients they need. This practice also helps prevent the spread of virus and tulip fire (Botrytis). (See Chapter 22 for more on this.) Aphids are the chief disease carriers so get after them early.

I would never put "broken" tulips into my garden, lovely as they are. A few in which the pattern of different colors in the flower is determined genetically (Cordell Hull, American Flag) are safe. The others are infected with the same virus which triggered tulipomania. While this is not fatal to some varieties (Zomershoon is still cultivated, although it has been infected for more than three centuries), other tulips may degenerate quickly once they contract the disease, and lilies may also succumb to this virus.

In climates where aphids appear early in the season in quantity, the virus may spread abundantly, according to the Bulb Research Laboratory in Lisse, Holland, which is supported by the Dutch bulb industry. They warn us to maintain a good distance between virus-infected tulips and others. Many American pathologists suggest keeping them out altogether. They are most grown for flower arrangements in the manner of the Old Dutch Masters.

After Care

We have already emphasized how important the formation of good foliage is in replacing annually the food a bulb needs to produce flowers in a subsequent season. In the tulip, which matures its leaves far quicker than the narcissus, for example, you must not remove any of the basal leaves when cutting flowers, and it is better not even to cut stems so long that the secondary leaves are sacrificed. If you need long stemmed tulips for cutting, raise them new each year in special rows rather than deplete your garden scheme. Short stems of course can be picked anywhere. Remove all withered flowers and never allow tulips to set seed.

Because their leaves disappear relatively soon, it is easier to put up with maturing tulips than with some other bulbs. You can avoid even temporary untidiness by hiding them behind burgeoning clumps of perennials like peonies, iris, phlox, chrysanthemums or Shasta daisies. One of my favorite screens is the little-known perennial, *Amsonia tabernaemontana*, whose clusters of pale blue stars contrast beautifully with most tulip tints (Color Plate VIII). Its luxuriant foliage grows quickly to between 2 and 3 feet. Low annuals like pansies, alyssum and forget-me-nots are often interplanted with tulips; while they look lovely in bloom together, the annuals are not big enough to take the curse off the browning tulips. Leave enough room between tulips and screening perennials to allow free passage of air and sunlight through the bulb foliage.

SO MANY KINDS

Investigating the extended tulip section of a big bulb catalog can overwhelm the beginning gardener unless he has some idea what to look for. Most bulbmen list tulips by type

10. Early tulips are massed in beds in the Keukenhof gardens maintained at Lisse in Holland by the Dutch bulb industry. Here for three months each spring visitors can see a display of millions of spring flowers in both formal and informal plantings (Malak of Ottawa).

and season, including height and color for each entry. A few even subdivide each class by color, and most indicate those varieties best for forcing. Plan what you want and need on paper, then scan the catalogs for what is available in your price range. The least expensive varieties are usually vigorous growers (when you are buying from a reputable dealer), but they may also be older varieties; this is not necessarily bad either. Briefly (with examples of each in parentheses) we can summarize the tulips thus in approximate order of bloom:

Early

SPECIES—Emperor and water lily types etc. (Chapter 6).

EARLY SINGLES—forcing; short stems, long-lasting flowers for foreground of garden (Keizerskroon, Pink Beauty, De Wet).

EARLY DOUBLES (PEONY-FLOWERED)—forcing; short stems, very long-lasting flowers make masses of color in quantity in foreground (Maréchal Niel, Peach Blossom, Schoonoord).

Mid-Season

MENDEL—forcing; lovely colors (Orange Wonder, Her Grace, Apricot Beauty).

TRIUMPH—wide color range; many have taller stems than Mendels; these two classes are most important to bridge the season between early and late varieties (Blizzard, Red Matador, Sunmaid).

DARWIN HYBRIDS—a new race no garden should miss (Chapter 6).

May-Flowering

DARWINS—most popular tulip; self-colors and bicolors, many fine pastels; long stems, globular blossoms (Glacier, Charles Needham, Aristocrat).

BREEDERS—often tinted with second color, includes browns, gold, bronze and purples; tall, stiff stems, cup-shaped flowers (Chappaqua, Southern Cross, Indian Chief).

COTTAGE—brilliant colors, many flushed with another shade; flower cups often more open, petals may be pointed, tall stems (Rosy Wings, Mrs. John T. Scheepers, Carrara).

LILY-FLOWERING—reflexed and pointed petals make this form of cottage tulip the most graceful; long lasting on tall stems (Mariette, White Triumphator, West Point).

PARROT—heavily laciniated, twisted petals, many bicolored or partly green; shorter stems; better for arranging than garden decoration; several hundred years ago one writer termed them "monsters," but in the modern vernacular they are "sick" (Fantasy, Faraday, Blue Parrot).

FRINGED (CRYSTAL, BEARDED)—regular, cup-shaped flowers with lacey petal edges; heights vary even within same variety, but lovely for garden use if clumped by one color (Sundew, The Skipper, Gemma).

BOUQUET—multiflowered; as many as ten blooms on a branching stem but averaging five; few tulips can compete with these their first spring for mass color and accent, but branching habit retained only by deep-planted bulbs; some varieties open one shade and end up suffused another; also known as MULTIFLORA, CANDELABRA, BRANCHING, BUNCH-FLOWERED or TREE tulips (Rosemist, Georgette, Wall-flower).

LATE DOUBLES—long lasting on taller stems than early doubles; give partial shade; many hues, some bicolors (Eros, Mt. Tacoma, Uncle Tom).

BROKEN TULIPS—feathered and flamed survivors of the virus-infected tulips which drove Holland wild 300 years ago; usually listed as REMBRANDTS, striped and flaked red and white; BIZARRES, yellow ground with streaking of red to brown; BYBLOEMENS, white ground with lilac, rose or purple markings; may bring virus to your garden.

CAPSULE VIEW OF TULIPS

By judicious choice of various types including species, you may have bloom for nearly three months.

Every color and hue except true blue, many bicolored or edged with second tint; plant in clumps of one color.

Flower forms diverse: blooms may be oval, reflexed, globular or double; stems may be short, tall or branched; petals may be round, pointed, twisted, convoluted or laciniated.

Give sunny site where water never stands in soil.

Plant in late fall 6 to 7 inches deep for exhibition beds where they are to be dug up annually; for long-time garden growing set as deep as you dare in your soil: this may be as much as 12 inches in well-drained loam.

CHAPTER 6

Species Tulips Are Different

Generalizations are impossible in the world of the species tulips. Here are bulbs for the gardener who seeks something unusual and likes to experiment. Only a few of the biggest bulb houses offer extensive lists of the species tulips. Those who trouble to hunt up sources for them will find a new realm of infinite variation in size, hue, height and beauty. Most of the species bloom in March and April when the weather stays cooler and so yield color over a satisfyingly long period.

Ancestors of our garden tulips, the species need early fall planting in clumps about 6 inches deep and in places where they will not be disturbed.

Most of them require full sun and do best where they get only minimum moisture during the summer months and where the soil is thin and rocky like that of their homelands in mountainous areas of the Mediterranean and Asia Minor. Treated thus, many will become much more permanent garden inhabitants than their better-known cousins. All but a few are small and dainty, perfect for the rock garden, and the majority bloom before and during the daffodil season when the big garden tulips are still just pushing their buds toward the wayward spring sunshine. Most species are still so little-planted in American gardens they are sure to arouse interest and exclamations; but one of them, the dazzling Red Emperor, is seen everywhere!

All I have grown are remarkably in tune with the weather and open their blooms only when the sun is out and the thermometer is above freezing. A drop in temperature or a cloudy day finds them tightly closed for protection. Those planted to the east will fold up their petals each day as soon as the sun has moved far enough to cast a shadow over them, and all species will be shut hours before sundown. Many exhibit green, olive or brown on the reverse of the petals, which is most confounding until they open to reassure you with bright yellow, pink or white flowers.

Variation Abounds

Anyone who becomes enamored of the *tulipas* (as they are sometimes called) is immediately struck by the great variations. Some like the fosterianas (the Red Emperor belongs to this group) and the kaufmannianas produce big blossoms which taper in the bud but open almost flat. Others have tiny blooms, like the bifloras and turkestanicas. Many species tulips bear from two to eight flowers per stem. Some have twisted petals, some are starlike when open and others resemble oval or round goblets.

Foliage ranges from emerald green (*T. saxatilis*) to almost blue-green (*T. clusiana*) with many of the others curiously streaked with brown. Flower hues are often vivid, and heights vary from a few inches to nearly 2 feet. There is a species tulip for almost any place in your garden.

"Why, then," you may ask, "are they not more widely grown?" Undoubtedly because as a class they are not as showy as garden tulips like the Darwins nor as easy to grow or to work into the traditional border. And for some inexplicable reason we tend to stick up our noses at wildlings and favor the colossal hybrid every time.

The characteristics that make the species tulips so endearing to the enthusiast were deliberately bred out of the race which fathered the modern exhibition tulips. While still loving our Darwins, we can add interesting notes to our gardens by taking advantage of the very species habits which earlier generations of gardeners spurned.

Thus the exceedingly short stems of *T. tarda* make it ideal for the rock garden, and the small flowers of many others recommend themselves to this same use. The nodding, informal green and yellow heads of *T. sylvestris* fit in beautifully with the other plants of a lightly shaded woodland, where the Darwins would look out of place even if they could prosper there. Sylvestris is the one species that tolerates some shade.

Paradoxically, while most species tulips will continue to flower well for many years after they are established, they do not always bloom the year after planting. This in direct contrast to the garden tulips which are always their best the first spring after planting. I have heard of species tulips which finally bloomed after so many years of sulking that the gardener had forgotten them. How many of us are patient enough to wait until they have made themselves at home or to continue experimenting until we find conditions under which they prosper.

Finally, a kind of vicious circle keeps the tulipas from the public eye. Since they are not widely-grown, few gardeners are likely to meet them and be tempted. Being less in demand, the bulbs receive less attention from commercial growers so supplies remain short and prices high in comparison with the more popular types. Of late, prices have been slowly dropping, and the Dutch bulb growers report a spectacular increase in species tulip sales which bodes well for the future.

Tulipa Hybrids

Exciting new developments are just now taking place among the species tulips, due I am sure to the tremendous recent acceptance given to the Red Emperor and related hybrids which bring such bright, dependable early color to our spring gardens. Here is a compromise between the nearly-wild and the big exhibition types. The breeders are now crossing various species with each other as well as with the more popular tulips, and some of the resulting progeny create delirious gaiety weeks before the Darwin, cottage and breeder types come into flower.

Such tulips as Gudoshnik, Holland's Glory, General Eisenhower and Oxford are the results of crosses between the Darwins and the Red Emperor family. They bloom later than the emperors and earlier than the Darwins and have fine body and height. Gudoshnik (Golden Freckles) in my garden last spring stopped everyone who passed with its glowing color, tall, straight stems and general sturdiness no matter what the weather. It bloomed ten days after the White Emperors and seventeen days after the Red Emperors.

Astounding colors are found among the so-called Peacock tulips, hybrids from *T. greigi* x *T. kaufmanniana*. They have foliage mottled with brown and are almost too gaudy when planted in the mixtures usually sold. Selections are sure to become more frequent in this class, and then it will be possible to plant them in clumps of one kind where they will provide vivid splashes of reds and yellows, some selfed and some in color combinations that have to be seen to be believed. There are already some named Greigi Hybrids, and this is a class to watch for in the catalogs; prices are already coming down.

I have one catalog which lists twenty-eight Kaufmanniana Hybrids and nearly that many with some *T. fosteriana* heritage.

The Hageri Hybrids bear smaller flowers on stems seldom higher than 8 inches in odd shades of dull red, greenish-black and various yellows.

No one can predict where this hybridizing between tulips will lead, but it is sure to bring us future introductions to decorate our gardens with new forms and colors earlier in spring than we had ever hoped for even a few years ago.

Recommended Species

KAUFMANNIANA (water lily tulip, Color Plate IV) seldom exceed 8 inches and bear large, single, tapered flowers which open almost flat in the sun. They weather well, are very early and dependable. My favorites are: *T. kaufmanniana* (the type) with yellow-centered creamy flowers, marked pink on the reverse; Shakespeare, the most gloriously-colored of all—a blend of apricot, cream and red; Gaiety, which exhibits an orange base on its creamy open flowers and is so short it practically rests on the leaves; Berlioz, a fine yellow. Others include shades of buff, pink, red, orange and yellow, often in combination. When spring is cool, this type lasts three weeks (March–April).

FOSTERIANA include the justly famous Red Emperor (registered name: Mme. Lefeber) whose dazzling scarlet flowers with a golden base took America by storm. They weather well but do not like heat. Bulbs multiply and continue to flower for many years although gradually decreasing in size. Plant this family 6 to 9 inches deep for best results. White Emperor (correctly Purissima) is just as impressive but a week later and survives more heat. Golden Emperor is the newest member of the family. Fosteriana Hybrids mentioned earlier bridge the season between the species and the garden tulips (March–April).

GREIGI tulips will soon be as well known as the Emperors. The enormous hybrids in yellows, oranges and reds vividly color the early garden. Some do not care much for the brown or purple foliage mottling, but the flowers excite everyone. Ideal for rock gardens and foreground since they seldom exceed a foot. Buy only named hybrids and plant separately by color (March–April).

BIFLORA and TURKESTANICA (Color Plate IV) are almost identical with small white stars borne in clusters about 8 inches high. They have yellow centers and prominent redbrick anthers and are perfect for the sunny rock garden. Turkestanica is the first tulip to flower in my garden every year, but biflora is more floriferous. Other growers report the opposite; there is obviously some confusion, a common occurrence among lesser-known bulbs. Give a dry summer site and do not disturb. In cool weather they last nearly a month (March–April).

SYLVESTRIS (*Florentina odorata*) are wayward darlings. Their petals are green and yellow outside but pure canary on the inside even to the anthers, and their 16-inch stems arch so the flowers nod. They remind me of the lily tulips and must have been one of their ancestors. They will take a little more moisture and shade than most species so are good for naturalizing but must have some sun. They are a treasure if happy, but often several years pass before they are prolific of bloom. Be patient, for to me they are the only tulips with a real perfume! Heat and direct midday sun cut their flowering period short (April–May).

TARDA (*Dasystemon,* Color Plate V) love a sunny bank facing south where their white-tipped yellow stars open wide whenever the sun shines. In size they are midway between the tiny biflora and the big kaufmanniana. Each bulb produces several flowers, but each is borne on its own 4-inch stem. Every other petal is colored pinkish-brown on the reverse. They remain in good shape for at least two weeks (April–May).

CLUSIANA (candystick or lady tulip) have endeared themselves by their dependability and beauty. Seldom higher than 12 inches, they show cherry-red and white strips on the outside of their blooms, which close tight every night. Inside, they are white with a purply-red base and black anthers. When open they resemble shallow goblets. Fine for the rock garden, they also flourish in moister sections of my garden (April–May).

CHRYSANTHA is the tiniest of all. Flowers are scarcely an inch long, bright yellow inside, striped red and yellow outside and seldom 6 inches high. Unfortunately they are chary of bloom, but give them a spot where they can be seen if they do flower and where they will not have to compete with coarser plants (April).

VIRIDIFLORA tulips are the so-called green types. They are startling in arrangements, but not recommended for garden purposes even though they last extremely well in all kinds of weather. The very green that excites the creative artist makes them less effective in the garden, so if you wish them for designs, grow in cutting rows. Artist, Pimpernel, Viridiflora and its improved form (*T. viridiflora praecox*) to my mind are the best with petals artistically waved and streaked with green.

Groenland (Greenland) is rose, cream and green with a shallow goblet shape (April–May).

Even Rarer Species

By the time you have tried half of these, you will qualify as a fancier:

T. *acuminata* (*cornuta, stenopetala*, spider tulip)—18 inches, long, thin, twisted petals in yellow and red (April).

T. *batalini*—6 inches, chrome yellow with deeper yellow center (April).

T. *eichleri*—12 inches, medium-sized crimson flowers with black base and yellow margins (April).

T. *linifolia*—8 inches, scarlet cup-shaped flowers with black bases (April).

T. *marjoletti*—18 inches, one of the latest with cream and pink blooms (May).

T. *persica* (*breyniana patens*)—7 inches, another late yellow with a bronzy reverse and several flowers on a branching stem (May).

T. *praestans*—9 inches, several orange-scarlet flowers on a branching stem. Fusilier and Zwanenburg are good named varieties (March–April).

T. *pulchella humilis*—4 inches, a real rarity with violet-pink crocus-like flowers having a yellow base. The variety, Violet Queen (*pulchella violacea*), is very early and has red-purple flowers (February–March).

T. *saxatilis*—12 inches, often bears more than one pink-lavender flower to a stem, yellow bases; hard to establish; foliage appears very early so protect from rabbits and frost (April).

T. *sprengeri*—12 inches, the last to bloom with a reddish interior and yellow-green reverse; rare (May–June).

CAPSULE VIEW OF SPECIES TULIPS

They bloom mostly in March and April.

Great variety available in size, height, color and shape.

Species require sunny undisturbed spot which remains dry in summer and where soil is not too rich.

Plant most 6 inches deep as early in fall as bulbs are available.

Be patient until they have had time to become established.

Hybrids of species usually give more spectacular, dependable bloom than the type.

CHAPTER 7

A Host of Carefree Daffodils

Who does not love the merry daffodils? Their nodding heads whisper of spring and poet's songs, of a world reborn after its winter sleep. Promising sunshine tomorrow, they laugh at inclement April. And with all their beauty and all their apparent fragility, they remain hardy, pestfree and virtually carefree, multiplying with all the abandon of the rankest weed. How could any gardener help but plant them?

The wonder is not that they are so fruitful nor so varied nor so easy to grow, but that so few gardeners know much about them! Every catalog lists more than just the big trumpets, but only fanciers appreciate the extent of form, season and color available.

Granted the big golden trumpets are beloved. Not one bit more, though, than the tiny perfect yellow trumpets of *Narcissus jonquilla simplex,* just one stalk of which perfumes a whole room. Or the gardenia-like clusters of Cheerfulness, the apricot cups of Louise de Coligny, the bright clusters of orange and white where Geranium vies with primroses, or the chaste whiteness of Mount Hood. How compare the delight of February Gold above a late snow with *N. jonquilla gracilis* which may close the season in late May?

What is a daffodil, then? Or are all these daffodils? Technically, yes. The botanical name for them all is *Narcissus,* but years of common usage have imprinted the word "daffodil" indelibly in our springtime vocabulary. It is a fine Old English term you need not hesitate to use for any member of the tribe. The genus belongs to the amaryllis family.

The Greeks Loved Them

Unlike the tulips of the previous chapter, there is no great mystery about the early history of narcissus. We do not know where they first appeared or who discovered them of course, but we do know the narcissus is native to that great Central European and Mediterranean region so long inhabited by man. Some species have been found in Spain, France and Portugal, a few in China and Japan, but it was in ancient Greece that we know the narcissus first came into its own. References are rife in Greek literature, and the coming of spring was associated constantly with "Persephone's flower."

In some undated time before Homer an unknown Greek explained the creation of the narcissus thus:

> Earth, by command of Zeus, and to please All-welcoming Pluto,
> Caused narcissus to grow, as a lure for the lily-faced maiden.
> Wonderful was it in beauty. Amazement on all who beheld it
> Fell, both mortal men and gods whose life is eternal.
> Out of a single root it had grown with clusters an hundred.
> All wide Heaven above was filled with delight at the fragrance,
> Earth was laughing as well, and the briny swell of the waters.[1]

From this and other quotations we can guess their narcissus was closer to our jonquils or the cluster-flower tazetta daffodils than to today's giant trumpets. Of the six species native to Greece, one is *N. poeticus,* which grows in the marshes of Pharsala and flowers in May, much later than the others. So seriously did the Greeks take their narcissus that in the last

---

[1] "Hymn to Demeter," trans. William Cranston Lawton, The Greek Poets, ed. Nathan H. Dole (New York: Crowell, 1904), p. 95.

century the poet, Achilles Paraschos, was judged guilty of exceeding poetic license for a famous verse on picking narcissus in May. Apparently all Greeks did not know Pharsala!

The Egyptians left bunches of dried narcissus in funerary wreaths, and the practical Romans later raised narcissus in greenhouses for the decoration of patrician homes and banquets. No less an authority than Liberty Hyde Bailey suggests the Latin term, *Narcissus,* was inspired by the poisonous or narcotic effects of the bulb taken internally rather than a pretty reference to the foolish boy of Greek mythology who drowned while admiring his own reflection in the water. Writing in the first century after Christ, Pliny thought the same. No doubt this dangerous effect kept the daffodil out of the garden lore of the Middle Ages, where most flowers are mentioned only for their medicinal or edible properties, but the flowers themselves spread over Europe. When better times brought an opportunity for men again to enjoy flowers for their beauty, the daffodil came once more into its own: the gardener's joy and the darling of the poet—from Robert Herrick of the seventeenth century to Amy Lowell of the twentieth. Shakespeare mentions daffodils over and over as common components of an English spring.

In our own day men seldom call their sweethearts Daffodil as did both ancient and Romantic poets, but the word is so strongly entrenched in our sensibilities that it has served in such extremes as to name a British naval vessel and to designate a kind of angel-food cake! Apropos of our business, it is one of the very best bulbs for gardens.

Why Grow Them?

Aside from their undeniable beauty, daffodils have other things to offer. They are virtually pestfree. If you are careful to plant only healthy bulbs, you may well enjoy daffodils in your garden all your life without encountering bugs or disease connected with them, particularly in the northern states. Nor need you fear the voracious attacks of hungry rabbits. The tender tips of tulips and crocus may be eaten to the ground, but never those of daffodils, which is one reason they are so popular for naturalizing, and the bulbs are immune to rodents too.

Moreover, daffodils increase in beauty and number for years without more effort on your part than an occasional feeding of bonemeal. This is a blessing for those of us whose backs and budgets demand our gardens develop over a period of years rather than in one fell swoop. I counted the buds just now on a planting of Mount Hood which is about to flower for its second year. The original five double-nosed bulbs are yielding nineteen white trumpets. I cannot wait to see what happens to Binkie a year from now because my favorite bulb dealer sent three triple-nosed bulbs last fall which are already producing eleven blooms by my kitchen door! It pays to buy from a good source, doesn't it?

When to Plant

All daffodils benefit from early planting. Order by August if possible. In the ground by mid-September at the latest, the narcissus has enough time to put out roots and get acclimated for a stay of years. This early planting is particularly important for those which flower first in spring. You can plant them later if events so dictate, but you will get earlier, better flowers if you get them in during September. My order for Lent lilies (a form of *N. pseudo-narcissus*) was not delivered until late November one time. They were popped into a spot I had saved for them, but that first spring they failed to deliver color early as I had hoped.

How to Plant

Most daffodils should be planted 5 to 6 inches deep from the top of the bulb itself rather than from the slender neck. Small sizes or heavy soil suggest slightly shallower depths. Even the small species should go 2 to 4 inches deep, depending on the bulb size. Shallower planting encourages an increase, which is advantageous with expensive, new varieties you are anxious to propagate. Deeper planting means the bulbs stay in place years longer. It is wisest too for plantings where the summers are very hot. Place them as far apart as you can for the effect sought: for immediate effects, put them about 4 inches apart; for an eventual garden grouping 6 to 8 inches apart; where naturalized on a large scale, they can easily go a foot apart.

The ground beneath the bulbs should be friable for root development, and a tablespoon of bonemeal can be mixed in well there, but never let it touch the bulb. Water well after planting to get them started and repeat weekly if the fall is dry. Additional moisture is also beneficial if late spring is very hot and dry, since the bulbs after flowering are busy storing food for another year.

They grow best in soft, fertile loam, but the various hybrids are so undemanding they are often mistreated; I have seen them with tips bent and bruised from the effort of emerging through hard clay. Few bulbs can tolerate wet conditions, but some daffodils will put up with considerable moisture while they are growing roots in fall and leaves in spring. (The King Alfreds around my birdbath have prospered through years of extra wetting.) Most others do magnificently on gradual slopes,

11. The foliage of plumy bleedingheart already adds grace to a planting of Narcissus Laurens Koster in partial shade. Soon the rose blossoms and ferny leaves will hide the ripening daffodil foliage. This bleedingheart often goes on blooming into November in author's garden.

and this is partly because such situations allow them to bake during summer dormancy.

Where to Plant

Although most daffodils are hardy all over the United States, those which bloom latest, such as the *N. poeticus* varities, do not do as well in the South. In cold sections the bulbocodium and some of the jonquilla and tazetta types will not prosper. The only way to find out for sure is to test a variety or species in your own climate, but obviously your garden will look better if you concentrate on those best suited to your area. The less dependable are fun to try on the side. The yearbooks of the American Daffodil Society (ADS) are helpful for those seeking varieties for less temperate sections. Bulbs of the earliest types and those of dubious hardiness deserve a protected spot.

Obviously, daffodils will fit somewhere into almost any garden, but some are more effective in certain places. The tiny species types like *N. triandrus albus*, the bulbocodiums and the many species hybrids like Beryl, Hawera and Kidling need an intimate setting such as the foreground of a rock garden or a special small nook of their own where they will not be overlooked. The big trumpets can hold their own in almost any situation. Later-flowering daffodils last longer if planted to gain a little shade during the hottest part of the day if you live where late April turns scorching.

Those with narrow rushlike foliage like *N. jonquilla simplex* can go anywhere since they are unobtrusive after flowering. The "pink" and "red" daffodils produce their best color if grown in partial shade, but they need sun half the day anyway.

Daffodils with heavy foliage are easier to work into the back or middle of the garden where their drying leaves are partially hidden. I do not find the neat bluish-green foliage unsightly until it begins to yellow. By then it is flopping toward the ground where it can be tucked behind other plants if it offends the perfectionist. This is surely better than tying it into tortured knots. Rather than solving a problem, this creates another since these gruesome things are much harder to hide than a few loose leaves. Moreover, they do not dry as fast, and I would think leaves so mistreated less likely to do a proficient job of manufacturing food for the maturing bulb.

Few flowers look their best lined up in a row; daffodils are not one of them. Plant these informal flowers always in a group. With only three bulbs you can plant on the points of a triangle and get a lovely effect. With more bulbs, strive to plant them more densely in the middle of the group, with a few bulbs straying singly to the side, for extra charm. Some gardeners achieve a casual effect by tossing a handful of bulbs into the air and planting them wherever they fall.

I cannot conceive of any reason for buying the so-called naturalizing selections of unlabelled narcissus. No matter how fine or carefully balanced the mixture, it can never be better than a hodgepodge. Where naturalizing has been done on a large scale in public gardens or estates, you will always find the daffodils planted by the variety since this ensures masses of the same color at the same time in one area. The horticultural experts who do the planting know they will get more effect from a dozen bulbs of one kind planted together than from half a hundred of the mixture. Labelled collections are good buys if they contain varieties you want.

To naturalize an area place a dozen bulbs of an early type here, a dozen of a later variety there, a handful of a different class to soften the lines of a rock. (On a large estate, you can plant groups by the hundred.) Each year a group or two are added, and each year past plantings will be lovelier as these dependable flowers multiply. That is the only way to do it, and you can invest as little or as much as you want over as many years as you desire.

Transplanting

You may ask about now: When should I transplant daffodils? Unless you are a glutton for work, I would answer: only when bloom begins to fall off or the size of the flowers falls below your standards. Usually this happens when the bulbs have increased until they crowd each other. Sometimes it means they are not getting enough sun. This often occurs in new gardens where small trees and shrubs suddenly begin to take hold and spurt upward and outward to reach mature growth. The daffodils which once did beautifully begin to falter from lack of sunshine since they do their best only when receiving plenty. The only narcissus I have lost were those left too long in such deepening shade.

We speak of naturalizing daffodils, but this does not mean they are shady woodland flowers. They will blossom only if they are planted where the sunshine penetrates while they are maturing their foliage. Since this often takes a long time (I have had green foliage on February Gold at the end of July), they will luxuriate only on the southeast, south and southwest sides of trees or large shrubs, never in the center of a copse of trees where shade is intense. Remember not to mow daffodil meadows until after the foliage has matured. After it withers, fill in the holes left in the soil by the big stems to protect the bulbs from insect damage.

Eventually, any daffodil planting will need dividing, but I have had bulbs which were deeply planted 6 to 8 inches apart go eight and ten years without bloom falling off, although flower size dropped. Fanciers dig their bulbs more often because they are trying to increase supplies of more expensive varieties quickly or to produce very large flowers for exhibition.

When you judge it necessary, the best time is when the foliage has turned brown but has not yet begun to disintegrate, so it serves as a guide to each bulb. Use a large fork and plunge it several inches away from the foliage. Then pry toward the bulbs, and they should come up without injury. In dry weather, water well the day before to soften the earth. The largest bulbs go back into the garden; smaller sizes may be used for naturalizing or planted in cutting rows for a year or two.

If bulbs must remain out of the ground for a while, leave for several days in a light, airy, rainproof place first to dry. They may then be stored in a cool, well-ventilated place until late summer planting. It is easier to separate the bulbs after they have dried a little. I prefer to put mine right back into the ground rather than storing. That way they get an early root start. I have never forgotten the time I inadvertantly disturbed some King Alfreds in late July. They had already started growing new roots—proof positive that early planting is best!

What to Plant?

Aye, there's the rub. If you love them as I do, the question might better be, "Where to stop?" There are so many in the catalogs, and each has its merits. Having told you there is more to a daffodil spring than the big yellow trumpets, I must once more admonish you against trying to grow one of each variety. Like all bulbs, they look best planted in clumps of one kind.

Before we delve deeper into the world of daffodils, let us look for a moment at the official classification of the American Daffodil Society. While it is specifically intended for orderly

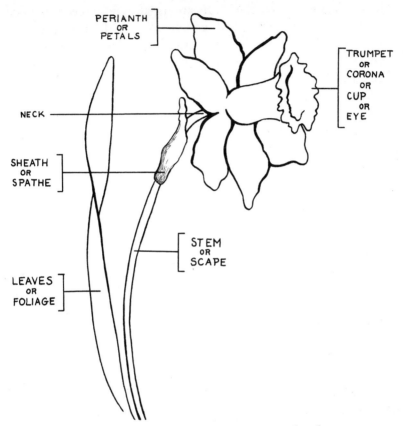

FIG. 8. This labeled daffodil illustrates the terms that botanists use to describe the parts of a flower.

presentation of show entries, it is useful as a guide to just what differences exist. Examples of the more important classifications are given in parentheses. I have tried to include mostly bulbs which are reasonably priced, although at least one in each group ranks high in the latest ratings of the ADS.

Bear in mind that this book is primarily written for gardeners. The varieties, therefore, are usually those recommended for outdoor growing. Those which take the highest prizes at shows are often unable to withstand garden conditions and weather. Most bulbs available are Dutch or English varieties, and their hybridizing has favored development of showy daffodils which are not always entirely satisfactory outside. Some of the American breeders in Oregon and Virginia may help reverse this trend with new blood lines more adaptable for our climates.

Official Classification

TRUMPET DAFFODILS (Division I), trumpet as long as or longer than perianth segments: (A) perianth and trumpet colored (Garron, Unsurpassable, Diotima); (B) perianth white, trumpet colored (Music Hall, Pres. Lebrun, Trousseau); (C) perianth and trumpet white (Mt. Hood, Beersheba, Mrs. E. H. Krelage); (D) any other color combination (Spellbinder).

LARGE-CUPPED DAFFODILS (Division II), cup more than one-third but less than equal to length of perianth segments: (A) perianth and trumpet colored (Carlton, Fortune, St. Egwin); (B) perianth white, cup colored (Mrs. R. O. Backhouse, Kilworth, Brunswick); (C) perianth and cup white (Carnlough, Dunlewey, Niphitos); (D) any other color combination (Binkie).

SMALL-CUPPED DAFFODILS (Division III), cup not more than one-third length of perianth segments: (A) perianth and cup colored (Edward Buxton, Apricot Distinction, Chungking); (B) perianth white, cup colored (Lady Kesteven, Blarney, La Riante); (C) perianth and cup white (Frigid, Foggy Dew, Cushendall).

DOUBLE DAFFODILS (Division IV), any color and type (Cheerfulness, Irene Copeland, White Lion).

TRIANDRUS HYBRIDS (Division V), several nodding flowers to a stem, white or pale yellow (Thalia, Tresamble, Moonshine).

CYCLAMINEUS HYBRIDS (Division VI), single yellow flowers usually nodding, narrow cup, reflexed perianth (February Gold, Beryl, Peeping Tom).

JONQUILLA HYBRIDS (Division VII), usually several yellow flowers to a stem, short cup, flat perianth, often fragrant (Trevithian, Golden Perfection, Cherie).

TAZETTA (POETAZ) DAFFODILS (Division VIII), usually several small flowers to a stem, fragrant (Geranium, Cragford, Laurens Koster).

POETICUS DAFFODILS (Division IX), one flower to stem, white perianth, small flat cup with red or green edge (Actea, Recurvus, Cantabile).

SPECIES DAFFODILS (Division X), varied wild forms (*N. asturiensis, N. bulbocodium, N. cyclamineus*).

MISCELLANEOUS (Division XI).

Daffodils in the Garden

Daffodil hybridizing has been going on for many years, as the above lists certify, and the flower has become so varied as to be confusing unless we use this system when we consider its importance in the garden. Each catalog contains various representatives of each division, and the most helpful ones use the official classification. You will not go wrong to follow the recommendations of your favorite bulb house. Low prices are a good signpost toward hardy, dependable varieties since they reflect such behavior over a long period.

THE TRUMPETS (I). My own preference is to plan a garden where the big trumpets in either yellow or white form the backbone as it were. They are bought and planted separately to make clumps of one color. Plant the trumpets at least 5 inches apart to allow for natural increase since most of these vigorous varieties reproduce themselves enthusiastically. Six of a kind are enough to start a swathe of color. Daffodils from the first three divisions produce lush, vigorous foliage, a consideration when you position them in the garden. You cannot go wrong, ever, with reasonably priced trumpets.

LARGE-CUPS (II). Here are fine contrasts, mostly for mid-season bloom, although Fortune, for example, is an early bloomer and Belisana one of the late ones. Many of these have wide, open cups quite different from the trumpets, but others closely resemble them. The difference is that the cups of this section are never as long as the petals. Stems are often nearly as tall as among the trumpets. Here you find the most colorful daffodils: red and orange combinations and the widely-touted pink daffodils. These latter are more apricot than pink and few of the newer types are better for the garden than the oldest, Mrs. R. O. Backhouse. Last spring, however, I saw the late-blooming Azalea, which I think the best of all. There are also fine pure white narcissus in this division, but they suffer as a class from susceptibility to basal rot. The hybridizers promise healthier varieties are being developed. Generally this division is vigorous and hardy. The main thing is to choose

FIG. 9. What is a daffodil? More than the giant trumpets, as these examples of various hybrid and species shapes and sizes graphically show.

colors which will harmonize with your own garden. Sometimes these daffodils are listed as "Weatherproof" or "John Evelyn Hybrids" in catalogs.

SMALL-CUPS (III). Here the cups are quite obviously shorter than the surrounding petals, making these a daintier narcissus, usually on shorter stems than the two previous sections. These too are mostly mid-season flowers although Polar Ice and Frigid are two of the latest of all daffodils. Many have white perianths with colorful cups, and there are numerous recent introductions, among them some pure whites. They are often fragrant and good for naturalizing.

DOUBLES (IV). No more long-lasting daffodils exist than these, but they should be mulched with some clean material like buckwheat hulls, since they are often bent to the ground by heavy rain. A canopy of high tree branches helps too. One of the prettiest is the white Irene Copeland, but there are good yellows like Twink, Texas, and Inglescombe. Many of this class have a few central orange segments. Several members of other divisions are also double and may be included here: Cheerfulness and its yellow sister are *tazetta* doubles, both among the finest garden daffodils in the world. From the species division are *N. telamonius plenus* (Van Sion) and the double white *N. poeticus flore pleno* (*N. odoratus*); the first is one of the earliest daffodils and the second one of the latest, though not reliable in cold climates. Many doubles are fragrant, most have lush foliage. Pink Cloud is a double pink, but still rare; White Lion and Golden Ducat are outstanding new doubles.

TRIANDRUS (V). For the rock garden, the foreground or a little niche of their own, these are ethereally dainty, with nodding small flowers and thin foliage. Stems are usually quite short, and bloom comes toward the end of the daffodil season. Mark these and all other grassy-leaved daffodils well to prevent weeding them out by mistake. I have done it twice, to my dismay! Most here are white flowered.

CYCLAMINEUS (VI). Heralds of spring! Heights here range from the 6-inch Little Witch to the 15-inch February Gold, with corresponding differences in the size of the flowers. These are among the very first of the genus to flower and have yellow petals reflexed in varying degrees. They deserve a warm, sheltered spot to bring them out early. The foliage is broader than in the previous section but never terribly obtrusive so plant them wherever you wish, preferably where you can see them from a window or along a well-traveled path.

JONQUILLA (VII). Probably the most fragrant of all narcissus. The foliage here is rush-like, so mark well. Heights range from 22 inches in the newer hybrid, Golden Perfection, to 9 or 10 in older types. They tend to bloom toward the end of the season. Most are yellow, but Topaz bears a white perianth and Cherie a pinkish cup and white outer petals. This class does best with full sun and is a favorite in the South.

TAZETTA (POETAZ) (VIII). These bunch-flowered daffodils are among the best for garden decoration, and most are delightfully fragrant. All bear more than one flower per stem, many have seven or eight, creating lovely splashes of color. Here at Philadelphia all have proven hardy without protection, but this strain is less able to withstand cold northern winters than others. For cutting they are ideal. The paper-whites also belong here, but are unsuitable for outdoor use except in the far South.

POETICUS (IX). Late flowering as a class and one of the hardiest types for northern gardens. All are marked with a contrasting rim around the central eye and are fine for cutting. They are most important for extending the season, fragrant and good for naturalizing.

SPECIES (X). As might be expected there are wide variations here. Some members of this group fathered hybrids of other divisions and are often cataloged with their progeny; i.e., *N. cyclamineus* in Division VI. Generally, all these are short-stemmed. One of the tiniest is *N. asturiensis* (*minimus*) which bears small yellow trumpets on 3-inch stems in earliest spring. Many of these like the bulbocodiums and *N. canaliculatus* are not reliably hardy in the far North, but you may be able to bring them through in a sheltered southern spot with a wall to the north. Some bear miniature flowers, others are less dainty with dwarf stems and fairly large flowers like the Lent lily, often cataloged as *N. lobularis* or *N. minor var. conspicuous*.

Many species do not flower as dependably as other divisions, being more liable to weather fluctuations, and in rich garden soil they often decide to multiply instead of flower. Make sure they do not have to compete with more vigorous plants for sunshine and space, never fertilize them, and plant the bulbs deeper than their size would indicate: 3 to 4 inches for the miniatures (often these are species hybrids) has worked for me; the smaller species bulbs probably should not go as deep in heavy soil, but there is a great deal of differing opinion among the experts. I favor 2 to 3 inches in full sun and thin, summer-dry soil because it more nearly approximates their natural Mediterranean habitats, but I have not grown them long enough to be sure. This treatment works, however, with the species tulips, which are also fleeting in rich garden situations. The tiny *N. cyclamineus* is a possible exception to the dry maxim; it is reported sometimes to grow in soil which is quite moist in spring.

Earliest planting is mandatory for all species narcissus. Many of the bulbs are tiny and must not remain out of the soil.

This is a division for those who desire something different and who like to take extra trouble to make a bulb at home, but it can be a lot of fun. Catalog descriptions often differ. This is partly because wildlings tend to greater variation than selected hybrids, but it also reflects the fact that this division is still little known and not widely planted, and the names are often guessed at by fanciers who pass bulbs around. As a rule the bulbs will bloom the first year, but keeping them in your garden may be a series of trials and errors until you hit on just the right spot for them. Many of this class were originally found in Spain and Portugal.

Beginners will find the garden hybrids of the species, many of which are cataloged as miniatures, easier and more dependable. They are often cataloged with the species, but the hybrid names are always capitalized. Rock gardens on a slope where there is full sun and perfect drainage are ideal.

FOR SPECIAL EFFECTS

Having advised you to anchor your garden with the dependable trumpets and then to fill in with what appeals to you from the other divisions, I have almost finished the daffodil story. It has been a tale of a flower which is important not only for its intrinsic beauty but also for its place in the garden as a whole. While the lovely whites and pale yellows are softening touches to act as foils for the brilliant colors of the species tulips, this ancient flower is too important simply to be relegated to the role of companion. Not the least of her reasons-for-being in your garden is to bring cheerful golden sunshine to a winter-weary world.

Fashions in daffodils change, as in everything else. An old variety bows before the superiority of a new introduction. A widely-heralded novelty fails to live up to expectations and is dropped from the catalogs. The most reasonable prices in a reputable dealer's catalog are a good index to the most dependable narcissus. These are the ones to start with, and there are good examples in each of the divisions. As you become more familiar with the genus, you will want daffodils for specific reasons and places, and you will want some of the current novelties just for fun. The following paragraphs suggest varieties for special uses.

Daffodils by Season

All gardeners enjoy displaying the first or the last of a particular flower. Some varieties listed here may be hard to find because they are newer introductions or older types no longer widely offered, but from my own experience and observations early and late at a trial garden, these will give you the widest range.

EARLY

N. telamonius plenus (Van Sion), Ada Finch, *N. lobularis* or Trumpet Major, February Gold, March Sunshine, *N. asturiensis* (*N. minimus*), Fortune, South Pacific, High Sierra, Sacajawe, Hollywood, Sweet Talk, Cornet, Shah, Jumblie, Jana, Barthy, Caerhays, *N. cyclamineus*, and Peeping Tom.

LATE

Cushendall, Jonquilla Helena, *N. poeticus flore pleno*, *N. gracilis*, Polar Ice, Cantabile, Hawera, Sun Disc, Lights Out,

Baby Moon, Silver Chimes, Bobby Soxer, Happy End, Frigid, Azalea, Belisana, Rose of May, Tittle Tattle, Ultimus, Rippling Waters, Geranium, Corncrake, Cheerfulness, Kidling, Zanita and almost all classed in Division IX.

You can stretch the seasons by planting the earliest ones in a protected, southerly spot and placing the latest in a colder spot.

Daffodils for Semi-Shade

All daffodils must have sun, but a few will do well with less than most. It must be a spot where there is plenty of light, perhaps under high branches, or where the sun shines in for about half the day. Those recommended for this semi-shade include: Moonshine, Glorious, Lady Kesteven, and Amateur. Among the species are *N. triandrus albus, N. juncifolius* and possibly *N. cyclamineus* and some of the bulbocodiums. I have had Cheerfulness and Laurens Koster do quite well for some years under these conditions, but they are never as good as in sunnier places.

Daffodils for Special Colors

GREEN

This is a newish fancy, particularly among arrangers, but in the garden they have a chaste, refreshing coolness. All the following have at least a suggestion of green or lemon-green at some time: Green Island, Emerald Isle, Arguros (St. Patrick), Cushendall, Zero and Grapefruit.

PINK

These will be more apricot than pink but certainly different: Apricot Distinction (Apricot Attraction), Apricot Beauty,

Azalea, Toscanni, Rose of Tralee, Louise de Coligny, Wild Rose, Pink Fancy, Mabel Taylor, Rosy Trumpet or Cherie. The hybridizers are working furiously on these, but the oldest, Mrs. R. O. Backhouse, and the moderately-priced Siam and Menton are still the outdoor gardener's best choice.

WHITE

Catalogs where classification numbers are given make it easy to pick out good whites: I-C, Mt. Hood, Beersheba, Mrs. E. H. Krelage for the garden and Cantatrice, Brough-shane for showing; II-B has many with fine white perianths, but Papillon Blanche especially appeals to me; any in II-C fill the bill but try Carnlough, Ludlow, Silver Lining; III-B contains Polar Ice and III-C again are all white with Frigid, Cushendall and Bryher among the best; white doubles include Cheerfulness, Irene Copeland, Snowball, Mrs. William Copeland and Daphne; many triandrus hybrids are white and many of the tazetta bear white perianths as do all of the poeticus; W. P. Milner is among the miniatures easiest to grow but try also Frosty Morn and Snipe.

RED, ORANGE

Brilliant cups make the following outstanding, although the reds are more nearly red-orange than scarlet: Rouge, Carbineer, Rustom Pasha, Bahram, Manco, Quirinus, Red Goblet, Red Bird, Red Marley, Red April, La Riante, Confuoco, Kilworth, Wodan, Scarlet Elegance, Geranium.

Daffodils by Height

Contrast is always interesting and by choosing from certain groups you can have both short and tall narcissus.

TALL

Almost any of the yellow trumpets but especially Stentor and Diotima; Mt. Hood and Mrs. E. H. Krelage are tall white trumpets. Most of the large-cups are also tall; noteworthy are Fortune, Jules Verne, Papillon Blanche, Kilmorack, Spencer Tracy, Yankee Clipper, Polindra, Revelry and Hopesay. Among the tallest doubles: Twink, Texas, Indian Chief. Golden Perfection and Lanarth are tall jonquils, Laurens Koster the tallest tazetta.

SHORT

Aprilis, a white large-cup; Silver Chimes, Moonshine, *N. triandrus albus* and *N. triandrus concolor* among the Triandrus; Beryl, Little Witch and March Sunshine among the Cyclamineus; Baby Moon, the campernelli, *N. jonquilla simplex* and *jonquilla flore pleno* among the Jonquils; among many species the bulbocodiums, *N. asturiensis*, *N. wateiri*, Little Beauty, *N. canaculatus* and *N. juncifolius*. Rosy Trumpet, W. P. Milner and *N. lobularis* seem dwarf rather than miniature. The ADS recommends among the best miniature hybrids of the various classes: Tanagra, Wee Bee, Goldsithney, Xit, Pencrebar, Frosty Morn, Hawera, Dawn, Beryl, Kidling, Demure, Halingy and Elfhorn.

Daffodils for Fragrance

All daffodils have a subtle fragrance of a sort, but if you wish to grow some just for this purpose, choose from the Jonquilla, Tazetta or Poeticus groups. These are the only real sweet narcissus, and undoubtedly it was from ancestors of these types that the old Romans manufactured their famous narcissus perfume.

Just to Be Different

Some of the following daffodils are no longer really novelties, having been accepted as fine additions to the garden, but each is different in some sense. No garden could support too many of them, some may not prove worth keeping or up to your standards. Use a few to add a bit of spice. While many are more expensive than the common yellow trumpets, none is outlandishly so. Read your catalog descriptions carefully and try three to six bulbs of whatever sound interesting. Later you can buy more of those which particularly appeal.

Spellbinder and Binkie, reverse bicolors whose cups slowly turn white as they age; Golden Castle, a yellow trumpet with a double cup; Hillbilly's Sister, the open cup is nearly as large as the perianth, and May Muriel which has an enormous flat crown; Rosy Trumpet and Torch, star-like perianths; Red Marley and Red Goblet, startling contrast of yellow and red; Wodan and Confuoco, brilliant color and huge cups; Peeping Tom and Cornet, very elongated trumpets.

Grullemans Giant, Broughshane, Stentor and Diotima, huge flowers; Pink Rim, Criterion, Kansas, Mother Catherine Grullemans, Limone, rare coloring often with contrasting edges; yellow Rex and white Flora's Favorite, extremely ruffled crowns; Johannesburg, triple frilled crown; L'Argentina, cup has radiating stripes of yellow and orange like spokes of a wheel.

Recently a new type of daffodil appeared, the result of subjection to ultraviolet rays which changed the chromosome count. Called de Mol's "orchid" daffodils after their Dutch breeder, they have cups heavily ruffled, cut and interspersed with the perianth segments. They grow 15 to 18 inches high and flower early to mid-season. They have an exotic look, but

12. A new type of narcissus, Del Mol's orchid daffodils have cups heavily ruffled, cut and interspersed with the perianth segments. Top: Artist; left, Elizabeth Bass; right, Mol's Hobby (Courtesy George W. Park Seed Co.).

we will have to try them for a few years before being sure how they do. They are classified in the miscellany of Division XI.

CAPSULE VIEW OF NARCISSUS

By planting various classes of daffodils, bloom may extend for six to eight weeks, but peak flowering is in April over most of this country.

Good whites and yellows of all shades and sizes are abundant; "pink" daffodils are more nearly apricot; "red" ones are mostly brilliant orange.

Flower forms vary: perianths may or may not be reflexed; cups may be large or small, sometimes frilled or very open; doubles exist in several classes; some varieties bear more than one flower per stem.

Choose a site which has sun at least half the day; narcissus like summer dryness, but during droughts give some moisture just after flowering and while rooting in early fall.

Plant as early in the fall as possible 5 to 6 inches deep from the shoulder of the bulb for most hybrids but only 2 to 4 inches deep for the smaller species bulbs; shallower planting stimulates increase of bulbs.

For ordinary garden effect space them 4 to 8 inches apart; in naturalizing they may go a foot apart.

CHAPTER 8

Fragrant Hyacinths: Outdoors and In

More fragrant than any of its early spring companions, the lovely hyacinth deserves closer attention than American gardeners have recently given it. If you treat them as plants rather than soldiers to be lined up stiffly in concentric circles or parade-dress files, the hyacinths contribute much beauty to the March and April garden, where they are the first major bulb to appear. Most of the early flowers are little things, so the foot-high hyacinth has a majesty badly needed as an accent during this time. And how delightful to enter a room perfumed by a stray stalk in a bouquet!

Like so many others of the lily family, the common hyacinth (*Hyacinthus orientalis*) is native to lands of the Mediterranean and Asia Minor. The big truss of the modern hyacinth, which has been intensively hybridized by the Dutch, bears little resemblance to the flower so often mentioned in ancient Greek poetry.

The historical clues I have found are tantalizing: its fragrance was noteworthy, Homer mentions the hair of Ulysses as "tight-curling as a hyacinth flower curls tight," and several other sources describe the flower as purple, a shade often confused with reddish tints by early writers. The flower is sup-

posed to have sprung up where Apollo had inadvertantly
killed the young boy, Hyacinthus, as they were playing quoits,
and its petals were marked with the symbol "ai" denoting the
god's grief. Just how this is connected with the Festival of
Hyacinthia celebrated by the disciplined Spartans of old I cannot image. Archaeologists suggest several other flowers for the
role of whatever the Greeks were describing, but we are
equally justified in thinking the flower the Greeks loved was
a smaller, looser form of the same one we plant, probably resembling the graceful French-Roman hyacinths more than the
big Dutch hybrids.

Introduced into the West only a few hundred years ago,
hyacinths were limited to the gardens of the wealthy for a
long time, and the Dutch had a limited speculation somewhat
like the frenzied tulipomania. Eventually the growers discovered that by "scooping" the underside of the bulb (making
a cone-shaped cut through its base) hyacinths would produce
offsets faster. (This process is described more fully in Chapter
19.) Nicholaas Dames, whom we met in the tulip story, improved this technique and also invented "prepared" hyacinths
for early forcing by control of storage temperatures. It was
only so short a time ago as 1910 that he electrified a December
flower show in Haarlem, Holland, with hyacinths in full bloom!
Today's gardeners know few more dependable bulbs for early
indoor forcing.

Pink at Last

For those who like color for its own sake in gardens, hyacinths are the one truly good source of early pink. How many
times last April did I peep out the window at the cheerful
warmth of a clump of Princess Margaret! There are many good
blues too, varying from lightest amethyst to dark royal shades.
L'Innocence is still the best of the whites, immaculate and

waxen with an exotic scent. Grow it alongside Red Emperor tulips to gladden the grayest of days. This startling planting remains extraordinary no matter how many gardeners copy it, mostly because it is so unlikely a color combination so early in the season. The newer white and yellow emperors offer further possibilities.

La Victoire and Jan Bos are the most brilliant of the red-rose shades and fine for a spot of color in early spring symphonies of blue and white. For a change of pace plant City of Haarlem, a creamy yellow, to contrast with bright early tulips or evergreens.

How to Plant

Stifle the terrible temptation to plant hyacinths in geometric patterns. Instead, place them in groups of three or four of the same color about 6 inches apart and 5 to 6 inches deep. This creates a bold mound of color and helps the hyacinths combat the weather. Simply place three short stakes on the periphery of the clump, then wind twine in figure-eights between stakes, catching the hyacinth stalks within each cross. They will thus support each other.

With some bulbs, it is wise to buy the largest you can obtain, but this is not true of hyacinths. Except for exhibition or indoor forcing, order second- or third-size hyacinths, the best outdoor investment because they weather more successfully. Even these slightly less expensive sizes often yield spikes so massive the stems snap in wind and rain. Planted in clumps, however, staking is easily accomplished and hardly noticeable. Counting the later secondary spikes which mature bulbs often produce, your hyacinths should give at least a full month of color. Even the fourth-size is worthwhile in the garden.

If the foliage receives plenty of sun well into late spring and if the bulbs get a dressing of bonemeal and dried cow manure regularly, hyacinths will provide lovely color and fragrance for at least five years after the original planting, but the trusses will be smaller and more graceful in subsequent years. This means staking is unnecessary. I think the smaller spikes in following years are prettier and far easier to use in bouquets. When the spring arrives that they do not give a good account of themselves, order new bulbs; but plant them in a different spot or replace the soil since it is likely to be deficient in the exact nutrients they need.

Grouped by color in clumps, hyacinths are stunning accents in any garden, big or small. They will soften the lines of a boulder, illumine a shrubbery planting and call attention to the focal point of a garden at a time when few other bold plants are available. I like them near the door to greet each caller with beauty and fragrance. Perennial candytuft is a fine companion. If possible, give them a spot protected from the wind.

Cultural Requirements

Hyacinths must have good drainage and sunshine at least half the day. They do better in full sun. A good loam is best, but I have had magnificent bloom from bulbs planted in clay enriched with peat and compost. Since they need time to develop good roots, plant them in early fall and water well once a week for a month if the season is dry. Here at Philadelphia we do not mulch our hyacinths; in the far north give them a light covering the first winter. To protect the bulbs, fill in the holes the heavy stems leave after they wither.

FOR INDOOR USE

Hyacinths are easy to force for indoor blooming either in soil or in water. Plant Dutch hyacinths early in September and keep cool (50 degrees F.) for at least three months for best results. Earliest plantings may produce flowers by Christmas, but are more likely to bloom in January and February. In soil, set the bulbs just beneath the surface. Keep in the dark (or cover with a paper cone) until the shoots are at least 4 inches high and the buds well out of the neck. Then bring to the light gradually and continue to grow in a cool spot. Such bulbs may be used in the garden afterwards if foliage is allowed to mature properly.

For water culture, you may like the special hyacinth glasses sold by bulb houses and garden shops. They resemble an egg cup, and the bulb is placed in the top half while the bottom is filled with water just to the base of the bulb. Rainwater is best, although you can use tapwater which has stood overnight. Add a few small pieces of charcoal to keep it sweet. For this forcing, select only the largest sized bulbs and discard after flowering.

Add water as necessary and keep glasses in a cool, dark place until the lower section is filled with roots. When the bud is at least 4 inches high, gradually admit light but keep growing in a cool room. You can also grow hyacinths in pebbles and water, but use bowls at least 4 inches deep to give adequate root room. It will take ten to twelve weeks for rooting and a month for the tops to develop.

"Miniature" Hyacinths

Several other types of hyacinths are more suitable and often faster and easier for indoor growing than are the big Dutch forms.

CYNTHELLA hyacinths are nothing but small-sized Dutch hyacinths and lovely for indoors in pots of soil since they produce smaller, more graceful spikes of bloom. Plant several bulbs to a pot. Pre-cooled bulbs give quickest results, and since they are hardy, you can plant them outside after forcing. Treat them just as you would the larger Dutch forms.

FRENCH-ROMAN hyacinths are quite another thing and probably the best of all for indoor forcing since they do not need as long a time to mature nor quite as cool a place once they come into flower. Each bulb yields as many as six fragrant, loose spikes. Pink and blue varieties are available, but the white is most popular. Give them eight weeks of dark, cool growing for rooting and three to four weeks more for top development. Bulbs planted early in October and forced about December 1 will give bloom for Christmas. Later plantings give even faster flowering. One knowledgeable gardener I know says she has not found it necessary to give them either darkness or coolest growing conditions for success, but I have always done so.

There are several small, tender novelties whose needs are similar to the French-Roman types. Planted early in September, Vanguard (blue) and Rosalie (pink) are easily forced for Christmas. Borah (blue) should not be hurried but responds well to forcing in January and produces a succession of short spikes for weeks. It seems to do best at an east or west window rather than in full sun, and all hyacinths in bloom should be removed from direct sun to prolong the flowers.

Neither the French-Roman nor the miniature novelties are reliably hardy except in frost-free locations, but I always plant mine hopefully in a sheltered southern exposure. This way there is nothing to lose, since they can not be forced two years in a row.

CAPSULE VIEW OF HYACINTHS

Dutch hyacinths are fine for early outdoor accents and the only good early source of pink and rose.

Plant early in good soil with perfect drainage and plenty of sun in clumps, never in straight lines.

Choose bulb size according to use: top-size for exhibition and indoor forcing only, second- or third-size for most gardens and bedding-size for mass effect.

No bulb is more easily forced for winter blooming, and the fragrance of most pink, white and blue varieties is strong and delightful.

The tender French-Roman varieties are usually sold by color rather than name, are quite distinct from the larger, hardy Dutch hyacinths and are the best and easiest for indoor use.

CHAPTER 9

A Revolution in Lilies

Revolution is a strong word, but it describes exactly what has been happening in the world of lilies. Yesterday's gardeners would not recognize today's lilies. Vigorous, spectacular hybrids in new colors and forms—most of them resulting from the work of American growers—are now available for the average garden. Thanks to their being grown under American climatic conditions, these bulbs are usually ready for fall planting long before the ground is frozen. Moreover, improved methods of propagation bring prices of new ones quickly down to reasonable levels and also keep the stock disease-free.

Heretofore we were limited to species lilies and their variations. Many of these wild lilies are difficult to grow and need special care and attention. Some were infected with virus and thus short-lived. Since most lily bulbs were grown in foreign countries, it was hard to obtain mature stock in time for our fall planting season. Unfortunately, too, these bulbs were often poorly packed for their long journey and arrived dried out, rotted, moldy or bruised.

World War II changed the picture, although hybridizing had already been going on here for some time. With bulbs from abroad no longer available, American growers concentrated on lilies, and the spectacular results are still far from final. Each year brings not only new hybrid introductions, but also better selections of previous strains, giving the gardener greater uniformity of color and form at lower prices. More on this later.

Lilies Begin to Cross

We are now reaping bountiful harvests from this hybridizing, but it took a long time for it to get started. The way was pointed out as long ago as 1867 when Francis Parkman, the historian who wrote *The Oregon Trail*, exhibited a hybrid of the species, *Lilium auratum* and *L. speciosum rubrum*. Parkman's lily electrified London, but over the years this clone died out, and for some years could not be duplicated. Old commentaries lamented the loss, but the cross has been made many times in modern hybridizing.

There was a period, however, when lilies seemed unwilling to cross except accidentally, as in the case of *L. x testaceum* (the Nankeen lily) which is a hybrid of *L. candidum* (madonna) and *L. chalcedonicum* (scarlet Turk's cap), both species long in cultivation. Here and there imaginative men still tried crosses. A Frenchman brought out the first gorgeous Aurelian Hybrids in 1928, and only a few years later Roy M. Wallace in Australia began the work which resulted in the striking Jillian Wallace, a re-creation of the cross Parkman made. However, it was the work of daring American and Canadian hybridizers that finally revolutionized lilies. By constant selection, by crossing and recrossing and then backcrossing with pollen from one of the original parents, by keeping exact records over a period of time and by painstaking attention to this data, they have created new races of lilies.

Why did they succeed where earlier attempts had failed? New methods of propagation and of storing pollen from plants flowering at different times plus improved techniques of raising seedlings were responsible. We must remember too how recently many fine species were brought back from the wild. For example, the regal lily was not found in China by Ernest Wilson until 1903.

Whatever the reason, suddenly, unrelated species would cross and produce viable seed, and the resulting hybrids were even more easily hybridized with each other. Jan de Graaff of Oregon is deservedly the most famous among a host of hardworking, imaginative breeders who have developed new hybrids so fine and different in vigor, color and form that they are rapidly replacing the species lilies. Where, for instance, there were once thousands of the old regal lilies sold each season, gardeners are now picking their white trumpets from among the new hybrids. Once-popular Centifolium Hybrids of the 1950's are already giving way to the Olympic Hybrids. In turn these have been subjected to further selection so that there are now pink, brownish (on the reverse), yellow and green strains as well as whiter examples of the original Olympics. Equally astounding developments have changed other types of lilies.

Further variations are now occurring from changes, induced through atomic radiation in the basic chromosome count so there are presently tetraploid lilies with even more stature and vigor. (This is a different technique than hybridizing.) For example, the tetraploid *L. longiflorum* (Easter lily) is stronger-stemmed with larger flowers having more substance than the type.

The excitement of this revolution is still a long way from dying down! After you have read here a basic introduction to the new lilies, your best source of information about the latest developments will be the current catalogs of lily specialists and the yearbooks of the North American Lily Society (NALS), an active group which also sponsors many informative shows. Study at least one new catalog each year just to get a complete picture of the wonders that are yours for the planting. And once you have seen and tried a few in your garden, you'll agree with me that soon many of the species will be kept alive only by sentimental gardeners and lily specialists. Fanciers will note I have listed only a handful of the best of the species lilies. This is because the hybrids are better adapted to today's gardens.

As Old as History

For a moment let us leave this wonderful new world of lilies and glance back into the mists of time. Lilies appear in some of the earliest records of man. Conjectures that the Biblical city of Susa was the original home of the madonna lily and took its name from their abundance thereabouts would put the earliest mention of the genus more than 4,000 years ago.

We are on firmer ground, however, if we start with pottery found on the island of Crete, where the lily appears to have been a favorite. Recognizable madonna lilies beautify vases dating from about 1600 B.C., and there are signet rings, beads and daggers with lily decorations almost as old. A charming seal (c. 1500 B.C.) found in a grave near the ancient Greek city of Pylos shows a woman offering lilies at an altar. There are early Mesopotamian designs which appear lilylike too, and the famous lion frieze in the Nineveh palace of that fierce Assyrian, Assurbanipal, contains representations of lilies which can be dated to the seventh century B.C. Far away from the old Mediterranean world we find prehistoric Siberian wall hangings with a design that certainly suggests a red lily.

Lilies appear in the Egypt of the Pharaohs too. We find flowers in funeral wreaths and even a madonna lily bulb tucked into a mummy case for food, medicine or as a rare treasure. A clay mould of a lily found in Egypt dates at least to 1587

B.C., and pieces of jewelry buried with mummies are shaped more like lilies than any native Egyptian plant.

Even today bulbs are eaten in China, and many authorities claim that the madonna lily became widespread through Europe because of its edibility and its medicinal properties in a salve. The history of those times is full of wars, forced marches and migrations, so the madonnas could easily have travelled far as food, medicine and mementoes of former homes. Since they need only the shallowest planting, even accidentally dropped scales could have rooted, as numerous experts suggest.

By comparatively recent Greek and Roman times, lilies were a favorite garland flower for heroes and for decoration. By the medieval period this lily had made its way all over Europe, where it was used both as medicine and food, as well as the symbol of the Virgin. Thus for millenniums mankind has loved the lily, but it is in modern times that the greatest achievements in breeding have come. Today, with the appearance of vigorous new hybrids, the lily is just beginning a career as a dependable garden inhabitant.

The Modern Story

Some of our most popular catalogs do not yet mirror what is actually available among the hybrid lilies, but the biggest bulb houses are beginning to carry a few selected types. Write and ask them to add others to their lists, or secure a catalog from a lily specialist. I have grown only a very small percentage of the new hybrids, and these have been vigorous and healthy. Some of the new hybrids have already performed so brilliantly under varied conditions that they have earned permanent stardom in the hybrid galaxy, but this is an unfinished story. No doubt many of today's hybrids will be replaced by even better introductions which they themselves will have fathered; reselection is constant. This is no reason to hang back from trying any of today's hybrids, although I would certainly start with those most reasonably priced, and in most cases this means buying strains rather than named clones.

Where to Buy

The world today needs fewer trade barriers and restrictions, so it is with regret I advise you to buy only American-grown lily bulbs, both species and hybrids. (Most of the best Canadian introductions are handled by American growers to avoid customs delay.) In some cases our bulbs are more expensive than lilies imported from Europe and Asia. Nevertheless, in the long run they are worth it. With plenty of fresh, new land available, adequate sanitation and inspection plus a conscientiously carried out program of raising disease-free stock from seed, American growers provide lilies worth any extra cost. Perhaps in time the Asian and European lily growers will be able to overcome the difficulties they face, but for the present imported stock often succumbs, not because the lilies are difficult, but because the bulbs were diseased or out of the ground too long.

Most important is the availability of American bulbs for fall planting. The value of this cannot be overemphasized. If you order early, it is seldom necessary to delay planting until winter has set in for most of the new hybrid bulbs from American sources, and fall planting is by far the best policy.

Most of our modern hybrids are grown on the West Coast. Modern transportation and packing have brought these within the reach of anyone in this country, and all the big bulb suppliers now offer them. Many of the Canadian lilies as well as some of their own introductions are being propagated by small nurseries in Vermont and other parts of New England, and the federal Department of Agriculture is also active in this field; theirs are among the very hardiest strains, although all growers report healthy lily bulbs have survived far greater temperature fluctuations than was thought possible a generation ago.

Those who garden where severe climatic conditions like drought, heat and cold hamper success will find reports in the yearbooks of the NALS to aid selection of those hybrids most likely to succeed. These yearbooks, available for a small annual membership fee, are also invaluable to amateurs interested in hybridizing. Some of our most fruitful breakthroughs have been obtained through the work of patient backyard gardeners.

Clones and Strains

In discussing lilies there are several terms to understand.

WILD LILIES are called the SPECIES and given botanical names. Through common usage many are better known by a popular name (*Lilium candidum:* madonna lily). They breed true from seed, so obtain species lilies which have been produced from seed to avoid introducing diseases which are transmitted by vegetative propagation like scaling.

Modern lily catalogs also offer NAMED HYBRIDS and HYBRID STRAINS. Bulbs sold as a specific named hybrid are all vegetative progeny of one certain lily which was found to be outstanding. This CLONE, as it is called, because of its unique color, flower size or shape was selected for perpetuating, and all bulbs sold under its name are in a sense part of the original. Since they have been reproduced asexually, every lily sold as Enchantment, Green Dragon or Jillian Wallace (to name a few famous clones) is exactly like the original plant selected. When first introduced, bulbs of named clones may be expensive. If they multiply well, prices gradually come down. Because they must be reproduced vegetatively, there is always a chance the bulbs of a clone can be diseased. Modern lily growers, aware of the dangers, rogue out any suspicious plants constantly to guard against this.

A HYBRID LILY STRAIN is the result of crosses between species or hybrids. A great many seedlings are raised from crosses between two known parents, and the resulting plants will vary as will their progeny from continued crossing. At any time during this process a clone may be selected for naming. Most of the results of a cross, however, are not worthy of this honor. At this point the breeder has a hybrid strain, such as the Aurelian Hybrids, which shows a tremendous variation in color, shape and growth habits. The Aurelians, for example, are the results of crosses between trumpet lilies and the re-curved *L. henryi*. Some of the seedlings look like one parent or the other while some have a new shape or color intermediate between the parents. Where a catalog description mentions much variation, you know that those hybrids have not yet been further selected.

Our American growers, applying the laws of inheritance first discovered by Mendel, have gone several steps further in most cases. Taking a general hybrid strain, they have SELECTED plants with the same general characteristics of color, shape, season of bloom or growth habit and bred to strengthen them. These may be listed as Selected Aurelian Hybrids, and some notation as to their outstanding characteristic will clue you to the difference.

From selected hybrids to HYBRID STRAINS is perhaps the greatest American contribution. More and more catalogs feature them, and we have already indicated these are the best buy for the average gardener. The well-known Fiesta Hybrids are a fine example. The original group is still available in many bright colors with some variation in flower form. For only slightly more per bulb, however, you can now purchase the Citronella Strain (lemon), the Bronzino Strain (browns and ambers), the Burgundy Strain (dark reds) or the Golden Wedding Strain (golden-yellow).

The advantages in planning garden pictures are obvious. Uniformity of color is much easier to integrate with other plants. There will be some variation in a strain, but it should stay within the color range. The slight differences in height, color or flower shape of such strains add charm. When further selection is done within a strain, you have even more uniformity, still at reasonable prices. The Sunburst Strain, for instance, was originally a selection of Aurelian Hybrids with flat star-shaped, only slightly-recurved flowers quite different from either parent. It has been subdivided into whitish, orange, yellow and pink strains, all with the same general flower form.

Lilies within a strain are produced from seed of known parents (selected from the results of known crosses, back-crosses and recrosses). The laws of inheritance being what they are, the breeder can continue to produce lilies within a strain from seed. This means bulbs remain healthy and prices reasonable because the growers have become so efficient at raising seedlings. In addition there is a continued improvement because the growers constantly select the most typical parents so that a strain is gradually strengthened. Often a strain is named for a famous clone whose flowers are used as parents. The strain is always cheaper than the clone.

Within the last few years the number of strains and clones offered has increased to a point where a lily catalog is a bewildering array, even to the experienced lily grower. For the

13. One of the lovely Heart's Desire hybrid lilies in an attractive quiet nook. Against the green of shrubbery, a single plant contrasts with the delicate foliage of ferns (Herman v. Wall).

gardener who just wants a few lilies, the situation is rapidly reaching a point of no return.

A revolution is always confusing, and the present state of lilies is so far from static you may well wonder what to choose. No formal horticultural classification of the genus has yet been adopted to help us, although Mr. de Graaff has proposed one which will be used by many of his dealers. I have adapted this to give you some idea of the breadth of present lily hybridizing. By selecting representatives from the various divisions, you will be able to adorn your garden with different types of lilies to spread bloom over the longest period.

Why a Classification?

The logical classification of dahlias and daffodils makes it much easier to describe members of those genera and also easier for you to find what you want in catalogs. Some such treatment for lilies is overdue. It is not possible to make such divisions at the beginning of intensive hybridizing; no one can predict just what may appear. When certain lines of breeding have developed, however, it becomes a necessity to the ordinary gardener, who should not have to take a course in genetics before choosing a dozen lilies.

Up to now most lily catalogs have listed lilies either alphabetically or under the breeder's name. The number of strains and named clones is already so great it takes hours to select them intelligently. The matter is further complicated by the wide range of colors, flower shapes, heights and forms of inflorescence among the hybrids. Moreover, different lilies may bloom as early as May and as late as November in various parts of the country. Few other genera spread flowering over so long a period. No one classification can take every point into consideration, but Mr. de Graaff's proposed system encompasses them all to some degree. With allowances for individual variances, those hybrids in Division 1 are earliest, with the flowering of subsequent divisions continuing the display up to those in Division 12 toward the end of the summer. (Species lilies—Division 13—extend the season both ways.) While envisioned as a horticultural listing to aid gardeners rather than a botanical system, it is founded on the general blood lines of hybrid lilies and thus automatically sorts them with some logic. Further subdivisions or more radical changes may be necessary if new lines develop.

More than one lily fancier thinks it is impossible to classify the new hybrids. Each breeder is convinced his representatives of a strain are better; each is jealous of his own prerogative in naming a strain and, of course, each hopes for a breakthrough in some different line with a new type of lily.

Each breeder also wants to sell bulbs, and perhaps this is where we as consumers ultimately will force them into group action. Already there is a fair amount of cooperation in the registering of new lily names. I know one thing: King Nonsense cannot refer to more than one specific clone or strain of lily any more than King Alfred can be applied to more than one daffodil if the gardener is to plant a bulb with any assurance of getting what he expects.

I am not listing here any clones. A current catalog is your best guide right now as to what is available. The representative strains I have listed are not inclusive, but they give you a jumping-off place and some conception of the pattern of hybridizing as it now stands. If the examples lean heavily toward de Graaff introductions, that is partly because he has done the widest breeding and partly because of course this is his basic proposal.

I do not present this as a conclusive systematizing of the lily hybrids. I only know that having struggled lengthily to clarify the picture for myself before writing this chapter, I can testify to the need for some classification and strongly urge the NALS and allied groups to adopt something soon. I acknowledge with gratitude Mr. de Graaff's allowing me to adapt his classification here. Of all those active in hybridizing lilies, he seems the logical person to bring order to the present chaos. At least here is a step in the right direction.

What to Buy

You cannot go wrong with any of the Mid-Century Hybrids, and there are named clones available everywhere in brilliant shades of red, yellow and orange to give color in early summer (Color Plate XX). The Martagon-Hansoni types are reported subject to basal rot, but they are beautiful and some clones in existence are thirty years old. I grew dozens of species madonna lilies at one time without any trouble from disease, but stock is not always healthy now; disease-free, seed-grown bulbs can be found, and hybrids are coming.

The Cernuum types are very hardy, but the pinks may be lilac or anemic. I have not grown the Bellinghams and am told they are not as easy here in the East as other hybrids; I would like to try the reported English hybrids of eastern American lilies. The Tetra Longiflorums introduced by the U.S.D.A. have been enthusiastically received by many and are reported hardy in Maine! Most of the Davidi Hybrids are very bright and reported very hardy for areas where spring has late frost.

The new trumpet lily strains which include pink, white, green and yellow selections are uniformly fine. The Aurelians divide into four main types, as Mr. de Graaff's classification shows. They fall mostly into white, yellow and orange shades but pinks have recently appeared, and the bicolors are exciting. I am partial to the Sunburst types, but the others are just as good. Almost every hybridizer has Aurelian Hybrids of some sort. Use the classification with the catalog as you order. The Aurelians are probably not as hardy as some other types in severe climates.

The late-flowering Tiger Hybrids are fairly new and bring vivid yellow, orange and red-orange shades to the midsummer lily spectrum.

Toward the end of the summer the new Japanese Hybrids from Division 12 reign wherever they are planted, and they are reported wonderfully hardy. (A few hybrids from this group flower earlier due to *L. rubellum* blood.) There are red, white and pink strains available, some with the gold band of the auratum parent, others with the spotted, reflexed petals of the speciosums. Make sure the bulbs you buy from this group are hybrid strains and not species variations, and you will be getting the very newest and most beautiful late summer flowers among the bulbs.

The greatest improvements have been made among the Chinese Trumpets, the Aurelian Hybrids and among crosses between the two species, *L. auratum* and *L. speciosum*, both garden favorites. This latter group is now being subjected to further crosses with several other lilies. Sometimes they are listed as Auratum Hybrids or as Speciosum Hybrids. It is really too early to limit ourselves to rigid terminology since so much selection and breeding is going on in this auratum-speciosum program. Most of the growers are naming only a few clones, and I think this will be good for our gardens. There is no reason not to think that in time these will show even greater improvement, but the selections now on the market are incredible in color and beauty.

Heights and Dates

Catalogs indicate considerable variation in heights and blooming dates of the hybrids. Climatic and seasonal variations account for some of this. A lily which reaches only 3 feet in the North or in field-grown trials may double its height under perfect conditions in more temperate gardens. There is of course always some variation in strains. The perfectionist should seek the uniformity of named clones. Usually lilies bloom later their first season, and a few take a whole year before making themselves at home. Because the lily story is still so new, even the growers do not always know for sure what maximum heights will be under varying conditions. You will be part of the story when you report how they did in your garden.

Bulbs of moderate size apparently transplant best although they may not yield as much initial bloom as the jumbos.

PROPOSED CLASSIFICATION OF LILIES

Division and dates of bloom	Name and Flower Description of basic species used in hybridizing	Description of Flowers and representative strains available
Division 1 (May–June)	Hollandicum Hybrids *L. dauricum* (early, upright cups, yellow to red)	Early, upright, cup-shaped, in yellow, orange, red; Hollandicum Hybrids, Coronado Hybrids, Golden Chalice Hybrids; named clones available
Division 2 (June–July)	Early Tiger Lily Hybrids *L. tigrinum* (orange, recurved)	Early, upfacing, pendant or outfacing flowers, more or less recurved; Mid-Century Hybrids; many named clones

Division 3 (June)	Martagon-Hansoni Types *L. martagon* (many nodding, reflexed flowers, mostly purple or white) *L. hansoni* (many nodding, orange, slightly recurved)	Wide range of color: white, yellow, orange, lilac, mahogany, spotted; many recurved flowers on tall, slender stems; Paisley Strain, Backhouse Hybrids; Painted Lady Hybrids; some named clones
Division 4 (June–July)	Madonna Lily Hybrids *L. candidum* (fragrant white trumpet)	*L. x testaceum:* buff; watch for others to be introduced
Division 5 (June–July)	Cernuum Hybrids *L. cernuum* (small, pink-lavender, recurved)	Many recurved flowers on branching stems in ivory, pink, lilac, amber shades, very hardy; Harlequin Hybrids, Patterson Hybrids; some named clones
Division 6 (June–July)	Native American Hybrids (West Coast species)	Rhizomatous bulbs; many nodding to semi-outfacing, more or less reflexed flowers in yellow, orange and red shades, spotted; some named clones
Division 7 (July)	Easter Lilies *L. longiflorum* (fragrant white trumpet)	All varieties and hybrids of the species, including tetraploids; tetras hardier than the type which is most used in forcing; Croft, Ace, Estate, Longiflora Tetra
Division 8 (June–July)	Davidi Hybrids *L. davidi* (many, small reflexed, pendant, mostly red)	Hybrids of this and related species with many nodding, reflexed flowers from yellow to maroon shades; Fiesta Hybrids (color strains sold), Preston Hybrids (named clones)

Division 9 (June–Aug.)	Chinese Trumpet Hybrids *L. leucanthum var. centifolium,* *L. sargentiae, L. sulphurum,* *L. regale* (white and yellow trumpets	Hardy trumpets in white, yellow, chartreuse, pink, some with darker reverses; Olympic Hybrids Pink Perfection Strain, Black Magic Strain, Sentinel Strain, Green Magic Strain, Green Mountain Hybrids, Carrara Strain, Shelburne Hybrids, Sulphur Hybrids; named clones in some colors
Division 10 (July–Aug.)	Aurelian Hybrids hybrids derived from crosses with lilies in Div. 9 and *L. henryi* (many, nodding, reflexed, orange)	White, yellow, orange shades widely available; pinks and bicolors are newer.
A. Trumpet flowers		Hybrids of strictly trumpet shape; African Queen Strain, Copper King Strain, Emerald Strain, Golden Clarion Strain, Moonlight Strain; some named clones
B. Bowl-shaped flowers		Hybrids with clearly bowl-shaped and outward-facing flowers; Heart's Desire Strain, Inspiration Strain, Golden Harvest Hybrids, Carnival Strain; some named clones
C. Pendant flowers		Hybrids with distinctly pendant flowers; Golden Showers Strain; few named clones
D. Sunburst flowers		Hybrids with flat-open, star-shaped flowers; Sunburst Strain available in selected

		colors of white, orange, gold, pink, also mixtures; many named clones
Division 11 (July–Aug.)	Late Tiger Lily Hybrids L. tigrinum and similar L. maximowiczi	Late-flowering hybrids like Div. 2 in yellow, orange, red; Grenadier Hybrids; some named clones
Division 12 (July–Aug., but a few may be earlier)	Japanese Lily Hybrids L. auratum (bowl-shaped, gold band on petals) L. speciosum (recurved, pink, red or white, spotted) L. japonicum (pink trumpet) L. rubellum (early pink trumpet) Subdivisions possible by flower shape or parentage	White, pink, or red flowers, often spotted, some have gold band on petals; some almost flat, others recurving; Potomac Strain, Jamboree Strain, Red Band Hybrids, Pink Glory Strain, Flying Cloud Strain, Angel Wings Strain, Imperial Crimson Strain, Imperial Gold Strain, Imperial Silver Strain, Parkmanni Hybrids, Atomic Hybrids
Division 13	All species lilies	(bloom time: May to December, depending on species and climate).

CHAPTER 10

Success With Lilies

With the modern hybrid lilies, it is not necessary to go to special lengths to provide congenial homes. They belong in the garden with the other flowers.

Perfect Drainage and Ventilation

Assuming you start with healthy bulbs, the key to success with lilies is drainage. You may read of wild lilies growing in running water; nevertheless in the garden they must have soil which drains perfectly so there is never standing water around the bulbs. The best idea is to give them a place on a slight slope. (Other ways to insure drainage are discussed in Chapter 2.)

Lilies do not like crowded conditions. Choose a site where the air is able to move—not where there will be wind damage but where there is good ventilation. Avoid pockets made by shrubbery or buildings where frost may linger, or locations where thick, overhanging branches make too dense a screen.

Humus and Soil Preparation

Constantly, wherever lilies are described, you will find the words "moist but well-drained." Humus in the soil is the answer

154

to the apparent paradox. Almost any plant grows better in soil full of organic material for this automatically permits better drainage, entrance of air and beneficial bacterial action in the earth itself; lilies demand such conditions. Considering the splendor of their display and their longevity when their needs are met, you should be willing to prepare their home at least as well as you might for roses. (Ways to add humus are detailed in Chapter 2.)

Before you plant lilies, dig the soil at least a foot deep to make sure it is not compacted. Add humus if necessary. This initial preparation is more important than any fertilizing or mulching you may do in subsequent years and needs to be done only once. No magic chemical will ever substitute as a soil conditioner for added humus and thorough digging so do not stint on it for lilies—or anything else you want to grow.

When to Plant

Fall is best. The earlier the better, and with madonna lilies that means August or September so they can make fall foliage. For other lilies, particularly if winter arrives early in your latitude, prepare soil early and mulch with piles of straw, hay or leaves to keep it from freezing until the bulbs arrive. Replace the mulch after planting to keep lilies from heaving the first winter. Since many American-grown bulbs are ready by October, this will not be necessary in most cases. Always water well after planting and repeat several times if the season is dry.

When bulbs come very late or unforseen events upset your schedule, pop them into large clay pots of soil and store for the winter in a cold frame or a cool place. Insure drainage with a layer of pebbles in the bottom of the pot (Figure 13). Gently remove the whole soil block and plant without disturbing the roots as early in spring as practicable, setting the bulb at the right depth at the same time. The soil in the pot should be moistened slightly during the winter if the pot does not get natural irrigation from the weather. I have had such dismal results with spring planting that I shall no longer do any. (Some of the big lily growers say they can store lilies well enough to make it worthwhile.)

How Deep?

Modern lilies do not need deep planting. It used to be they were planted a foot or more below ground level because some wild species had been found at those depths. Many of them were never seen again after burial!

Now all of the American hybridizers advise against setting the bulbs with more than 5 or 6 inches of soil above them. Given proper preparation, the soil above and below the bulbs will be in good tilth. This means the basal roots of the lily will be able to pull it farther down into the earth if necessary, and it also enables the stem roots which many types produce above the bulb to wander freely in the soil (Figure 1). The bulb which is perhaps set too shallowly can thus sink, but no chance exists for one originally buried too deep.

A good rule of thumb is to set the smaller bulbs with 2 to 3 inches of soil over them and the largest sizes with 4 to 6 inches. Try to plant at least three bulbs of one kind in each clump and put them from 6 to 12 inches apart. The big new hybrids should not be too close; smaller species need less space.

Sandy soil requires deeper planting than heavy clay soil. Severe winter temperatures suggest slightly deeper planting than where it is more temperate. Where summers are exceedingly hot and dry, some mulch is absolutely necessary to keep roots cool; use whatever is easiest, as indicated in Chapter 2.

Living plants either as groundcover or as foreground plantings tend to shade the earth around the lily bulbs and accomplish the same result in less torrid climates.

The important exceptions to these rules are *L. candidum*, *L. chalcedonicum* and their hybrids which are never planted deeper than 2 inches; 1 inch is sufficient in most soils. In every case follow the grower's directions for the latest and best advice.

Fertilizing

Like other bulbs, lilies will be healthier without too much artificial fertilizing, but the addition of small amonts of bonemeal (⅓ cup is enough for several square feet) in the fall or of a chemical fertilizer low in nitrogen (use sparingly) after shoots appear in spring is helpful. Scratch into the soil rather than just dumping on the surface. Old cow manure or dried manure may also be used in small amounts during the fall but never apply fresh manure to lilies and never allow it to touch stems or leaves.

Possibilities in Shade

Your catalogs will indicate lilies which grow in some shade; this will never mean more than light, high, changing shadow. No lily prospers without some sun. Many of the pink, red and orange varieties keep their color better if given a little protection from the midday sun. The shifting pattern of trees and shrubs is quite sufficient; shade cast by buildings or thick evergreen copses will be too much. Lilies cannot compete with thick tree and shrub roots.

Most lilies look best when planted with other growing things, partly because their tall stems need the tempering effect of lower-growing plants. This is especially true of the big new hybrids, many of which yield multiflowered candelabras or pyramids 5 feet or more above the ground. (Sometimes I wish the breeders would do more with dwarf lilies.)

When to Transplant

Once you have prepared the soil well, you will not have to transplant healthy lilies for some time if you have set them far enough apart. Never move them unless you have to, and then replant immediately. Try not to bruise the bulbs, and discard any which appear diseased or damaged.

If lilies are still growing when you must transplant, treat them like other plants, disturbing the roots as little as possible and watering and shading them afterward. It is much better to wait until the stalk has died down since this is when the lily is most nearly dormant, but do not leave plants or bulbs out of the soil even overnight. Mark the location of such transplanted lilies well and do not disturb for two seasons; they often sulk and make no growth at all for a year. Even with care I have had transplanted lilies just disappear forever so avoid transplanting as long as you can.

Mosaic, Virus and Tulips

Please don't let reference to virus keep you from growing the modern lilies. And if you once grew lilies that sickened after a year or two, by all means give today's hybrids a chance before you condemn the whole genus. (Chapter 22 contains first-aid suggestions for sick lilies.)

With hybrids field-grown in this country, you may garden

without ever seeing any of these diseases. A few general precautions will make it easier. Once more I repeat—buy only disease-free stock, and this is most likely to be obtained from American growers at the present time. For easiest gardening stick to the hybrids which have built-in vigor and resistance.

Never divide lilies and replace some in the same soil. Discard any which are badly bruised (a few injured scales can be easily peeled off). Throw away those which are rotten or contain spots likely to be the sclerotia of disease. Clean up all debris carefully and burn it after the foliage has matured to avoid carrying disease over the winter in the soil.

Where bulbs are just one facet of a garden, you might as well have fun and mix them as you wish. Mr. de Graaff reports he grows tulips right alongside his greenhouses and sees no reason to separate tulips and lilies or to worry about cucumbers and other related plants near them. Dr. Cynthia Westcott, the famous Plant Doctor, suggests not growing the three genera near each other.

Mr. de Graaff obviously knows more about lilies and tulips and related diseases than I do, but undoubtedly he also sprays systematically against aphids and botrytis. I do not. I feed and water my plants and try to give them congenial growing sites, and they have to get along with that. So far they have done well close together, but I plan to distribute future plantings so tulips and lilies will not be adjacent—an ounce of prevention as it were.

My thinking may be too conservative, but on the other hand, "Every known mottle virus of lilies transmits to and can be detected in tulip."[1] Moreover, the virus which breaks the color in tulips might be fatal to lilies so do not admit any of the "broken" tulips to a garden with lilies. Watch carefully in the

[1] McWhorter, Frank P., *Handbook on Bulb Growing and Forcing* (Northwest Bulb Growers Assn., 1957), p. 63.

spring for danger signs on your tulips and get rid of any you suspect before they infect other tulips or your lilies. Melons, squash and cucumbers grown near lilies may also transmit disease. Aphids are the main virus carriers so fight them constantly.

Rogue and burn any suspicious lily to keep disease from spreading. Once a lily has virus there is no cure, so be ruthless.

Finally, think twice about introducing species lilies into a garden where there is a big investment in the more expensive hybrids. Be finicky enough to inquire into the source of species lily bulbs before buying them; seed-grown types are the safest. This may seem like splitting hairs, but with seed-grown species you can be fairly sure they will not bring a disease in if they were grown by a reputable nursery. Some wild lilies are resistant to certain types of virus even though actually infected; they act as disease carriers. There is also more than one type of virus, and what is a mild infection in one species is death to another.

Even so it is possible to grow a great many without loss if the original stock is healthy. It is only common sense, however, to separate the different species if you have a garden big enough to support many of them. The general rules promulgated in Chapter 22 for all bulbs are important enough to the growing of lilies to warrant your giving them a reading before trouble enters.

This warning section had to be written in all fairness, but it is not meant to throw cold water on anyone. Nothing available today is more beautiful than the new lilies for the summer garden. I sigh over the catalogs and find that choosing those the budget will allow is one of my hardest autumn tasks. Each one is lovelier than the next, and no garden is complete without some.

THE SPECIES LILIES

Some gardeners will always plant a few of the more than one hundred wild species and their mutations, and not only for sentimental reasons. Many have an ethereal beauty and daintiness missing in the big hybrids. A number are important for early or late blooming since the present hybrids flower mostly during midsummer. Others have unusual color and form.

Even as I write this, however, I wonder how many of the species will be able to hold their own against new introductions which are hardier, healthier and sturdier because of their hybrid vigor. There are whispers of hybrid madonna lilies; and already the Painted Lady, Paisley and Backhouse Hybrids are nudging the ordinary martagons. Some of the Atomic Hybrids, they tell me, are incredibly early bloomers, and every hybridizer is working to stretch the bloom season at both ends.

The orchid-like show lilies (*L. speciosum*) and the gold-band lilies (*L. auratum*) were so very beautiful we kept planting them no matter what their foibles, but now there are hybrids which are being selected for their likeness to both types. The Potomac Hybrids and the Jamboree Strain may replace the speciosums while selections from the Imperial Silver and Imperial Gold Strains are much hardier than the auratums they resemble. One big lily grower told me he is removing all species auratums from his own garden. Crosses between these two favorite species have already produced beautiful lilies new in form and color.

Because our American lily growers have taken the trouble to grow many of the old species from seed so they would have disease-free bulbs for propagating purposes, I do not think the species will be entirely ignored. They are too lovely for such a fate now that there are dependable sources.

Even so there is no reason to lament their giving way in most gardens to the new hybrids, any more than there is sense in advocating that today's gardeners discard their healthy and colorful floribunda roses for the old June-flowering bushes. We still grow some of the old roses and certain wild daffodils and tulips, for example, because their form or season fills a specific need in our garden. The species lilies will play a similar role.

Below are some of the more important and beautiful species lilies, the most likely to remain in our affections, with notations as to particular needs.

EARLY

TURK'S CAP (*L. amabile*)—2 to 4 feet, late June; bright red, spotted black; full sun; about 4 inches deep; there is a lovely yellow form.

MADONNA LILY (*L. candidum*)—3 to 4 feet, June; waxy white, fragrant trumpets; plant no deeper than 2 inches in loam with a touch of lime as early as you can get the bulbs, so they can make fall foliage; botrytis-resistant strains are available; but many candidums harbor mosaic.

STAR LILY (*L. concolor*)—2 to 3 feet, June to July; vibrant red, star-shaped; plant in groups in full sun 3 to 4 inches deep; a fine yellow form exists.

TENUIFOLIUM or CORAL LILY (*L. pumilum*)—1½ to 2 feet, early June; dainty scarlet Turk's caps; often short-lived if left to go to seed but easy to grow from seed; well-drained soil, sun; 4 inches deep; named yellow forms available.

ROYAL LILY (*L. regale*)—4 to 6 feet, June to July; white trumpets with rose reverses; easy and dependable; 5 to 6 inches deep; fine yellow forms are mostly natural mutations.

L. RUBELLUM—1 to 2 feet, May or June; dwarf rose-pink trumpets; hardy but slow-growing; get healthy bulbs, plant in humus-rich soil and semi-shade; about 3 to 4 inches deep.

MIDSUMMER

L. FORMOSANUM PRICEI—2 to 3 feet, July to August; dwarf, early form; very susceptible to virus but easily raised from seed; full sun, well-drained loam about 4 inches deep.

L. HANSONI—4 to 6 feet, June; nodding, yellow-orange, recurved flowers, spotted brown; resistant to virus; give some shade; 5 to 6 inches deep.

L. HENRYI—5 to 8 feet, July and August; many orange, pendant, recurved flowers; light shade; 5 inches deep; a rare yellow form exists.

EASTER LILY (*L. longiflorum*)—2 to 6 feet, July; fragrant white trumpets popular for indoor forcing; various strains have different heights and hardiness; 5 to 6 inches deep; the Beltsville (USDA) tetraploid longiflorums are larger and hardier.

WHITE TURK'S CAP (*L. martagon album*)—3 to 5 feet, June and July, pyramids of dainty white, pendant caps; thrives in almost any soil in sun; one of the most permanent; 4 inches deep; so far no hybrid compares with this white form.

L. NEPALENSE—2 to 3 feet, July; pendant, emerald-white trumpets with brownish-purple throats are striking for arrangers but of little value for garden decoration; seems to be fairly hardy, moist, deep, well-drained soil; 4 inches deep; these bulbs wander.

L. PAPILLIFERUM—about a foot tall, July; eggplant-colored Turk's caps; rare and mostly for arrangers; give a warm, well-drained location; it seems to be fairly hardy; 2 inches deep.

LATE

L. DAURICUM WILSONI—3 to 5 feet, August to September; upright apricot cups; partial shade; 3 inches deep.

L. FORMOSANUM—5 to 7 feet, September to frost; white trumpets with purplish-brown reverses; sun or a little partial shade, may need extra water in dry summers; where fall is late, these may bloom until December but very susceptible to virus; 5 to 6 inches deep.

SHOW LILY (*L. speciosum*)—3 to 6 feet, August to September; frilled and reflexed in red, pink or white, often spotted, branching stems; cool, well-drained soil with plenty of humus and a touch of shade; 5 inches deep; white form bloom later than pink.

AMERICAN SPECIES LILIES

This continent has been particularly favored with a wide variety of wild lilies although most of them are in shades of red, orange or yellow. Conservationists and wild flower enthusiasts will find many of them difficult to cultivate; tolerance and habitats are quite limited in many cases. Described in detail are those considered easiest to cultivate. Several lily growers and wild flower specialists offer bulbs for sale. Never gather bulbs in the wild; only the botanist stands much chance of success there.

RARE SPECIES

L.	L.
bolanderi	*ocellatum*
catesbaei	*occidentale*
columbianum	*parryi*
fairchildi	*parvum*
fresnense	*pitkinense*
grayi	*rubescens*
humboldti	*shastense*
iridollae	*vollmeri*
maritimum	*washingtonianum*
nevadense	*wigginsi*

EASIER SPECIES

MEADOW LILY (*L. canadense*)—2 to 5 feet, July; pendant bells, yellow to deep red variations; moist, well-drained soil, sun or partial shade; 6 inches deep, often wanders.

WEST COAST MARTAGON (*L. kelloggi*)—2 to 4 feet, June and July; nodding, fragrant Turk's caps open ivory to light pink, mature purple, often have yellow stripe on petal, sometimes spotted; moist, well-drained, part shade; 2 to 4 inches deep.

L. MICHIGANENSE—2 to 5 feet, June and July; pendulous orange flowers, spotted; yellow forms exist; sunny, moist site; 5 to 6 inches deep.

L. MICHAUXI (*L. carolinianum*)—1½ to 3 feet, July and August; smaller, southern form of *L. superbum* but seems to be hardy north.

LEOPARD LILY (*L. pardalinum*)—5 to 8 feet, July; many Turk's caps of orange-crimson, spotted; easily grown in north-west, where it needs nearly full sun; multiplies rapidly by branching rhizomes; 2 to 5 inches deep.

WOOD LILY (*L. philadelphicum*)—1 to 3 feet, June and July; upright chalices, yellow to red forms, spotted; must have cool, acid soil, plenty of humus and well-drained, sun or partial shade; about 5 inches deep.

AMERICAN TURK'S CAP (*L. superbum*)—5 to 9 feet, July and August; many flowers, yellow to deep red, very hardy; easiest for gardens but keep soil on acid side; humus, moist, sun or light shade; 5 to 6 inches deep.

CAPSULE VIEW OF LILIES

Plant only healthy bulbs; hybrids are easier than species; hybrid strains are the best buys in most cases at the present time.

Lilies must have perfect drainage at all times of year; prepare soil well before planting.

Do not plant too deep: 3 to 4 inches is enough for small bulbs; 5 to 6 inches for large sizes; 1 to 2 inches for madonna, chalcedonicum and their hybrids which also need earliest planting.

Most lilies prefer slightly acid soil.

Fertilize sparingly; water well in droughts; cultivate

shallowly only after shoots emerge; protect spring shoots from frost; give summer mulch or shade roots with other plants.

Most lilies prefer sun; many hold their color and petals better with partial shade at midday.

Sanitation is important to keep lilies healthy. Keep tulips, lilies and cucurbits at a distance from each other if you are conservative and hate to spray; fight aphids to prevent the diseases they spread; there are sprays for Botrytis.

CHAPTER 11

Hardy Bulbs for Summer Bloom

Aside from the true lilies, there are only a few hardy bulbs for summer bloom, and some of those may not withstand a severe winter. However, they offer so much color at a time when the perennial garden is quiet that they are worth trying. Many are spectacular, fine for summer accent among lower-growing annuals.

Geography will help you decide which bulbs are most likely to succeed in your climate. Those native to this country (except Florida and other mild areas), to northern Asia and Europe or to the mountainous or southernmost parts of South America are hardier than those from the tropics or from South Africa. Exceptions are the hybrids, which are always more vigorous. Place of origin is given after the botanical name.

These bulbs are listed in the approximate order of hardiness. Most winter over at Philadelphia, but only the first few can survive without protection north of New York City or in rigorous inland climates. Some will not flower after a really bad winter, but may stage a comeback in subsequent years. Always give them a well-drained site. Those which cannot take your winters can be dug before frost and stored in peatmoss, sand or sawdust at cool but never freezing temperatures.

It helps to plant dubious survivors in a sheltered, south-facing position with a wall or thick evergreens for protection at the north. A location near the top of a slope is good since frost tends to stay later in the hollows. Winter mulching is advisable for the doubtful ones—several inches of salt hay, excelsior or dry leaves—held down by evergreen branches after the ground freezes. I try to plant all my doubtful bulbs in the same garden so one mulch job will suffice. This makes it easy to leave that area covered well into spring. Many of the doubtfuls will not flower if nipped by a late frost. The mulch keeps the roots cold and prevents early sprouting which is often the main danger. A temporary spring covering of burlap or an over-turned basket will save tender shoots or buds from damage if a late cold snap threatens.

All these bulbs need for nourishment is a tablespoon of bonemeal worked into the soil around each plant in the fall after growth stops and small amounts of dehydrated manure applied several times through the growing season; they can get along without regular feeding if grown in good loam.

IN ORDER OF HARDINESS

BLAZING STAR (*Liatris:* N. America) may be cataloged as gayfeather, but under any name it is a dependable late summer flower for bold accents. It may grow from thickened rootstocks or from tubers, depending on the species. The tall spires of fluffy flowers may reach 6 feet in some types, and it is hardy almost everywhere. Seed-grown plants are easily managed and will bloom the second season, but named hybrids and species are available from many nurseries. Liatris does best in full sun, but will blossom in light shade although the stems straggle.

¶ Cover liatris tubers with about 1 inch of soil and plant 6 inches apart; do not plant any closer because they increase in size, each giving more than one spire.

With age the tubers work to the surface, so reset in early spring if necessary. No pest or disease has ever bothered any of mine. The foliage is neat and clean, requiring little space.

White varieties tend to be later-blooming. I have had them in flower until October frost. However, the 6-foot September Glory is also late and a fine purple. *Liatris spicata*, Silver Tips, is a soft lavender-rose about 4 feet high for July and August. You will find some variation when you raise liatris from seed; botanists tell us the genus has become very mixed through hybridization. I have several whites which bear short branches of bloom on a tall spike and others of true spire form. The branching plants provide lovely flowers for small bouquets. Kobold, a non-branching purple hybrid less than 2 feet high, is best for small gardens, but every liatris I have ever seen is worthwhile.

Order plants for early spring planting. If you grow liatris from seed, mulch lightly the first winter to prevent heaving. Mature plants get no protection here.

GOLD STAR GRASS (*Hypoxis hirsuta:* N. America) is little known in gardens, but if you can acquire bulbs, you will be delighted with its hardiness and long blooming period —late spring and well into summer, sometimes until frost. The yellow flowers are seldom higher than 12 inches.

¶ Hypoxis will take lightest shade, prefers acid soil and goes about 2 inches deep and 5 to 6 apart in rock gardens.

MAGIC or RESURRECTION LILIES (*Lycoris squamigera:* Japan) are hardy in all but the most northern states. The popular name derives from their habit of producing clusters of lavender-pink trumpets on 2-foot stalks in late summer, after the lush, green, spring foliage has ripened and gone.

14. *Lycoris squamigera* is known as the resurrection lily because the flowers appear after the foliage fades in mid-summer (Roche).

¶ Lycoris does best with light shade, and the bulbs should go 4 to 6 inches deep and at least 5 inches apart.

Since they have no leaves when they bloom (Illustration 14), these "lilies" look best either toward the back of a border or interplanted with ferns or other plants which take some shade and have good fall foliage. Sometimes listed as hardy amaryllis or *Amaryllis halli*, the bulbs are usually planted in the fall; spring-planted bulbs often skip flowering their first year. Bulbs lifted just after the foliage has died in midsummer and immediately transplanted do best of all, but you can seldom obtain them commercially then. Leave them undisturbed indefinitely since they resent moving.

The related RED SPIDER LILY (*Lycoris radiata:* China, Japan) and the hybrid AMARCRINUMS will survive most winters at Philadelphia with a mulch, but they are not really reliable north of Washington, D.C. I am told that *Crinum bulbispermum* and the forms C. Cecil Houdyshel and C. Moorei are hardy into Ohio at least. Try them 6 inches deep and mulch for the winter.

Less hardy are the white *Lycoris alba,* the orange *L. sanguinea* and the yellow *L. aurea.* The same is true for the various NERINES and the other CRINUM LILIES. Even in the upper south these amaryllids benefit from mulching. In the far south and when grown in pots, most are planted with the top half of the bulb above the soil. In the north these tender and half-hardy bulbs may be pot grown for late summer bloom. Give them fertilizer and water while growing and flowering, keep them dry when dormant and store free from frost in the pots. Like most amaryllids the bulbs are best pot bound. Many will have to complete their leaf growth inside after frost.

THE BLACKBERRY LILY (*Belamcanda chinensis:* China), a member of the iris family, bears small, red-spotted orange flowers in graceful sprays about 3 feet high in August and September. Later the capsules split to reveal clusters of black seeds much used by flower arrangers.

¶ Set the rhizomes about 1 inch deep in rich loose soil in sun or partial shade and mulch lightly above Philadelphia.

Each foliage fan yields a branching spray of blossoms, only a few of which open at a time, so flowering is spread over several weeks. For good effect plant in clumps of at least three. There is a rare, later-flowering, pure yellow species (*B. flabellata*), and the Avalon Hybrids produce shades of apricot, yellow, orange and red, some of which are unspotted. Some catalogs still list the plant as *Pardanthus*. The rhizomes are usually planted in the fall, and belamcanda is also easily raised from seed and propagated by division.

FOXTAIL LILIES (*Eremurus*: Asia, Illustration 15) make dramatic accents in the early summer border, producing tall spires packed with hundreds of starry bells. Planted in autumn, they require a mulch the first winter. Where snow does not lie on the ground, it is wise to mulch every winter, partly to discourage too early emergence of shoots in spring. The brittle, fleshy roots resemble giant spiders and need careful handling to prevent breakage.

¶ Dig a wide hole, set the center tuber about 3 to 4 inches deep in average, well-drained soil in full sun and arrange the roots gently so they spread out horizontally around the tuber.

Since in time these lilies make a large rosette of sword-like leaves, place them several feet apart. A clump of three is spectacular at a distance but out of place in a small garden. The foliage browns quickly after flowering and disappears by midsummer. Foxtail lilies may not bloom the first season after transplanting so plant them where they may stay undisturbed for years. To prevent a late spring frost from damaging flower buds, cover emerging shoots with burlap or inverted baskets on questionable nights.

Easiest to work into average gardens is the 3- to 4-foot *E. bungei*, which bears yellow flowers in July, but it is not the

15. Foxtail lilies (*Eremurus*) are for dramatic accents in the early summer garden (Genereux).

hardiest. In June *E. elwesi* has pink flowers on taller stems; *E. himalaicus,* one of the hardiest, is earlier and has creamy white flowers on spires as much as 7 feet high; *E. robustus* is pink and may reach 8 feet in June. The slender Shelford Hybrids produce sturdy 3-feet stems of cream, yellow, apricot, pink, and orange bloom. The Tubergeni Hybrids with the same colors have even heavier spikes on stalks 8 to 10 feet high. All look best with evergreens as a background, and these protect the eremurus from the wind. Where slugs are rampant, protect the shoots with slugbait.

Eremurus may be raised from seed, but it will be at least three full years (often longer) before plants bloom. The younger roots are less hardy, but nurseries offer them at low prices, and these are easier to transplant without damage. Either way, your patience in mulching and waiting will be amply rewarded.

LILY TURF (*Liriope:* China, Japan) produces bluish flowers resembling grape hyacinths in summer and fall, but the shiny black berries which follow make these plants decorative much of the year since they last well into spring. They are related to the OPHIOPOGONS which are also called lily turf but are not quite as hardy and creep widely. Both types do well in sun or light shade and average soil.

¶ Hardy at least as far north as New York City, liriope should have its creeping rootstocks just beneath the soil with the tuberous roots extending vertically into the earth.

These plants make lush fountains of grassy leaves and are best kept away from smaller plants which they might crowd out. For edgings, *L. spicata* and *O. japonicus* are small and good. Under suitable conditions *L. muscari exiflora* has evergreen foliage and grows about a foot tall. There are taller species. Seed of several varieties is available. Several forms have variegated foliage.

RED-HOT-POKERS (*Kniphofia:* S. Africa) are still known to most of us by their old botanical tag: *Tritoma*. By any name (torch lily is another) they are a spectacular bloom for summer, 2 to 4 feet tall with long bright upright heads of tightly packed flowers which resemble small firecrackers.

¶ The tritomas are best planted in early spring 1 foot apart with about 1 inch of soil over the roots in full sun and soil that is well-drained but not too rich.

Oldest and most common are forms with flowers yellow below and red above, hence the nickname. There are exciting new and hardier hybrids in pure white, rose, primrose and combinations of these softer shades. The long, sharp leaves are triangular, more like a rapier than a sword, and form clumps. Bloom the first year is sketchy, but in time each rhizome will yield many blossoms over a long period. My mother grew the old types without protection for years just north of New York City, but in severe climates it is wise to give a sheltered position and mulch or store for the winter. The new hybrids (except the 5-foot W. S. Reeves) are hardier. Kniphofia make fine garden accents, and a selection of hybrids will spread bloom from June into fall.

Earliest of All is the apt name for one of the first to bloom, a coral-rose shade. Once established, White Giant blooms lengthily, Primrose Beauty is one of the best yellows and Rosea Superba is pure white, tipped rose. Many other named varieties are sold. The small-flowered types look better in most gardens and are daintier for arrangements, for which this flower is justly popular.

Although easily raised from seed, tritomas seldom flower the first season no matter how early you start them. Unless well-mulched, seedlings in the North are likely to heave and die during their first winter.

OXALIS ADENOPHYLLA (Chile and Argentina) is the only oxalis with any claim to hardiness. On stems 3 to 6 inches high during the summer come small rosy-lilac flowers among low, graceful foliage. It has not yet been widely enough planted to determine its northern limits. Mine did not survive.

¶ Plant this tuberous oxalis in the rock garden during early fall in a warm, sunny position about 3 inches apart and 2 to 3 inches deep.

JACOB'S ROD (*Asphodeline lutea*: Mediterranean) is the asphodel of the ancients, a spire of golden stars 3 to 4 feet tall and fragrant in June. It is little seen although quite hardy. The basal foliage resembles an onion, is evergreen here and never obtrusive. Plants are seldom available, so raise your own from seed started in late winter. Protect the first winter to prevent heaving. I have never been able to get bloom the first season.

¶ The bulby rhizomes work themselves down into the soil and do best 5 to 6 inches apart in light shade.

LILY OF PERU (*Alstroemeria*: S. America) offers clusters of fine yellow, pink, white and orange flowers, sometimes spotted, on stems which may reach 3 feet. The long, twisted tubers must be handled carefully to prevent breakage.

¶ Plant horizontally in partial shade and light soil 2 to 4 inches deep south of Washington, D.C.; farther north mulch and plant deeper.

Where winters are not too severe, these plants will sometimes survive, but bloom will be sparse and hardly worth the trouble. It is better to treat them as tender bulbs. The pure yellow *A. aurantiaca lutea* is the hardiest variety.

GIANT BELLFLOWER (*Ostrowskia magnifica:* Turkestan) is a member of the great campanula family but grows from a corklike tuber and bears large lilac bell flowers in early summer.

¶ Plant ostrowskia vertically 2 to 3 inches deep and 4 to 6 inches apart in a dry, sunny, sheltered spot.

With mulching I have been able to keep this plant successfully through a record-breaking Philadelphia winter, but it did not bloom. The leaves wither and disappear by midsummer. It is recommended for the temperate West Coast.

WAND BELLS (*Dierama:* S. Africa) have pretty pink and white, funnel flowers on thin stems 5 feet high above irislike foliage. A seldom-seen relative of sparaxis, it is reputedly hardy at Philadelphia, but I have always lost the seedlings during their first winter. Bulbs are almost impossible to locate, but seed germinates well so sow it very early to get plants mature enough to winter through; a cold frame would be handy the first year. There is a dwarf form, *D. intermedia,* which grows to 3 feet.

CHAPTER 12

The Tender Summer Bulbs

Among the tender summer- and fall-blooming bulbs, there is a multiplicity of riches. These come from the tropic or warm-temperate zones and range from the giant bells of summer hyacinths (*Galtonia candicans*) to the dainty umbels of lady's eardrops (*Bessera elegans*). There are whites and pastels as well as vibrant hot colors in one genus or another. Two of the most popular, gladiolus and dahlias, are separately treated later.

I have divided the bulbs here into early and late sections. Seasonal variations may cause one genus to lag, another to blossom sooner, but generally speaking those in the first group bloom before August 15 at Philadelphia, those in the second from then until frost. Where summers are long, calla lilies and other bulbs discussed in Chapter 16 are often grown in the open ground. Check the spring catalogs to see what is available in this group.

An over-enthusiastic gardener could easily plant a super-abundance of these tender bulbs. Except in the South, the frost-free Southwest and perhaps the mildest areas of the Pacific Northwest, they must be lifted each fall and stored indoors until spring. Planting too many will work hardship on busy gardeners since they must be handled twice each season.

179

Your vacation plans are to be considered too: choose bulbs that flower when you are home to see them.

Here where frost does not usually come until late October, I dare try any of them but I start most of them early indoors. Those like begonias and caladiums which need heat to grow are also started inside so as to have as long a decorative season in the garden as possible. None of these plants should go outdoors until the spring frosts are definitely over. South of Philadelphia, all these tender bulbs will do well. The late group are of dubious value where frosts end late and begin early. You can overcome this difficulty by growing in pots, but you will need indoor sites for starting them in spring and for maturing the foliage in fall.

Cultural Details

Because they make their complete growth cycle in a shorter time, these tender bulbs require more fertilizing than the hardier types. I prefer manure water, mixed according to the directions printed on the easily-obtained packages of dried cow manure; a cup per large plant in open ground or two tablespoons per bulb for smaller things; apply every two or three weeks from the time the shoots are several inches high until the foliage begins to yellow with maturity. In very wet weather when heavy rains may leach out the soil, fertilize more frequently than when rainfall is scanty. Never bring any manure into direct contact with stems or bulbs; the soil protects the roots from burning.

When in active growth in hot weather, these bulbs, particularly those in pots, require copious amounts of water. Never allow them to bake out. Those with true bulbs or corms are stored dry and cool for the winter at around 50 degrees F. Those with tuberous or fleshy roots should be packed in sand,

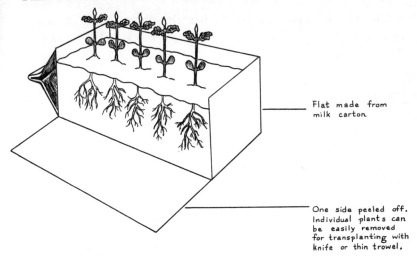

Flat made from milk carton.

One side peeled off. Individual plants can be easily removed for transplanting with knife or thin trowel.

For Starting Bulbs or Seedlings on Windowsills

FIG. 10. Easily obtained and disposable, quart and half-gallon cardboard milk cartons make fine flats for starting bulbs and seedlings early in the house. Wash them well first and punch holes in the bottom for drainage. A layer of pebbles in the bottom insures perfect drainage. When transplanting, peel off sides of carton for least disturbance to roots.

sawdust, or peatmoss to prevent dessication, or they may be stored with some soil adhering for the same result. All need storage above freezing but not at house temperatures. Choose the coolest part of the basement.

Empty cardboard milk cartons are handy for starting those to be transplanted later (Figure 10). Cut one side off to make a shallow box for small bulbs like begonias and achimenes. For large roots like cannas, remove just the top of the carton and use one per root. These containers take less space in the house than round pots. When transplanting time comes, peel the sides away and plant without disturbing the roots. Choose a cloudy day for the job, and give them extra water for a few days to combat shock.

For Pots and Patios

Where the season is short, many summer-flowering bulbs are planted in clay pots and started early in the house. They are placed outside only after nights are warm. Where fall frost is early, they can then be brought back into the house to finish flowering and maturing. Such treatment is also decorative for a patio and outdoor living room, but my bulbs never do as well in pots as in the ground. (Many of the bulbs in Chapter 16 do well in pots, however.)

Choose containers in scale with the eventual plant. A big, tall canna is out of proportion to a small pot. Deep pots also give the big bulbs and tubers a better chance to get the moisture and food they need. A pot 12 inches deep is not too big for a dwarf canna, clivia and the like.

After shoots are several inches high, pot-grown plants must have feeding in slightly smaller amounts than advised for those grown in the open ground. Continue every two weeks until the flowers open, when fertilizing should be decreased. Reduce water, and never feed a plant which is dormant, resting, or beginning to brown in maturity.

Never let pot plants, particularly those growing in full sun, lack for water when growing. Set them in a shallow saucer to conserve moisture, or sink the pots to the rims in soil. Leave an inch of space above the soil surface in the pot to facilitate deep watering and make at least a daily inspection in blistering weather. A pebble mulch looks neat and retards evaporation from the soil. Bulb pans, those pots which do not taper toward the base, are more wind-resistant. Attractive pottery and red-wood containers can be used to conceal clay pots.

FOR SHADY POSITIONS

Achimenes   Caladium
Begonia (tuberous)   Gloxinia (porches only)

FOR POTS IN SUN

Bessera   Habranthus
Calanthe   Haemanthus
Canna (dwarf)   Hedychium
Chlidanthus   Lapeirousia
Clivia   Milla biflora
Cooperia   Oxalis
Crinum   Vallota
Eucharis   Zantedeschia
Eucomis   Zephyranthes
Gloriosa (give support)

FOR EARLY BLOOM

ACIDANTHERA (tropical Africa, Illustration 16) should be more frequently grown in our gardens. This is one bulb which gives secondary flowers. Although often termed a late bloomer, *A. murieliae* planted early one May gave me continuous color from July 9 to early September. Similar to gladiolus, the foliage is neat, 3 to 4 feet high, and takes little room, so clumps fit easily into the border. The flowers are whitish with a purple-brown center blotch and a faint spicy perfume.

¶ Plant acidanthera corms outside in full sun after mid-April when the soil is warm, about 3 inches deep and 4 to 5 inches apart in garden loam.

16. Acidanthera yields a faint, spicy fragrance and unusual flowers over a long period in summer (Genereux).

Bloom begins at the base of the flower stalk and continues until the last bud at the top opens. If faded flowers are removed, side shoots soon appear to repeat the process. Each flower is several inches wide and has a long, arching tube so it may be picked separately. Acidanthera last well in water and make graceful arrangements due to the curve in the flower tube. The similar *A. bicolor* is creamier and may have a stronger fragrance.

After the shoots are about 3 inches high, I give at least one good feeding of manure water, a mulch of grass clippings plus extra water in dry weather. Before frost, I gather and store, as for gladiolus. Propagation by offsets is rapid.

TUBEROUS BEGONIAS (Illustration 17) as offered for summer growing are hybrids of various species, all from warm climates. They come in tints of white, yellow, pink, red, and orange and in many forms. They are for lightly shaded places, the north side of a house, or under the high branches of trees, or for pots on porches. In catalog lists, you will find large, tuberous begonias which resemble roses, camellias, daffodils and carnations. These are best on porches or in sheltered spots where the effect of wind and rain are minimized. There are some with picotee edges of contrasting color, others with ruffled or fringed petals, as well as smaller-flowered pendant types for hanging baskets. Where summer is very hot, these plants are never as good as in cooler climes.

¶ Start begonias early in the house in all but the entirely frost-free areas, and do not set out until the weather is reliably warm. For starting begonias use flats or pots with half an inch of drainage material in the bottom. Fill the rest with rich soil containing plenty of humus and press the concave tubers, round side down, into the soil until just their tops protrude. Leave 3 inches between tubers. Water well once, then sparingly until the shoots (which are found only on the hollow top) are well up. Keep in a warm place in semishade. When shoots are 3 to 4 inches high, transplant carefully, lifting out the whole block of soil so as not to disturb roots. Grow on in pots until outside conditions are warm and settled.

I leave mine in pots all summer since it is easier to take them up in fall, but plants can be put in the open ground. Choose squatty pots at least 5 inches deep. When transplanting, set the tuber deeper than it was for starting, so almost an inch of soil covers the hollow top where feeding roots will grow. Begonias need plenty of water during growth and benefit from liquid manure every two weeks until midsummer. Tubers can also be planted in open ground after frost, but you will have a shorter period of bloom.

Begonias need rich, porous loam with a good amount of humus and perfect drainage. In hot, dry weather syringe foliage gently with the hose. To get bushy plants, pinch out the main stalk about the time the first buds show color, especially with the large-flowered types. Stake those with large flowers and choose a spot where they will have good air circulation. I do not pick off the smaller female flowers (they have a thick, triangular swelling just below the bloom) since they give additional color to the plant. Remove these, however, as soon as petals drop to prevent seed from maturing, since this checks flowering.

You will be much more pleased if you plant your begonias in groups of the same color and type than if you buy a mixture. Individually named tubers are often quite dear, but types by color are no more expensive than in mixture. For garden use I prefer the multiflora types which come in three sizes: multiflora, maxima and gigantea or grandiflora. The grandifloras are similar in form and size to the standard camellia types. The multifloras bloom earlier, give more flowers per plant and are less subject to weather damage than the more frequently grown large begonias. Some are double. Multiflora begonias started inside in late March flower here by early June and seem more floriferous in our blazing summers.

17. Tuberous begonias are favorites for shady summer gardens either in pots or directly in the ground (Courtesy Brown Bulb Ranch).

Most stock available on the East coast is from abroad, but some catalogs offer American-grown tubers. These give me more satisfactory results, but prices are higher.

CALADIUMS are plants of tropical America and related to the jack-in-the-pulpit. They produce a calla-like flower which has no decorative value and should be quickly removed, but their heart- or arrow-shaped leaves make fine accents in partially shaded places. The various types all have some green in the leaves but are more or less variegated with white, cream, red, or pink. They look best planted in groups of at least three of the same color, and striking effects are obtained by juxtaposing contrasting groups. Named varieties are widely sold and more uniform in size and color than those offered merely by color. Buy only first-size tubers for sure results. A few new dwarf caladiums with lancelike leaves seldom taller than 10 inches are now available.

¶ Start caladiums indoors in early spring so the leaves will be luxuriant by out-door planting-time and also so they will have a long growing season. Otherwise the tuber may not store up enough nourishment for subsequent years. Place 2 inches deep in damp peatmoss, water sparingly and keep warm (70 to 85 degrees F.). Shift to pots 6 to 8 inches deep when shoots and roots have made good growth. Use a rich, porus loam with plenty of humus.

Caladiums thrive in hot, humid weather. Move them outdoors to a partially shaded, well-drained site after nights have become warm. Give plenty of water and weekly applications of liquid manure while growing. They do equally well whether transplanted from the pots to a bed or left in the pots, but sink the latter to the rims in soil to conserve moisture. In the fall gradually give less water and bring the big tubers in before frost. Store for the winter in the pots or in some dry material, choosing a warm, dry spot, about 60 degrees F. Very small tubers are not worth saving.

Whatever other shades you try, include always some of the delicate white-leaved caladiums such as Candidum, White Christmas, Aaron or Sea Gull for a cool summer picture.

Related tropical foliage plants like the enormous ELE-PHANT EAR (*Colocasia esculenta*), the ALOCASIAS and the XANTHOSOMAS are similarly treated though the last two are too large for the average garden. All are often grown under glass.

CANNAS, (color plate XII) with flowers in lovely pastel shades on dwarf plants are regaining a deserved place in American gardens. The newer types have florets several inches wide and closely spaced on stems seldom more than 4 feet high. With their clean, luxuriant foliage, they are stunning for accents, each plant sending up successive trusses of flowers over a long period.

¶ In the North cannas are best started early in the house about a month or six weeks before outdoor planting. I use an upright half-gallon milk carton for each root, setting it just under the surface in a mixture of good loam and peatmoss. Grow in full sun and water well. After danger of frost is past and good shoots have formed, set plants outside. Standard cannas go 1½ to 2 feet apart, dwarf types may be closer. Peel off the carton and plant so the top of the root is 3 to 4 inches below the surface of the soil. Give several summer feedings of dried cow manure worked into the soil surface and extra water during dry periods. After frost blackens foliage, remove it to within 6 inches of the root, dig and dry off, leaving some soil adhering. Store upside down in a cool, shaded place. The next spring the rhizome may be divided before planting, but leave several eyes to each piece.

Few summer-flowering plants offer more than cannas, and the new rose, pink, salmon, cream, and yellow shades are delightful. Started indoors in mid-April last year, mine gave continual bloom from late July until frost. Unfortunately, they are most attractive to Japanese beetles, which feast on the flowers; in heavily infested areas, it may be wise to forego cannas. The fleshy roots are grown as food by the Indians of tropical America where cannas are native. A few cannas sport reddish foliage, but most of the newer varieties bear good green leaves which are dramatic enough.

Probably the best of the new cannas belong to the Grand Opera Series, most of which seldom grow taller than 3 to 4 feet. My standard favorite is Eureka, a cream tinted with salmon and sporting handsome bright green leaves. It blends in well anywhere. I found Pfitzer's dwarf cannas disappointing and not worth their inflated price. A new race of very dwarf cannas only 18 inches high may be grown from seed to flower in one season if started early indoors.

SUMMER HYACINTH, (*Galtonia candicans*) from South Africa has impressive spikes of pendant, white bells which rather suggest a dwarf yucca. With its wide fleshy leaves and 3-foot flower stalks, galtonia is fine for accents in the back of the border or amid shrubbery.

¶ Sometimes cataloged as *Hyacinthus candicans,* the big bulbs are planted after the nights warm up in almost any sunny place about 3 inches deep and 5 inches apart.

Those set out in mid-May last year began blooming July 17 and lasted nearly a month, a time when the garden needed flowers. This was at the height of the worst Japanese beetle invasion we have ever had, but none touched the galtonia nor did any other pest. Although the plant has no fragrance I could detect and is somewhat ungainly with the big, green-tipped bells set far apart on the thick stalk, I came to love it for its immunity if nothing else!

Galtonia has proved hardy without protection here at Philadelphia. If it will not winter through your climate, you may store dry and cool; but many prefer to plant new bulbs each year.

PERUVIAN DAFFODILS (*Hymenocallis calathina* Illustration 18) are among the prettiest of the summer flowers. Often listed as ISMENE, they yield clusters of graceful, white flowers on 2- to 3-foot stems, and the amaryllis-like foliage is neat and green all summer, decorative of itself. Since this bulb flowers very quickly, do not plant it until the soil is warm and there is no chance of frost. June is time enough here; earlier planting may kill the flower buds.

¶ Place hymenocallis about 3 inches deep and at least 5 inches apart in rich, well-drained loam and full sun.

Give a dose or two of manure water after flowering. Dig bulbs before frost and store upside down in some dry material. The roots should be left on and merely trimmed slightly the following spring. Offsets blossom in a few years if grown separately until they reach flowering size.

Larger flowers and taller stems mark an improved form of calathina, Advance. Sulphur Queen has soft, yellow flowers; *H. festalis* has graceful, thin petals and a spidery appearance; *H. harrisiana* is the earliest and only about a foot tall. The family is noted for its fragrance.

Some of the North American hymenocallis are even more lovely, and those listed as *H. americana* and *H. occidentalis* will survive winters outside quite far north. In the far South the native *H. coronaria* is widely grown. Many of these wildflowers are popularly called basketflowers or spiderlilies.

18. Peruvian daffodils (*Hymenocallis*) are fragrant, and the glossy foliage remains attractive all summer (Genereux).

PANCRATIUM MARITIMUM is an old-world relative which is treated as for ismene. ELISENA LONGIPETALA, which bears very dainty white flowers on 2- to 3-foot stems, is another near-relative. It is reported hardy with protection to New York City. Bulbs of both are scarce and hard to find.

MEXICAN STAR (*Milla biflora*) is native to our own Southwest but not hardy in the North. Its flat, fragrant, white

flowers are borne on branching stems nearly 2 feet high and
are larger than silver dollars.

¶ For best results start milla early indoors in pots of rich
loam, placing the bulbs 2 to 3 inches deep and several inches
apart.

Water once, then only sparingly until growth is well along.
They will bloom sporadically several times during the summer.
For this reason they are best grown in pots which can be
moved about for decorative purposes. The bulbs may be left
in the pots for the winter and kept dry and cool while dormant
in a frost-free place. Repot only when they become crowded
and give several light feedings with manure water during the
summer.

In the North the same treatment is recommended for the
RAIN LILIES (*Cooperia*) and the ZEPHYR LILIES (*Zephyranthes*)
of which some species are native to our Southwest as
well as South America and Mexico. The latter is the home of
the similarly-treated LADY'S EARDROPS (*Bessera elegans*)
which bear umbels of nodding little coral and orange flowers
with blue anthers on 20-inch stems. The various HABRAN-
THUS, most of which have pink flowers, also do best in the
North with this technique.

All these members of the amaryllis family should be planted
1 to 3 inches deep, depending on the size of the bulb. They
can also be given gladiolus handling, but the results are not
as rewarding. With a heavy mulch and a sheltered position the
hardier cooperia and zephyranthes may be wintered outside almost as far north as New York City, but it is risky.

Bulbs of cooperia are hard to find. They produce fragrant
funnel-form flowers 4 to 9 inches high, usually white with red
or pink tinting; *C. smalli* is yellow. The atamasco lily is the
most famous of the zephyr lilies and much naturalized in our
South where it is native. Bulbs of others easy to find include:

Z. *candida,* white and the latest to bloom; Z. *citrina,* yellow;
Z. *rosea,* pink; Ajax, cream. They resemble large open crocus
never higher than 10 inches.

Bulbs of the iris family which should have the same pot
treatment in the North include: LAPEIROUSIA CRUENTA
(*Anomatheca*), FREESIA, CORN LILIES (*Ixia*), WAND
FLOWERS (*Sparaxis*) and BABIANA, all described in Chapter 17. Specially treated bulbs are offered for summer-flowering. The last four do best where summers are not too hot. In
the South they are all planted in the fall and bloom in early
spring outdoors.

OXALIS bulbs are cheap and often flower two weeks after
planting. I can think of no other reasons for growing them
outdoors! They are tender, bulbous relatives of the pesky,
yellow sorrel which I am constantly weeding out of the garden,
and the leaves and flowers look just the same but somewhat
larger. There are white, red, pink, and lilac varieties.

¶ Plant oxalis in pots 2 inches deep and an inch apart, water
once and keep dark and cool until growth starts; then bring
to full sun, increase water and feed sporadically when in
active growth. They are often grown as house plants, but
need lots of sun.

The one good exception is *O. adenophylla* of Chapter 11
which probably should be treated as a tender bulb in the
colder sections.

FOR LATER BLOOM

ACHIMENES would be more popular if it did not take so
long to come into flower, for the flat but petunia-like blossoms
are large and striking. They are for partially shady places and
come in bright colors from white through various pinks, reds

and oranges with several good purples and at least one fine deep blue.

¶ I started the tiny achimenes tubers (which resemble pine-apples) an inch deep in a mixture of loam and humus in a warm place during late March, but bloom did not begin until late August; try starting them earlier.

The bulbs are watered once, then kept barely moist until growth shows. Give them only a few hours of sun, water regularly and transplant outside to a shady place only after the nights are warm. In the South they may go into the ground and need be only a few inches apart for carpeting. They produce a fountain of green foliage and are also good for hanging baskets. Each flower lasts almost a week if not damaged by wind or rain. Never let them lack for water. They are sometimes listed as widow's tears.

Before frost bring the pots in to enjoy further bloom (reduce water when flowering ceases) or dig the bulbs, leaving some dirt around them, and store cool. The tiny tubers may increase prodigiously.

Southern growers offer many achimenes by name or color. Blue Beauty (Mexicana) is one of the largest and a vibrant color. Purity is pure white, there are many good reds and pinks and a few with pansy-like markings. They are not easy for the north because the slightest touch of cold affects them adversely.

TIGER FLOWERS (*Tigridia*) are another Mexican native, a bright flower with upfacing triangular-shaped blooms having spotted cups and rising about a foot from miniature gladiolus-like foliage. The flowers last only a day, but each corm produces several over a period of time. They like sandy soil and are often seen at the seashore.

¶ Plant tigridia during early spring 2 inches deep and 3 inches apart in a sunny well-drained spot.

Often they do not flower the first year, probably because bulbs were undersized. You can start them early from seed, and a few may blossom the first season. With mulch they are sometimes hardy to Philadelphia, but treat as gladiolus in severe climates. Leave some soil on the bulbs or store in dry peat to prevent dessication.

Most catalogs list *T. pavonia* only in mixture, but it is much more effective planted by color. There are varieties predominately white, red, yellow, pink and orange. Sometimes listed as SHELL FLOWERS or FLAME FLOWERS, they were sacred to the jaguar cult of the ancient Aztec Indians and thus have been in cultivation for many centuries. Tigridia looks pretty in the rock garden.

MONTBRETIAS (*Tritonias* and *Crocosmias*) are easily identified as gladiolus relatives, with similar sword-like leaves, but they seldom grow as high. The open flowers of these South African relatives are also smaller and more graceful than gladiolus, and the stems arch and branch. Bloom here is in September and October, and the outward-facing montbretias make gay spots in the fall garden.

¶ Plant in a warm sunny position during early spring 3 to 4 inches deep and 2 to 3 inches apart in well-drained soil.

Do not be surprised if they take forever to sprout. I have had delayed early May plantings show their first shoots from late June to late July! With a light mulch they may come through winters at least as far north as Washington, D.C., but in the North they are best handled as gladiolus. I adore them but doubt their usefulness where frosts begin early.

Again they look best in groups of the same color, but it may

19. Tigridia flowers last only a day, but each bulb produces several (Roche).

not be easy to find named varieties. They include yellow, orange, rose, red and salmon.

TUBEROSES (*Polianthes tuberosa*) have been the despair of northern gardeners because they either refuse to produce their waxy white flowers or are often caught by frost. My own experiment may cast some light on the problem because bulbs planted outside on a southern slope in mid-May after the ground was really warm bloomed before those begun inside in late March. The secret is I think to pick a very warm spot for these Mexican natives. My indoor pots were grown in a cool basement window; I suspect any kind of a chill sets them back.

¶ Buy the biggest bulbs you can and plant tuberoses in full sun 3 inches deep and 6 inches apart in good loam either outside after the weather is really settled or inside at a warm, sunny window.

Although the double form is most usually seen, the single type is more graceful, and both are lovely for the August and September garden. Heights vary from 2 to 4 feet. The fragrance indoors is too sweet for me, but many love it. Tuberoses often will not blossom the second year, probably because they have not had a long enough growing season and the new bulb is too small.

GLOXINIA (*Sinningia*) are started exactly as achimenes and sometimes take just as long. Oftentimes gloxinia planted in November for early spring indoor bloom (Chapter 16) do not come into their own until summer. In such cases they may be taken outside but only to a well protected shady place like a porch. The leaves must not get wet, and I keep mine inside. The species, *G. maculata insignis,* takes a little sun and does not mind an occasional wetting so it is better for outdoor use, but it requires forever to produce its fragrant blue bells. The slipper gloxinias have slender flowers on longer stems than the more common types.

GINGER LILIES (*Hedychium*) are simply beautiful, with short spikes of fragrant flowers, but they take too long to come into bloom for northern gardens.

¶ Mine were started inside during mid-April like a canna, but never blossomed, although the foliage was luxuriant.

Fertilize as for cannas and never allow them to lack for moisture; they are sometimes even grown around ponds. In favorable climates they may grow as high as 6 feet with many side shoots. South of the Carolinas they are often left in the ground all year. The roots may be divided like cannas. Types: *H. coronarium,* white; *H. gardnerianum,* yellow with a touch of red.

CHAPTER 13

Gladiolus Can Be Graceful

Gladiolus have as wide a color range as any bulb flower you can grow. Probably only tulips can give you as many shades for indoor and outdoor decoration. This flower ought to be as popular for summer growing as the tulip is for spring. That it is not is the fault of those who ought to be most interested in its popularity—the specialists and the commercial breeders.

Spurred by competition, these two groups have devoted their efforts to developing huge trusses of flowers closely spaced along a towering spike. As one of my dirt-gardening friends remarked: "The modern skyscraper-gladiolus is fit only for big funerals and cathedral weddings!" What a shame such an intrinsically lovely flower should have taken such a course. (I sometimes wonder if the modern hybrid lilies may go the same way.)

The Charming Miniatures

The battle, however, is not finally lost. There are graceful gladiolus, and it is time we gardeners ignored the giants, some of which reach 6 feet in the garden, and searched the catalogs for the miniatures. One, Little Pansy, was recently the first miniature to gain All-America selection; there will be others.

I had not grown gladiolus in years, but I planted some mixed miniatures with the hope I might find something nice to say about a genus I had crossed off a dozen years ago because of its size. How wonderful to report there are delightful gladiolus on a scale for small houses and in a range of colors and forms I predict will widen as we give the breeders new hope. Gladiolus with widely-spaced flowers are often classified as informal; these are the prettiest, but most varieties still have closely-set florets since this has been the favored type.

Among the miniatures I grew were ruffled, hooded, and wide-open blossoms, and one with long thin petals which was the daintiest of all. Some were of one color, others had a center blotch or picotee edge of contrast. More than half produced two short spikes, which were a delight. These are the gladiolus for average gardens, and a mixture is a good way to become acquainted. Then write for one of the gladiolus catalogs in which they are listed by color. Choose those that suit your own garden and house, and plant at least six of a kind so you will have a good effect at one time. These small gladiolus are found under these headings: Primulinus, Butterfly, Tiny Tots, Gladiolus elegans or Miniatures. The Baby or Early-flowering types are also small (Chapter 4) and hardier so you can safely plant them in fall. They are through blooming by late June, however, so you will need the tender miniatures to continue the show.

Classification of Gladiolus

Members of the iris family, gladiolus have been in gardens since classical Greek and Roman times. With such long hybridization, the modern types bear little resemblance to the species which are native to the Mediterranean region and

Africa. Even the hardy ones with Latin names are not really wild. In catalogs, you will find double varieties in some colors. Botanically, gladiolus grow from corms rather than true bulbs.

The official show classifications concern themselves only with size and color. As reported by the North American Gladiolus Council these are:

Miniature	100—florets under 2½ inches
Small	200—2½ to 3½ inches
Medium	300—3½ to 4½ inches
Large	400—4½ to 5½ inches
Giant	500—5½ inches and up

The code number as 100 refers to size. For judging and in some catalogs this includes two digits which describe color. Thus Bo-Peep is 331, a medium in a salmon shade with conspicuous marking of another color. These details are unimportant to the gardener, but rigidly observed in shows. In a helpful pamphlet the NAGC lists several thousand varieties with color keys and the average number of growing days necessary for each bloom. This pamphlet is available for a small fee to those who wish to know about exhibiting.

In the Garden

The first three sizes are best for garden use, needing no staking and providing the most graceful spikes. Some catalogs suggest varieties for early or late summer bloom. The NAGC list is helpful for such information. A few varieties require more than one hundred days for bloom, some need only fifty to sixty days. Many of the early ones are small-flowered. Most gladiolus average between seventy and ninety days. Larger

corms take less time to flower than smaller sizes so plant
different sized corms to automatically get bloom over a longer
period.

Early bloomers include Carlake, Glenwood, Heidi, Lavender
Petunia, Lullaby, Red Petunia, Rose Pavilion and Truly Brown.
Among the latest to flower are All Out, Autumn Gold, Banner,
Brown Bomber, Crinkles, Sables and Yellow Smoke.

Where gladiolus must be dug every fall, it is easier to grow
them with annuals like zinnias and marigolds or in cutting
rows. There is always the danger in the perennial border of
disturbing roots or trampling shoots of other things. (The
actual hole for a glad may not be large, but you have to have
room to work.)

Here at Philadelphia, gardeners often leave gladiolus in
the ground over the winter in a sheltered spot, although the
practice is not recommended for expensive or rare varieties.
This is probably the northern limit. Whether you can treat
them thus in your climate is a matter of trial. Make sure the
site has perfect drainage, give a protective mulch and test
some common varieties first. Where this will work, the
gladiolus is lovely in the border, with its spikes contributing
a fine vertical line. Such plantings must be dug and divided
every three years or so since the corms increase to the crowding point. When resetting, choose a different site and use bulbs
of different sizes to prolong bloom. The smallest corms and
cormels may be grown for a few seasons in cutting rows if
you wish and soon reach blooming size.

The cormels must be soaked several days before spring planting and set only about 2 inches deep the first year. The best
sizes for garden use are #1 and #2 graded corms, but #3
often gives satisfactory bloom. Good corms have high tops;
flat or concave tops are the mark of old corms.

How to Plant

Gladiolus may be started outside as soon as frost is out of the ground. Many gardeners make plantings every few weeks until late June so as to have continuous bloom. This is all right in the cutting garden but rather a job in borders where it is easier to use different sizes of corms.

Gladiolus like reasonably fertile soil and full sun. Remember this if you place some in the border lest they be too shaded by neighboring plants. Dig the site well and plant corms about 4 to 6 inches apart and 3 to 5 inches deep, the shallower depth being for clay soil or small corms.

At planting time a light application of an all-round fertilizer not too high in nitrogen may be placed a good inch below the corms where it cannot burn roots, but I do not do this, preferring to wait until buds are forming. Then, if anything, I give a teaspoon of dried cow manure and one of bonemeal for each plant and scratch it into the soil. For exhibition blooms, fertilizing before planting is more important.

Thrips are a real problem in some areas. (See Chapter 22 for preventive measures.) Corms from a reputable dealer are seldom infected. By keeping the weeds down, I have grown newly-purchased gladiolus without any spraying and had no trouble, but gifts of extra corms from well-meaning friends obviously had not been treated before storing and failed miserably. With a good spray program I might have saved them. To circumvent disease, rotate gladiolus in the cutting garden, using new ground each time you plant.

Exhibition gladiolus must be staked to prevent wind damage and insure straight stems. For garden use the smaller classes do not require it, but the heavy giants need help. They often are beaten to the ground by heavy rain and wind. Hilling with several inches of earth around the plants about the time the buds begin to show helps support them.

During early growth gladiolus must never suffer from lack of water. In time of drought soak the soil deeply every few days. Mulching helps, especially since the plants themselves cast almost no shade.

Harvesting

After flowering is finished, keep foliage growing until it turns brown or is damaged by frost. If you are leaving the corms in the ground, cut off old foliage to the ground and in cold areas mulch well. Otherwise dig corms carefully, cut foliage and let dry about a week in a frost-free place. Then clean, discard withered old corms, check largest corms against rot and disease, dust with 5-percent DDT powder to thwart thrips and store in ventilated bags in a cool but not cold dry place.

Usually you will have enough natural increase among the corms, but for propagating a particular variety, save small cormels at digging time and treat as suggested. Label stored varieties if you plan to use them for landscaping effects.

Where to Buy

Because they are so easily grown and propagated, gladiolus bulbs are among the least expensive summer flowers. A great many are raised in small nurseries in this country, and Dutch production has been increasing. While it is often smart to buy from nearby dealers whose stock tends toward the best varieties for your climate, the reputation of such growers is important, for it is your only sure protection against pests and diseases on the corms.

Such dangers are less likely in stock bought from the big bulb dealers and gladiolus breeders who regularly submit to voluntary inspection and dust harvested corms so as to be able to ship stock from state to state. If you fail with gladiolus bought from a nearby farm or variety store, order the next year from one of the well-known dealers and plant the corms in a different part of the garden.

CAPSULE VIEW OF GLADIOLUS

Gladiolus are half-hardy in temperate climates; but store rare varieties in frost-free spots.

Colors and forms vary widely; choose smaller sizes for garden use.

Thrips and fusarian rot can be troublesome; see Chapter 22.

Plant as soon as the ground can be worked for early bloom, 3 to 5 inches deep and 4 to 6 inches apart.

Succession plantings may be made up to sixty days of your fall frost date, depending on the number of days required by a particular variety.

CHAPTER 14

Dahlias for Lavish Display

No summer bulb offers more color over a longer period than the dahlia, which has come a long way since the sixteenth-century Spanish conquistadores discovered it in the Mexican gardens of the Aztec Indians. While many a modern gardener groans over the heavy, dinner-plate blooms and plants that demand staking, he considers only half the story. Today there are miniature and dwarf dahlias in a variety of forms and colors, and there is quality seed available too from which you can have a garden full of color in just one season. Unlike many other summer bulbs and tubers, dahlias have been hybridized for centuries. Even before the coming of the Europeans, the Aztecs had selected forms and colors to such an extent that botanists are still not certain which are the true species.

Before choosing types, decide what role dahlias are to play for you. Do you want landscape accents, cut flowers or exhibition material? The miniatures, the dwarfs or the dainty pompons will be perfect for summer color in the garden or in front of shrubbery, where plants can get sufficient sun and nourishment. These types are also perfect for cutting. The huge blooms of the A classification, however, are useful only as novelties for shows. Sometimes they can be made into arrangements, but they are seldom in a good scale with modern furniture and rooms.

Official Classification

Because there is so much variation in flowers, the official classifications of the American Dahlia Society, quoted here by courtesy of that group, are best to describe what dahlias offer for your garden. These terms are used in all shows sponsored by Society affiliates, and abbreviations for the classes are in most catalogs.

Dahlias are first divided by flower size (good catalogs also list the height of the bush in feet). The following abbreviations are official: A—large, over 8 inches in diameter; B—medium, 4 to 8 inches; BB—4 to 6 inches; Ba—ball, 4 inches or over; M—miniature, under 4 inches; M Ba—miniature ball, 2 to 4 inches; Pom—pompon (for exhibition must be under 2 inches in diameter); Dwf—dwarf, varieties of low bush growth.

There are fourteen color divisions that are determined by the predominate color or colors on the face of the petals. These are easy to follow, but the following abbreviations may be confusing to newcomers: Au—autumn, blends and suffusions of gray, tan, yellow, pink and lavender; Fl—flame, blends of yellow including scarlet-red or orange-yellow; Bi—bicolor, two distinct colors on the face of the petals; Dk Bl—blends of low brilliance; Lt Bl—blends of lighter tints; Var—variegated, two or more distinct colors, at least one in contrasting flecks, dots or splashes.

Finally, the form of the flower has become so diversified that classifications with appropriate abbreviations were made for quick identification. (An example of each is included): (Definitions—ray: flower petal; disc floret: the small tubular flowers in the center of the flower; ray floret: incomplete florets in a ring around the edge of the disc; double: flowers have multiple rows of petals and show no disc; involute: the petal curves toward its face or front surface and often appears

Pompon

Collarette

Single

Anemone

DAHLIAS
COME
IN
MANY
SHAPES

Orchid

Straight Cactus

Formal Decorative

FIG. 11. Dahlias vary greatly in size, shape and hue. There is one to fit any garden or color scheme.

tubular; revolute: the petal curves toward its back surface
and often appears tubular; incurved: the petal tip gradually
curves inward toward the center of the flower; recurved: the
petal tip gradually curves outwards and backwards toward the
stem of the flower; margin: the edge of the colored part of
the petal.)

SINGLE (S)—open-centered flowers having only one row
of petals, with margins flat or nearly so regardless of the number
of florets (Candlelight).

MIGNON (MIG)—single dahlias; the plants approximate
18 inches (Mies).

ORCHID-FLOWERING (O)—flowers as in single dahlias
except that the rays are more or less tubular by the involution
of the margins (Imp).

ANEMONE (AN)—open-centered flowers with only one
row of ray florets, regardless of form or number of florets, with
the tubular disc florets elongated, giving a pincushion effect
(Vera Higgins).

COLLARETTE (COL)—open-centered flowers with only
one row of ray florets, with the addition of one or more rows
of petaloids, usually of a different color, forming a collar around
the disc (Tribune).

PEONY (P)—open-centered flowers with two to five rows
of ray florets with or without the addition of smaller curled
or twisted floral rays around the disc (Bishop of Llandaff).

INCURVED CACTUS (IC)—fully double flowers with the
margins of the majority of the floral rays fully revolute for at

least half their length and the tips of the rays curving toward the center of the flower (Oakleigh Champion).

STRAIGHT CACTUS (ST C)—fully double flowers with the margins of the majority of the floral rays fully revolute for at least half their length, the rays being straight, slightly incurved or recurved (Edna D.).

SEMI-CACTUS (SC)—fully double flowers with the margins of the majority of the floral rays fully revolute for less than half their length and the rays broad below (The Cardinal).

FORMAL DECORATIVE (FD)—fully double flowers with the margins of the floral rays slightly or not at all revolute, the rays generally broad, either pointed or rounded at tips, with outer rays tending to recurve and central rays tending to be cupped; and the majority of all floral rays in a regular arrangement. (Jersey Beauty).

INFORMAL DECORATIVE (ID)—fully double flowers with the margins of the majority of the floral rays slightly or not at all revolute, the rays generally long, twisted or pointed and usually irregular in arrangement (Great Lakes).

BALL (BA)—fully double, ball-shaped or slightly flattened, floral rays, blunt or round at tips and quilled or with margins involute for more than half the length of the ray in spiral arrangement; flowers 4 or more inches in diameter (Alice J.).

MINIATURE (M)—all which normally produce flowers not exceeding 4 inches in diameter (pompons excluded). Subdivided into miniature single, peony, cactus, decorative and ball.

POMPON (POM)—same as ball but not more than 2 inches in diameter (Margaret Williams).

DWARF (DWF)—applies to size of plant without regard to form of flowers.

Although at first glance these classifications may seem complicated, they are necessary if any sense is to be made of this genus. Exhibitors must pay strict attention to the classes; for the rest of us it is also the most convenient way to separate the hundreds of varieties. In no time you will be translating the catalog's "Diana Maxine, M StC Y" as a yellow miniature straight cactus dahlia.

For Cutting

With such a multitude of colors and forms, dahlias are one of the finest summer flowers for cutting, from mid-season until frost. There is a trick involved, however. They wilt unless the cut stems are placed immediately in hot water. Only a few minutes in this conditioning are necessary, but I usually let them stay overnight in the water, which gradually cools. Gathered just before maturity and treated thus, dahlias last for days in arrangements, particularly if the water is changed daily. If a cut bloom wilts prematurely, snip off an inch of stem and plunge again in hot water. This should revive it.

For garden effect limit yourself to a few harmonizing colors to prevent a spotty effect. Like other flowers, dahlias look best grown in groups of similar colors. For cutting, choose the hues and sizes which best suit your indoor decorations.

Disbudding and Pinching Back

When you grow show dahlias, disbudding is a necessity to bring out the size and proper shape of the flowers and to secure long stems. You will observe that the buds tend to grow in threes. If the two side ones are carefully pinched off, the central bloom will be better. Repeat this process as the plant produces more stems; allow only the terminal bud on each to mature.

For the gardener who wants mainly color from his dahlias, a little disbudding is advisable, but never on the scale practiced by exhibitors. With the dwarfs, especially those raised from seed, I keep the flowers picked and pinch off some buds whenever I cut bouquets. Be sure to leave one stem coming, usually the outside one of a pair. This insures future blossoms.

Sometimes when a tuber is planted, more than one shoot appears. For best bloom remove carefully all but the strongest one. If you are more interested in the shape of the plant and in getting a multitude of flowers rather than a few exhibition blooms, pinch off just the tip of the plant after it has produced several pairs of leaves. Make sure that at least two good side nodes remain below the pinch. This will produce bushier plants which look better in the garden. I have not found it necessary to pinch back dwarfs or most miniatures.

The Way to Stake

All flowers in the A classification and the largest in the B need staking as protection from wind. To prevent injury to the tuber, place the stake at the time you plant the tuber. Dwarfs require no staking. Give the large miniatures a short stake which will be quickly hidden by the bush. For binding use strips of torn sheeting, which will not damage the stems.

Watering and Mulching

Natives of the South, dahlias are used to sudden tropical downpours so I always water mine at midday. It does them no harm and helps prevent unsightly mildew which often attacks plants that are wet toward sundown. When in active growth, they need plenty of water in dry weather. Rather than daily sprinklings give less frequent deep waterings.

Light surface cultivation is advocated by many dahlia enthusiasts, especially in clay soils. Dahlias will never grow well in baked or compacted soil, but take care lest you injure feeding roots. I prefer to mulch my plants, particularly those growing in heavy soil. Make a shallow cup around each bush first to aid watering when it becomes necessary. Where dahlias are on display, use ground corncobs or buckwheat hulls for a neat mulch. In my cutting garden, I utilize hedge and grass clippings or even weeds.

How to Plant

Do not plant dahlias until the ground and the nights have warmed up and there is no danger whatsoever of frost. Our last frosts here usually occur in mid-April, but we gain nothing by planting dahlias earlier than the last week of May. North or south of Philadelphia adjust dates accordingly. After tomato planting is about right. Tubers for exhibition blooms at fall shows are planted later than those for garden display. If your summers are short, start tubers early indoors in pots or milk cartons. (When transplanting these, or potted green plants from a dealer, or seedlings, harden them off in a cold frame or some protected place. Then move them on a cool, cloudy day, water well, and protect from direct sun until they are acclimated to the outdoors.

New tubers will come properly divided and showing an eye much like that of a potato, often already sprouted. Do not injure this bud. Old tubers must be divided, a job which can be confusing at first. The easiest method is to spread out the undivided tubers and cover with several inches of moist loam or peatmoss about a month before planting time. Keep in a cool, dry place, sprinkling occasionally if the loam gets dry. The day before planting, carefully uncover the tubers; bud eyes should have sprouted enough for you to see them easily.

For best flowers, plant only a single tuber for each bush. It must have an eye which is found only on the stem part of the tuber. Use a sharp knife or pruning shears, make a clean cut and leave the divided tubers in a cool, dry place overnight to air-dry the cuts. You may dip each cut in disinfectant if you wish. Start your surgery with the top tubers which are the easiest to cut out with part of the stem still on. In a big clump of roots you probably will not be able to salvage those at the bottom (Figure 1).

Soil where dahlias are to go should be deeply dug in advance, down a foot anyway. Its condition is the single most important requirement for success. The site must be well drained, the soil must contain humus and should be nearly neutral rather than heavily acid or alkaline. The plants need sun at least half the day.

You can mix fertilizer containing potash and phosphorus (but no nitrogen) in the soil two weeks before planting. Or you can place a handful of fertilizer in the bottom of the hole when you plant, covering with soil so it cannot touch and burn the roots. Sparing amounts of nitrogen fertilizer may be used later to promote foliage growth and large flowers, but too much nitrogen delays blooming and seems to reduce the vitality of the tubers. It will be better to use too little fertilizer than too much.

Large-flowered dahlias should have at least 4 feet between bushes while dwarf plants may go as close as 18 inches. In any but heavy clay soil (which is better loosened with compost and peat), place tubers flat in holes 5 inches deep and cover with 2 to 3 inches of soil. After growth begins, fill in with additional soil.

Harvesting and Storing

The first hard frost blackens dahlias. You can salvage an extra few days by covering the bushes with burlap or old sheets the first nippy nights, but these warmth-loving plants succumb to real cold. Leave alone for a few days so all the sap can drain into the tubers, then cut down the stalks and leave the tubers in the ground a week to give the stems time to bleed.

Choose a sunny day for digging and use a long-tined fork. Insert it a foot away from a bush on all sides, then gently pry up the clump so tubers will not be ripped off. This is more difficult if the soil is very wet or very dry. Shake most of the soil from the tubers and leave them in the sun for several hours to dry. Leave undivided, pack them carefully in flats, boxes or peach baskets and cover with some material to prevent shriveling during storage. Vermiculite is probably best, but sawdust has been used and polyethelene bags are reported good. I use ordinary garden loam for this purpose although there is some risk of insect or disease damage.

Place the tubers in a cool but not freezing place. Use the coolest part of the cellar and cover with newspapers to prevent warmth from entering since they do best at about 40 degrees F. With such care, it is seldom necessary to do anything more but check occasionally to see if the roots are still plump. Dahlias grow from tuberous roots which must not be allowed to dry out. A light sprinkling of water once or twice may be indicated through the winter. Should rotting occur, discard bad tubers and provide better ventilation and perhaps a cooler spot. Do not forget to label the tubers. A tag may be tied through or around the stems or a separate box used for each variety.

It is impossible not to increase dahlias. If properly grown, every single tuber will have produced numerous progeny by fall. In subsequent years each new tuber will yield exactly the same flowers as the original, and since you cannot use more than one tuber per bush, the supply easily outgrows planting space. This is one reason so many farm wives make pin money from these flowers. They sell extra tubers in spring and cut flowers in summer.

Dwarf Dahlias from Seed

It is even more fun to raise dahlias from seed as outlined in Chapter 18. A few years ago only the seed of the Coltness Hybrids (singles) and Unwin's Dwarf Hybrids (doubles) was easily obtained. Now you can find it for most other types too, usually in mixtures, sometimes in color blends. In the North start seed early in the house about a month or six weeks before outdoor planting time.

Since dahlias do not come true from seed in these mixtures, there is no telling what may result. A few plants may not appeal either in color or form; cull these out. Most of them will provide marvelous flowers for cutting, and a handful at least will be just the right size and colors for your house. These are the ones to mark. In the fall as many as half a dozen tubers will be produced by one seedling so you will have a fine collection of dahlias tailored just to your desires. Planted the next spring as tubers, they usually flower earlier.

Unwin's Dwarf Hybrids produce the best seedlings. They make short plants with semidouble or double flowers, although a few singles may occur. They seldom reach more than 36 inches in height, many are lower, and they give a multitude of blossoms. These dahlias are easily integrated into the summer garden, where they offer dependable color until frost. If you dislike the giant monsters, try a packet of these smaller dahlias before you ignore the genus.

You can treat the dwarf dahlias as annuals. Sow fresh seed every spring and don't bother with harvesting and storing. The only trouble is there is always some lovely seedling you want to perpetuate!

CAPSULE VIEW OF DAHLIAS

These are warm-weather plants, cannot tolerate any frost, but they are the most floriferous, dependable summer bulbs.

Colors, flower forms and sizes are extremely varied.

Give a warm, sunny site with well-drained soil containing plenty of humus; water well but fertilize sparingly.

Dahlias from seed show considerable variation; tubers and green cuttings come true to type.

Set tubers 5 inches deep, but gauge the distance apart by size of flower and bush; cover at first with only 2 to 3 inches of soil and fill in to grade level after growth begins.

CHAPTER 15

Bulbs for Autumn Color

Every year more gardeners are discovering that the autumn bulb story is not confined to planting for spring flowers. Beginning in late August and continuing almost into winter, a half-dozen dependable bulb groups offer fine garden color.

Although they share the same blooming season, they are unrelated. The tall late liatris belong to the great composite family, the colchicums are related to the lilies, the autumn crocus are cousins of the iris, the hardy cyclamen are primrose family members, sternbergia and *Allium stellatum* are hardy amaryllids and the hardy begonias belong to the family of the same name. Between them they offer a wide range of color.

Some summer bulbs like dahlias, tuberous begonias and cannas perform better as the nights grow cooler, and the montbretias, tuberoses and belamcandas often delay flowering until early fall. So there is a wealth of color available for the autumn garden.

Again I have listed these bulbs in the approximate order of blooming. They are reliably hardy at Philadelphia. With care in placement, most should survive in all but the coldest parts of our country, but flowering for some will depend on the season; early frost may cut them short.

Liatris and hardy begonia are planted in spring. Plant the others just as early as you can obtain bulbs. This means your

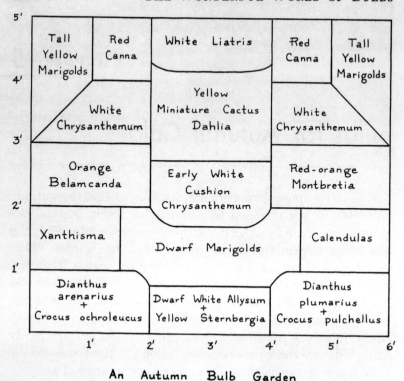

An Autumn Bulb Garden

FIG. 12. This garden can be planted before you go away on vacation. Mulched well, it will be gay all fall. In severe climates choose autumn crocus and the types of chrysanthemums that flower early in fall. Xanthisma and calendulas are late-blooming annuals that self-sow freely.

order should be mailed in early July. Shipment will be in August, and do not delay a moment in getting them into the ground so they can put down roots and produce flowers before snow!

Like other bulbs, they bloom a little later the first year after planting. Only trial will determine which of the autumn crocuses, fall cyclamens and colchicums can produce in your particular climate. Try first those which are known for early flowering. South of Washington, D.C., and in other temperate climates the latest autumn crocus or cyclamen is often closely followed by the snowdrops and the first spring crocus to make a full circle of bulbs, but most of us must resign ourselves to a period of winter in the garden when the evergreens and berried shrubs reign alone.

Cultural Details

Suggestions for the welfare of each of the fall-blooming bulbs is given below under each name, since their requirements differ widely. The liatris and hardy begonia will have begun growth in early spring and benefit from one good feeding of bonemeal and dried cow manure after the shoots are well up. Scratch about one tablespoon of each per shoot into the soil and water well.

The other fall bulbs make foliage *after* the flowers and need bonemeal in about the same amount. Apply it after the leaves have begun to show and again in the spring after frost leaves the ground. Always water August-planted bulbs deeply immediately after they are set out and weekly thereafter if the season is dry. When there is drought in late summer, water all areas where such bulbs are planted to encourage their awakening.

Since the foliage of sternbergia, colchicum and autumn crocus is a factor in the spring garden, take that into consideration when you place them, and mark locations well, since the leaves disappear in the summer. Careless cultivation can injure them. Those that bloom without foliage need a groundcover to set them off.

IN ORDER OF APPEARANCE

HARDY BEGONIA (*Begonia evansiana*) decorates the shady garden with dainty pink fountains nearly 2 feet high beginning in August. The leaves resemble those of the tuberous begonias, and the small gold-stamened flowers are similar to those of the fibrous type.

¶ Plant the little bulbs in the spring in moist, humus-rich soil about 1 to 2 inches deep and 6 inches apart.

Where it is at home, this plant spreads. Take care not to cultivate the area around it in spring, since it is often late in emerging, sometimes waiting even into July. Many stem bulbils are formed each autumn. You may store them and plant in spring, but most gardeners let them fall and plant themselves. I mulch my hardy begonias lightly; with such treatment they survive at least as far north as New York City in sheltered places.

A native of Java and China, this plant reaches its peak here in mid-September. The first cold snap discourages it even before frost, and it needs some wind protection. Sprays last well in bouquets, and a rare white form exists.

LIATRIS has already been covered in Chapter 11. Order September-flowering hybrids for the fall garden or grow your own from seed. My white (from mixed seed) has always been later than any purple varieties.

HARDY CYCLAMEN for bloom in summer and fall is similar to the spring-flowering types, but generally less difficult. The flowers are dainty and long-lasting, usually pinkish and only a few inches high.

¶ Give these cyclamen a shady spot with plenty of humus in well-drained soil and plant as early in summer as you can obtain the tubers, not more than 1 inch deep and about 6 inches apart in clumps of at least three.

Most catalogs suggest deeper planting, but I have found bloom more dependable at an inch. I add a little soil after the shoots begin to emerge. Where winters are cold and snow cover unreliable, mulch well with small evergreen boughs after the ground freezes. A touch of lime seems to their liking. I dry eggshells, crush them and spread around my cyclamen several times a year.

The easiest and hardiest is *Cyclamen neapolitanum* which bears either pink or white butterfly flowers on 4- to 6-inch stems beginning in early fall and often extending into December here. Try this one first, for if it will not do well, the chances of the others are doubtful. Earlier, often in midsummer, comes *C. europaeum* with fragrant rose-red flowers; *C. cilicicum* has fall-blooming pink flowers with crimson markings. All have attractive foliage, which appears after blossoming begins and is often mottled with silver. Leaves last through the winter.

After the foliage dies down, topdress with leafmold. Tubers may be left almost forever, growing slowly larger and producing more flowers each year—the reason they are planted far apart even when small. These cyclamen are propagated only by seed so let them alone as long as they do well. They resent moving and sometimes do not do well for a season or so afterwards. Try to get at least medium-sized bulbs. I doubt they will prosper in severe winters.

MEADOW SAFFRON (*Colchicum*) leaves me with mixed emotions. The double hybrid, Waterlily, (Color Plate XIV) is as beautiful as anything in my autumn garden, but the singles look terribly naked.

¶ Plant them as early in August as you can obtain the bulbs, about 4 inches deep and 6 inches apart in deep loam and half-shade (do not delay on receiving or they will flower in the bag!).

The bulbs of *C. autumnale minor* and *C. autumnale album* in Color Plate XXVI were overplanted with common thyme, which may soften them when it has had time to grow into thick mats. Some gardeners suggest using the big heart-shaped foliage of *Brunnera macrophylla* with colchicums, but ours sometimes is fall-blooming, and its blue flowers clash with lilac colchicums. It would be fine with the white form, which seems the most floriferous anyway. I noticed the foliage of *Muscari armeniacum* was 8 inches high when the colchicums flowered. Another year I shall plant a bulb or two of that with each colchicum; they should complement each other.

Waterlily was overplanted with one plant of annual alyssum which gave a beautiful effect, but its growth is graceful enough alone, since the big fluffy lavender flowers are produced on stems of varying heights. It is worth twice its present cost. There are numerous other hybrids, but none approaches this double. I intend to try a smaller double, *C. autumnale roseum plenum,* in preference to any more of the singles.

The spring foliage is neat and interesting, but quite tall so keep them from the forefront of a garden. Catalogs sometimes make much of the fact that these big bulbs will bloom indoors if left on a saucer unplanted. I cannot think of anything uglier, and the color then is a washed-out sickly shade.

STERNBERGIA LUTEA (Color Plate XVII) deserves a pretty nickname, for it is a sunny gold flower for the Fall garden when gray days are returning. Unlike many of the other hardy autumn bulbs, it produces neat foliage to set off its 5- to 6-inch-high cuplike blossoms which appear in September and October.

¶ Set the bulbs about 4 inches deep and 4 to 5 inches apart

on a well-drained slope facing south where they will get as much winter sunshine as possible.

Established bulbs bloom earlier than those freshly-planted, and the farther north you live the more important it is to get them into the ground as soon as you can obtain them, usually in August. New bulbs often do not flower the first year in northern climates. In the South this amaryllis is reported to multiply rapidly, but here the increase is very slow so a planting may be left alone for many years except for a fall feeding of bonemeal. When necessary, transplant after the foliage browns. It remains green and handsome here all winter and long into spring. I particularly recommend it for rock gardens. There is a rare spring-blooming form, *S. fischeriana.*

AUTUMN WILD ONION (*Allium stellatum*), an American wild flower, would be lovely with sternbergia in the rock garden. Its lilac clusters are borne 8 to 18 inches high. The bulbs are rare.

¶ Plant them about 2 inches deep in well-drained sites if you locate a source.

AUTUMN CROCUS are just what the name implies: crocus that bloom in the fall. These offer a lovely last defiant gesture for northern gardens, even blooming *between* frosts, but they are not as easy to work into the picture as the spring crocuses because most of them bloom without foliage.

¶ Plant autumn crocus in groups with a groundcover in late summer in well-drained sites 2 to 3 inches deep and not too far apart so they will form drifts.

Where September and October are still likely to have hot spells, the earliest-blooming autumn crocus benefit from light shade at midday, but farther north they want full sun and a protected location with good circulation of air to combat frost.

Where winter comes early, first try those cataloged as September–October flowering, although I have seen fall crocus in the snow at Syracuse, New York.

Dianthus foliage is a fine foil for the nakedness of the tubular crocus flowers, but any low groundcover should do. Get the bulbs into the ground as early as possible the first season.

My favorite is *C. speciosus albus,* an early pure white with bright orange stigmata, which seldom exceeds 4 inches in height (Color Plate XVI). For later bloom the white *C. ochroleucus* is even daintier. Blue speciosus forms often reach 10 inches, are early flowering and much like each other: violet-blue with darker veining and orange stigmata (Color Plate XVIII). I prefer *C. pulchellus,* which flowers at the same time, looks much the same but has shorter stems. Sometimes it has eight petals instead of the usual six and looks like the gold flowers on an ancient crown found in the famous royal grave at Ur in Mesopotamia.

Variable both in color and bloom time, *C. zonatus (kotschyanus)* has a bright orange mark in the throat. The white to lavender flowers look washed out and do not open as well as other types.

Lavender and violet crocuses include the venerable saffron crocus (*C. sativus*) which also has a white form; *C. medius,* a mid-season lilac which in my garden produced a short ruff of foliage to go with its flowers and has fine short stems (Color Plate XIX); and *C. asturicus atropurpureus,* one of the very latest.

CAPSULE VIEW OF HARDY FALL BULBS

Integrate these fall flowers with whatever else you expect in color from late August until hard frost.

Hardy cyclamen and begonia as well as the colchicums need

some shade when the weather is hot; plant with some shelter from wind; soil should be moist but well-drained and full of humus.

Autumn crocus, sternbergia and liatris want full sun and like a dry spot in summer; toward the top of a bank that faces south is best to stave off frost and get the most of winter sunshine.

Plant as early as bulbs can be obtained and water well afterward to get them growing as soon as possible.

Those which flower without foliage must have a groundcover to look their loveliest.

CHAPTER 16

Bulbs Make Fine House Plants

Did you ever consider bulbs as house plants? A few are noteworthy for their ability to grow and flower well under house conditions and to bloom during the winter when we need them most.

Any bulb which naturally flowers in summer heat or which is native to a hot climate (caladium and amaryllis, for example), is a possibility for your winter living room. Bulbmen are becoming adroit at controlling growth cycles so some bulbs of tender summer beauties can be offered for planting in early fall. When ordering, choose those listed as "pretreated," "stored" or "cooled" since these have been specially prepared for winter flowering. (The forcing of half-hardy and hardy spring bulbs for earlier bloom indoors is discussed in the next chapter.)

Proper Indoor Conditions

Without a greenhouse, indoor gardening is a matter of ingenuity. Before ordering bulbs, survey your house to determine how you can simulate proper conditions, for the climate of your house definitely governs what can be brought to flower in it during the winter months. You can manipulate temperature and humidity to some extent, two factors the outdoor

228

gardener must leave to chance. But a cyclamen will grow only in a cool room, and a caladium must have heat. In addition, all plants need sunshine (or artificial light) in varying degrees. The architecture of your house (the number of sunny windows and the plan of the rooms) plus the heating system dictate what bulbs you can grow indoors and where you can grow them.

While these tender bulbs need warmth and protection from drafts, they do not tolerate a drying blast of heat from radiator or register. Most thrive at a sunny window where room temperatures remain fairly constant during the day, and not much above 72 degrees F., and do not fall much below 60 degrees at night. Heated downstairs rooms usually qualify.

Humidity is particularly important in midwinter, when the furnace is constantly on. Plants do well set in trays filled with an inch of pebbles to which just enough water is added daily to wet the pebbles but not enough so pots stand in water. To increase humidity in very cold weather, pour boiling water into the tray, but do not let this virulent dose touch the pots. If your house is not automatically humidified, pans of water on top of radiators or by hot air registers will help. A plastic bag loosely tied around a pot makes a temporary greenhouse for plants in special need of higher humidity, but give them a daily interval without the bag and turn the bag inside out before replacing it (Figure 13).

Water in the morning to avoid fungus troubles, and sometimes from the bottom as well as the top to encourage deep root growth. A long-spouted watering can makes for less spillage. Have the water lukewarm and give enough to keep the soil from being dry but not enough to make it stay wet. Plants with large leaves need more water since there is greater evaporation through the foliage. Sunny days mean bigger

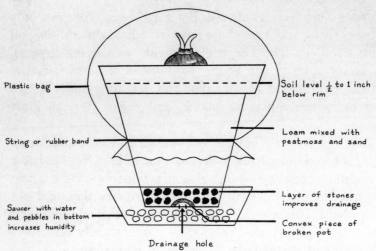

Planting in Pots (cross-section)

FIG. 13. In potting bulbs give good drainage. The layer of stones at the bottom and the piece of broken pot over the drainage hole insure this. Leave space below rim of pot for ease in watering. To increase humidity, set pots on pebbles in saucers or trays with water added below the level of the roots. Use a plastic bag as a miniature greenhouse for those bulbs in special need of humidity, but remove it at least once a day for ventilation; turn bag inside out each time so it will dry and not cause rot.

drinks than in cloudy weather, and small pots dry out faster than big ones.

Most plants benefit from an occasional syringing at the kitchen sink. Lay pots on the side and hold foliage under a lukewarm stream from the tap. Then keep plants out of direct sun until the leaves dry. Gloxinias and achimenes, whose leaves resent wetting, may be dusted with a small paintbrush if leaves become dusty.

Sun-loving plants like ornithogalums and gloriosa lily want southern windows during winter, a western exposure is next best. Plants needing less sun like gloxinias do nicely at eastern windows. Draw curtains back during the short days of December and January. As sunlight gets stronger, close glass curtains at midday only or move plants back from the pane. Plants coming from darkness or shade should be advanced gradually toward direct sun. Turn plants daily to develop straight stems and foliage.

On very cold nights plants close to window glass may suffer frostbite. Move them back or insert heavy cardboard between plant and pane as protection.

Soil and Potting

A mature bulb from a reliable source should bloom the first year if grown correctly, no matter what soil you give it. However, to get the loveliest flowers and to prepare the bulb adequately for its job the following year, this all-purpose mixture is suggested:

> 2 parts good garden loam
> 1 part clean sand
> 1 part domestic peatmoss
> 2 cups bonemeal per 5 gallons soil
> 2 cups dried cow manure per 5 gallons soil

Mix ingredients well several days before planting. Do not try to prepare too large a quantity at once. A wheelbarrow is a good mixing bowl, pails or tin cans are fine for measuring and a trowel or gloved hands easiest for stirring. Always prepare more than you will need, and store some indoors for winter needs. Add more sand for clay soils, more peat for light sandy loam.

I do not bother sterilizing the soil myself; for a rare bulb, I buy a package of a sterilized prepared mixture. Clay pots are still the best, I think. Scrub old ones clean and pour boiling water over them. New pots must be soaked overnight before using. The squattier bulb pans are ideal, but not mandatory. Non-gardeners are often happy to dispose of gift-plant pots so you can often assemble a fair collection over the years by judicious foraging.

Before planting, place a curved piece of broken pot over the drainage hole (Figure 13). Depending on the depth of the pot, spread from ½ to 1 inch of coarse gravel or small stones over the bottom. Then pour in some soil, place the bulb in position and fill in more soil, pressing it gently around the bulbs and firmly at the pot edge. Leave ½ to 1 inch of space at the top to receive water.

Bulbs in pots smaller than 3 inches top diameter dry out so quickly it is better to use a larger container. Immediately after planting, place pots in a tray of water and let them stay until the top soil feels damp. Then remove and store for rooting.

Kinds of Fertilizing

The loam and small amounts of bonemeal and manure you add to the potting mixture get your bulbs off to a good start. After the first leaves unfold, plants need additional nourishment. If you have only a few indoor plants, there are prepared fertilizer powders easy to mix and use according to package directions.

Liquid manure is my own preference. With one of the dried types like Bovung, you can mix a gallon as directed and keep it covered in a cool place. Always stir well before using. The smell vanishes quickly. Heavy feeders like amaryllis and gloriosa get a good drink of this once a week, at least from the time the first bud shows until the foliage is well developed; some gardeners start earlier. Then feedings are cut to every two weeks until the foliage matures. Other bulbs are fed every two weeks. Give no fertilizer when plants are resting.

Amounts vary with the size of the plant and the pot, but you are better off to use too little than too much. A good rule of thumb: 2 tablespoons maximum for a single bulb or one per bulb in a pot containing several. Do not let manure water touch foliage, and do not apply enough to saturate the pot. Water well the next day. Pour manure water on the surface of the soil rather than in the drainage saucers. With a fork, gently and shallowly loosen the surface soil occasionally to prevent crusting.

Cut off old flowers to promote further bloom and lessen the drain on the bulb. Remember that next year's bloom depends on your keeping the foliage growing as long as possible after flowering is over.

CHINCHERINCHEE (*Ornithogalum thrysoides,* Illustration 20) has consistently yielded more loveliness than any other indoor bulb I have grown, and plants given away as presents have proved amenable in other surroundings. The record of the plant before me is the best testimony. It produced its first starry white flower at the bottom of a triangular raceme last year on December 30. As each flower dried, it was removed from the raceme, which was still unfolding on February 24 when I cut it for a bouquet! More withered florets were removed while it remained on the table, but on March 4 the last flower, at the very top of the stem, began to open. That is not the end! The same plant by Feb. 14 was showing two additional well-developed racemes. The first flowered March 1, the second March 4. On April 8 two more buds showed so we cut the March blossoms for the table. On April 25 these last racemes were also cut for a bouquet. What other indoor bulb can match a record like that? The name chincherinchee comes

20. Star-of-Bethlehem (*Ornithogalum umbellatum*) is so rugged
it can become a pest, but the myriads of white flowers are welcome
in problem sites where other bulbs might not survive. Here two
pots of the taller, tender *O. thrysoides*, still in bloom at the end of
May, were brought out to show the family resemblance. This is my
least demanding, most floriferous bulbous house plant. Author's
garden.

supposedly from the sound of the wind rustling through the dried flowers of this South African native.

Plant bulbs early in the fall (September) just below the surface of the soil. Water sparingly until foliage begins to grow. I keep them away from direct sunlight but at a light window until good foliage has formed, then I place some where they will get as much sunshine as possible in hopes of getting early bloom. Others are held back until after Christmas, then given the same treatment, and even the most laggard usually shows buds by Easter. These last to bloom may continue into the summer. The amount of sunshine seems to have some effect on how soon they blossom, but there is great variation.

After danger of frost is past, set plants outside in a sunny place to finish blooming and mature their leaves. When foliage withers, I turn pots on the side and leave under a bench in a dry, sunny place until time to repot. Mature bulbs often produce bulbils on the surface; these are planted closely in a flat and kept growing all winter at a window. Some will usually blossom the following winter. I started my stock from seed (see Chapter 18).

A tender relation of the hardy star-of-Bethlehem, *O. thrysoides* has flower stalks seldom higher than 18 inches. The individual stars are about the size of a quarter, have a green or yellow center and odd golden stamens. The only thing missing is fragrance. The variety, *O. aureum* is similar but has yellow flowers and tends to be shorter; *O. arabicum* has a black central pistil and white flowers; *O. saudersi* bears pure white blooms. Stems of both are at least 2 feet tall. The last two reportedly require colder conditions than *O. thrysoides* and are not nearly as dependable.

GLORY LILY (*Gloriosa rothschildiana*) provides from a dozen to eighteen brilliant red-and-yellow, reflexed and waved, lilylike blossoms for at least a month. These are fine to cut and for corsages. Small tubers will not bloom reliably.

Handle the brittle tubers carefully to prevent breakage. From September to November plant singly in a 6-inch pot with the growing tip just under the soil. Tilt tuber slightly if too long for the pot. Water well and keep in a warm place, which need not be dark, until a shoot appears. Then give full sun, fertilize weekly from time sprout reaches 2 feet until bloom stops, then every two weeks until foliage ripens.

The glory lily climbs by leaf tendrils so provide a light support. A vigorous tuber easily reaches 6 feet, but you may shorten this by gently training shoots to bend on a trellis. Once well started, gloriosa grows 6 to 8 inches per day! The first time we watched in disbelief as this Jack-in-the-beanstalk plant passed the top of our short trellis without pausing. Two subsequent additions to the trellis were necessary before we realized we would have to curl the plant's leader or knock a hole in the ceiling!

The tendrils have a barbous end which easily hooks on string so you can use light plant stakes for the uprights and bracing of your trellis and green string for most of the verticals and horizontals. Our plant stretched a single thin stem to nearly 5 feet before branching. Allow foliage to ripen at the window, then rest the tuber in the pot in a warm place for several months before repotting for another year. Offsets should be carefully removed and planted separately.

Other varieties: *G. superba*, like above but petals are frillier; *G. virescens*, dwarfer, orange; *G. carsoni*, tall, flowers purple, edges yellow. Give same treatment to LITTONIA MODESTA KEITI, a similar climbing tuber with orange bell flowers.

AMARYLLIS (*Hippaestrum*) cause a great stir in bloom with immense trumpet blossoms, but since an individual scape (flower stem) seldom lasts more than a week indoors, buy the biggest size you can get in the hope of getting more than one flowering stalk. Two to four flowers are born in an umbel on each scape in vivid shades of pink, scarlet, salmon and dark red, and there are also pure white and striped forms. Named varieties are too expensive for any but the fancier, but most bulb houses offer moderately-priced bulbs by color. Small-sized amaryllis bulbs offered as "bargains" are hardly worth window space.

They bloom best if rootbound. Use a shallow clay pot no more than 2 inches larger in diameter than the bulb and plant with a third to a half of the bulb above the soil surface. Water well just once, then keep in a shaded, moderately warm place with only an occasional watering until growth starts. Bring to full sunlight and warmth and resume regular watering. Fertilize with manure water every week from the time the flower scape shows until foliage is lush, a period of some months. In a window these plants must be turned daily to keep the flower scape growing straight.

After flowering is finished, cut off the scape and keep the plant growing in full sunlight until there is no danger of frost. Then plunge the pot to the rim in a partially shaded site outdoors where the plant will continue to grow well into late summer. Water as needed unless there is *heavy* rain. Bring it in before frost. Reduce water and leave it on its side in a cool but frost-free place until late fall. If foliage dries up, withhold all water until time to start growth again. Evergreen species will need sparing amounts of water during this period and will not lose all their leaves.

Unless strict attention is paid to aftercare, these bulbs will not store enough energy for subsequent blooming. Allowed to grow as described above, they can continue to flower for years.

When buying new bulbs, make sure you get "stored" bulbs for early winter flowers.

With your own bulb, peel back dry outer layers of skin some time in late November to see if there is any green color on the bulb itself, an indication of readiness for another growing period. Do not repot unless the container is broken. Just scrape away the top layer of soil without disturbing roots and replace with fresh soil. Let half the bulb remain above the soil as before. In repotting, lift out the entire root mass, soil and all, and place new soil over the bottom of a larger pot. This will let the bulb rest at the same level as before. Add fresh soil around the sides and replace the top layer of soil. The cycle now begins again.

More exotic members of the same family are similarly treated. Most of them bloom naturally in late spring or summer. They are wonderful for the gardener who is limited to a window or terrace garden. New methods of storing make it possible to have some bulbs for winter flowering. The hippaestrums are the easiest members of the family for winter bloom, but their relatives are interesting for the gardener who likes something different. Those with evergreen foliage grow on indefinitely; they need regular fertilizing when not resting and should not be kept so dry they wilt.

They include: CHLIDANTHUS FRAGRANS, which has umbels of fragrant yellow trumpets on 10-inch scapes; SPREKELIA or JACOBEAN LILY (*A. formosissima*) which bears unique single crimson flowers on 18-inch stems; AMAZON LILY (*Eucharis amazonica* or *grandiflora*) with evergreen foliage and clusters of fragrant white, daffodil-like flowers on 24-inch stems (keep from direct sunlight); SCARBOROUGH LILY (*Vallota speciosa* or *purpurea*), also with evergreen foliage and scarlet umbels of trumpet flowers on 2- to 3-foot stalks; ZEPHYR LILIES (*Zephyranthes*) which have pink and white forms and bloom several times a year if given alternate periods of growing and dry resting; and CLIVIA MINIATA which has evergreen leaves and clusters of scarlet-and-yellow trumpets on a 12-inch stem. Clivias are mostly too big for ordinary windows.

CHIVES (*Allium schoenoprasum*) keep green company with a variety of winter-flowering bulbs on my southern windowsill, and I make no excuses for them. We allow the outdoor patch to wither with the frost, then watch for a thaw in January. One year a small clump was dug and potted, soil and all, the day ofter New Year's. Watered well and gradually acclimated to heat, it was then placed in sunlight and sheared for the first time January 16 to enliven buttered potatoes. The foliage grows lush all winter no matter how often we cut it for seasoning salads or vegetables.

In sections without our early winter thaw, put up a clump of chives after the first hard frost and place in a protected outdoor spot where it can easily be found after a month's rest. Bring gradually to light and warmth. Pots sold in grocery stores in early spring can be planted outside after frost to become the nucleus of a luxuriant hardy patch if you do not have one.

CALADIUMS provide decorative foliage for indoor growing, in shades of white, green, cream, pink and red. Start them in September (when bulbmen have special tubers available for winter growing) in a flat of sphagnum moss or sand in a really warm spot (70 to 80 degrees F.). Water sparingly until growth begins, then pot in the regular soil mixture, adding a little extra peat and covering tubers about 2 inches. They need lots of water, liquid manure every week after growth starts, and an eastern window. High humidity is their greatest indoor demand. By mid-June the plants are usually ready for resting. Store dry in the pots in a warm place like a sunny garage until the following fall (see Chapter 12).

TUBEROUS BEGONIAS and GLOXINIAS (*Sinningia*) are favorites for summer color in shady places (Chapter 12). By purchasing specially treated bulbs, you can bring them into winter bloom, but the average home is not quite ideal for such a venture, probably from lack of humidity. There is evidence too that these plants respond unfavorably to the short days of early winter.

Buying begonias and gloxinias in bloom from a florist is easier. Treat gloxinias as you might African violets; water thoroughly but not often enough to saturate soil completely, keep the foliage dry, increase humidity and feed with liquid manure every two weeks. If contented, they bloom all winter, but give them several hours of artificial light from late October until March when daylight lengthens.

Begonias need more moisture than gloxinias and benefit from a misty spray on the foliage in heated rooms. The multiflora types described in Chapter 12 bloom best indoors.

To bring either into bloom indoors during winter, order stored tubers early and start in September in flats or pots of mixed peatmoss and sand or in sphagnum moss. Push them into the rooting medium with the round side down until the flattish tops just show above the surface. Water well once and keep the soil just moist but never saturated while sprouts develop. A moderately warm and light but not sunny place is best. When several leaves form, transplant carefully to 6-inch pots, adding peat to the standard soil mixture, and setting bulbs about an inch deep.

In the waning sunlight of late fall and early winter, place plants in a south window but not close to the pane. One of my favorite nurserymen advises a fluorescent light or a 60-watt bulb 2 feet above the plants after they begin to grow to supplement the winter daylight. By stretching their day to 14 to 16 hours, you are most likely to get midwinter bloom. Move plants to eastern windows when the days begin to lengthen, toward the end of February.

Rest potted gloxinias in the house during the summer and water just enough to keep them from drying out completely. After the begonias have finished flowering, taper off the water gradually. When foliage is brittle, cut it off and leave tubers in the pots in the basement until the fall when the cycle begins again.

VELTHEIMIA VIRIDIFOLIA would be worth growing on the windowsill just for its foliage. The long, glossy, basal leaves are curiously ruffled and form a bright green rosette. The stiff 24-inch flower stalk can be expected in January from early fall planting and reminds me of a giant tritoma. The tubular florets are dusty rose and remain in good shape for three weeks if the plant is not subjected to too much heat.

Use a 6-inch pot and plant as early in fall as bulbs are available. Place each bulb so the top third is above the soil; water sparingly until growth begins; then fertilize weekly and water well. Place in a sunny window away from heat sources so the temperature stays under 65 degrees F. Keep the foliage growing as long as you can. Store cool in the pots after it matures and replace only the top layer of soil in the fall. The roots seem to resent disturbance but need careful repotting every other year.

CALLA LILIES (*Zantedeschia*) with their waxen flowers provide exotic cut flowers and make impressive pot plants, but the most commonly found types are rather large to accommodate on the average windowsill. Plant tubers in 6-inch pots as soon as available in fall with the top just beneath the soil surface, water sparingly and keep cool and shaded until growth starts. Then move to a sunny window away from radiators. All callas need constant watering during active growth, weekly applications of manure water as soon as a sprout shows, and high humidity.

The big arrow-shaped leaves are spectacular in arrangements, but do not remove more than one at a time from an individual plant if you wish to keep tubers in condition for another season. Cut aging flowers religiously, to encourage further blossoming. Keep the foliage growing as long as possible; pots may even be sunk in a sunny part of the garden to complete the process after frost. Store dry in the pots in a cool place after leaves turn brown, and repot every year. Unless you can give them high humidity, I do not recommend callas for indoor use.

The giant white form, Z. *aethiopica* reaches 3 feet in pots; Z. *elliottiana* is nearly as large with yellow spathes and white flecks in dark green foliage. Much better for your window are Z. *godefreyana,* a small, prolific white; Z. *rehmani superba,* a dwarf pink; and Z. *albomaculata* which has creamy blooms with a purple throat and white mottled leaves. A half-hardy curiosity often sold as the black canna (*Arum pictum*) for indoor use bears black-purple flowers with a green tube inside. I cannot see why anyone would want it around.

CAPSULE VIEW OF HOUSE BULBS

Buy the best bulbs you can get to insure fine bloom.
Increase humidity in midwinter.
Water and fertilize faithfully, but do not overdo either.
Let foliage mature fully to guarantee satisfactory bloom next year.

CHAPTER 17

Forcing Bulbs for
an Early Spring

Do you, too, long desperately for the colorful flowers of spring while the world is still trapped in winter? With forethought you can enjoy daffodils, hyacinths, tulips and a'host of little bulbs indoors ahead of schedule without benefit of a greenhouse. Tenderer sorts like freesias, cyclamens and lachenalias are also possibilities.

None of these bulbs, however, is for your living room. We have already discussed some important needs of bulbs in the house. While sharing those general requirements, this group must have *a cold place for rooting and a cool site for flowering*. I have divided them into the half-hardy bulbs which must never freeze and the hardy spring bulbs which can be forced early only after a really cold period for rooting.

Even after roots have formed, these bulbs will bloom only in a room where the temperature seldom exceeds 65 degrees F. A range from 50 to 60 degrees most of the time will allow you to grow the greatest variety. A sunny window in a cool bedroom or an unheated sun porch is what you seek. A location that stays nearer the 45-degree limit most of the time is too cold for the tenderer bulbs; one continually near or above 65 degrees is too warm for the hardier types. Choose your bulbs according to what your house offers.

Buy the largest and best bulbs you can for forcing, and load the scales in your favor by choosing the earliest-blooming types; most catalogs suggest suitable varieties. Fed and allowed to mature their foliage naturally, hardy bulbs may later be planted out in the garden and usually flower after one year of recovery. If they are given plenty of sun, water, and fertilizer until their foliage browns and are stored fairly dry and warm during the summer, many semihardy bulbs like freesias and sparaxis may be repotted and grown inside again, but only if the bulbs are large and plump; the little bulbs usually need at least another year of growing before reaching flowering size. Bulbs grown in pebbles or water should be discarded, but you can wash and reuse the stones.

Perhaps the nicest thing about doing your own forcing is that you can select just the right colors to suit the decoration of your own house. Buying pots from a florist, you must settle for whatever he has. The enthusiastic gardener will admit, too, that there is a thrill of accomplishment in raising your own spring window garden.

HALF-HARDY BULBS

The bulbs in this category should not be subjected to freezing ever. From August to November plant 1 inch apart as many bulbs as will fit a bulb pan or low pot. Store in a *cool place* around 50 degrees F. (my cellar is just right) to make roots. If you cannot provide natural darkness during this period, cover pots with paper.

When you can see roots through the drainage hole of a pot (Fig. 13), expose the potted bulb gradually to light. Rooting may take only two to three weeks for paper-whites, freesias and lachenalias, longer for others. Whenever these have good roots, they can go into a room where the temperature seldom rises above 65 degrees and does not fall below 45 degrees.

All do best grown on in a cool room even after they come into bloom. None makes so striking a plant (except the cyclamen) that you long to show it off, but all provide lovely cut flowers for weeks, even months if kept growing cool. (Cyclamen may last from Christmas to Easter.)

PAPER-WHITES (*Narcissus polyanthus* or *tazetta*) are the most popular and dependable of the half-hardy bulbs for indoors. They are so bent on blooming, you can grow them in pebbles and water although I use regular potting soil for mine; it seems to produce better flowers. A well-grown bulb will give one to three graceful, perfumed clusters. Soleil d'Or is all yellow, the Chinese Sacred Lily creamy white with lemon centers. In the dark days of winter from December into March their brightness is a delight in our northern homes.

Allow about five weeks for paper-whites. Those rooted just before Thanksgiving will give bloom by Christmas. A deep mixing bowl (or a really handsome container if you wish) of paper-whites just coming into flower makes a wonderful present for a neighbor. Later plantings yield even faster bloom. Wait until the third week of October before planting any to give the bulbs time to mature thoroughly. They may then be planted in succession for constant color, but start the last batch before the end of February since the bulbs lose their vitality after that. Store bulbs as cool as possible (but not freezing) to hold them back until you are ready to plant. Bulbs subjected to heat before planting seldom blossom at all.

Use a container at least 4 inches deep to allow for adequate root development and big enough to accommodate at least three bulbs, although even one alone looks nice in a pretty

21. A few paper-white narcissus and some geranium leaves make a quick and pleasant arrangement in midwinter (Roche).

bowl. Spread a few pebbles in container, place the bulbs, then add more stones to within ½-inch of the top of the bowl. Set the bulbs so their top two-thirds remains above the pebbles. Fill the bowl with enough water so that it just shows among the top stones (do not float the bulbs) and place in a cool, dark location. As water evaporates, add more, but after the first time, pour only enough to raise the water level among the pebbles to the base of the bulbs to prevent rotting.

At first the bulbs may be pushed above the pebbles by the growing roots. Gently press them back as best you can and pour extra pebbles around them. In soil, plant bulbs deeper so that only about a third shows above the surface; here they are less likely to push themselves out as roots develop.

No matter how strong the shoots may be at the top, do not remove pots from the dark until a good root system shows. You know it is adequate when rootlets protrude from the drainage hole. With bulbs in pebbles, carefully poke aside the stones with a pencil to check progress. There should be a good root mass at least two inches below the surface. Meanwhile the foliage will begin to lengthen.

You can bring pots gradually to light in succession over a period of about two weeks, but you can only hold them back so long once they have produced a good root system. Plant only a few pots at a time unless you plan to give them away. Keep the unplanted bulbs in an opened bag in a cool, dark place and plant some every ten days for a long period of bloom.

Do not bother saving bulbs to force for another year. Start each year with fine new stock. However in *mild* climates those grown in soil will often establish themselves in a sheltered spot outdoors if the foliage is allowed to mature properly.

FREESIAS have been my favorite indoor flower since my mother first brought them into my young life as part of a bouquet. I adore their perfume, and they come in warm shades of gold, orange, pink and bronze as well as cream and white. Bluish varieties are less attractive to me.

Requiring about twelve weeks to come into bloom, freesias can be planted as early as August and as late as November to give a whole winter of delight. They require plenty of sun, and a temperature that seldom rises above 60 degrees F. Since their foliage is scraggly, they are fine for growing in an unused room where they stay cool while you cut them. Pick the raceme when the second trumpet begins to open. A planting will continue to flower for about six weeks, so time your batches accordingly.

Place the corms pointed end up and just below the surface of the soil in bulb pans or narrow boxes which fit a window sill. Water well once, then store in a shaded spot at about 50 degrees F.; shoots straggle less if plants are not kept in the dark too long after they emerge. Do not place in sun until good roots show in the drainage hole, and water sparingly from the bottom until a strong root system is formed. When growing, freesias need plenty of water, fertilizing every two weeks and good sun.

On the windowsill, freesias need support. I use two or three stakes to a pot and wind the twine in figure eights between stakes and around the thin stalks.

LAPEIROUSIA (*Anomatheca crueta*) should be treated much like freesias and also needs staking. It bears a few brilliant red flowers blotched with crimson in a loose raceme, and I have flowered it in a cool, sunny living room window where the temperatures are higher than those suggested for freesias.

Kept in the pot and moved outside to a mostly sunny spot in the garden, lapeirousia often gives further bloom during the summer. Allow foliage to dry naturally, withholding artificial watering after it flowers, but leave it exposed to the elements until repotting in September. The winter flowers are sparse but very gay.

CORN LILIES (*Ixia*) and WAND FLOWERS (*Sparaxis*) are also grown like freesias. They are not as free-flowering nor as dependable under home conditions. They have no fragrance and their flowers do not last as long as freesias. Many of the colors, however, are exciting. Ixias range from white, yellow, pink and red to purple shades, often with a contrasting eye, and are borne in racemes. Sparaxis bear single, larger flowers in brilliant shades of orange, red, yellow, lavender and white with odd markings of another color. A few have short spikes of flowers. BABIANA is similar to freesia but not so tall.

CAPE COWSLIP (*Lachenalia*) is grown like the freesias and is one of the easier indoor bulbs. It comes quickly into bloom, often in six weeks from planting, and bears many pendulous, tubular flowers along a 12-inch stem. The foliage may be mottled with brown. The graceful flowers last up to three weeks in water. Buds blast if plants are brought into a room warmer than 65 degrees F., and the plants require copious watering just before and during flowering. Decrease water afterward and allow foliage to dry gradually.

Readily located are bulbs of *L. aurea*. The buds are red, and the immature yellow flowers tipped with the same color like the tiny firecrackers we used to call lady crackers. Eventually they turn almost entirely yellow. Other varieties are orange, red and yellow, often edged with green, red or purple.

CYCLAMEN (*C. persicum giganteum*) hold a special place in my heart because for many years my husband has brought me one annually to mark some holiday. You too will love the exquisite flowers, which look like hovering butterflies in shades of white, pink, rose and red. They make fine cut flowers, often lasting longer than two weeks in water, and this should be their use in the ordinary home.

Truth is, the cyclamen brought into a warm winter house dies quickly. It prospers best in a Spartan environment where temperatures rarely rise above 60 degrees. I grow it in my cold bedroom. Treated thus, it provides beautiful flowers for cutting and sharing as bouquets. Often delicately mottled silver, the heart-shaped leaves suggest valentines and they last well in arrangements.

Paradoxically, I use warm water for my cyclamen. It is placed on a layer of pebbles in a deep saucer or bowl, and water is poured into this container until the level reaches just above the base of the pot, so the plant can drink some while the rest remains to increase humidity. In a cool room, do this only about every other day. Feel the surface of the soil if you are in doubt because the cyclamen needs a lot of water during growth. Many gardeners prefer to pour tepid water at the top, but unfortunately many florists set the tubers too deep, thus opening the door to rot.

If a cyclamen is to spend any time in a living room, the only way you can hope to keep it alive is to pour a little boiling water in the saucer several times a day. Even with this care the plant will not perform well if it is otherwise exposed to dry heat. The technique, however, allows you to show one off *temporarily*. Try to purchase a plant with just a few flowers out and a myriad of developing buds for months of bloom; keep it in a cool room. Choicest plants are available around Christmas time, but some florists will have a few for Valentines. Give them an eastern window. They cannot take the sun at a southern window and often prosper at northwest and northeast exposures.

While not always successful, I try to garner a second year of bloom from my cyclamen. To do this, feed the plant 1 tablespoon of manure water every week, pouring it on the soil and continue until the last flowers open; then reduce feeding to every two weeks. Keep the fertilizer away from crown of the plant and do not give more than this amount. When spring frosts are over, put the pot outside, on its side in an eastern exposure, protected from summer sun by shrubbery. It needs no artificial watering.

In August or even before, new sprouts appear. Now carefully remove the tuber with some soil adhering, and in the regular potting mixture, reset it with the top just above the soil surface. Bring inside immediately to acclimatize it before the heat is turned on. Grow cool in a saucer as before and fertilize every week after leaves begin to grow. If no flower buds have formed by the middle of December, give it up as just one of those things and invest in another cyclamen from the florist. There are double, fringed, and ruffled varieties, but none is as lovely as the more common single.

HARDY SPRING BULBS

You cannot really "force" a bulb to do anything. It takes just so long for it to rest, develop roots and then finally send up a flower bud. The cycle must always take place, but indoors you can hasten the process by simulating appropriate conditions so a bulb will bloom sooner than it might if left outside to its own devices. We who live where there is no winter bloom outside derive a satisfaction from indoor-blossoming spring bulbs that no resident of the tropics could possibly understand. We talk about "forcing," but what we are actually doing is cutting short the spring waiting period. The bulb must have time to make good roots under cold conditions first; then we speed things up by offering it somewhat warmer weather while it is still winter outside.

It is not easy for the home-gardener to force pots of hardy tulips, daffodils and the like into bloom before their normal time. Nevertheless, it is not as difficult as some experts would have us believe, nor does it always require as much effort as the old-timers say. I have successfully used two shortcuts, but here first, briefly, is the time-tested technique.

Trenching Method

Plant bulbs of hardy spring flowers in clay pots during September or October, setting them about 1 inch apart and just under the surface of the soil. Dig a narrow trench 2 feet deep in a northern or eastern exposure and line the bottom with 6 inches of gravel, cinders or stones to insure drainage. After a thorough soaking, place the pots close together in the trench. Cover each with an inverted pot before filling between and over them with several inches of peatmoss or vermiculite. Next spread a 10-inch layer of straw or leaves and hold it in place with branches. Leave pots undisturbed for two to three months to form roots. Under the mulch they will be cold enough to root but will not freeze hard. Where rodents are a problem, line the trench with hardware mesh.

Long labels stuck into each pot make it easier to find what you seek when you come to bring the pots from the trench to a warmer spot for forcing. Veteran gardeners arrange pots so those to be brought in first are at one end. By the time they uncover the far end of the trench, they have reached those they want last.

From the trench move the pots to a dark place where it is still really cold but above freezing. Keep the soil moist but never wet. A cold section of a cellar or garage is fine for this stage. Here the bulbs remain until a good root system shows in the drainage holes. When this sign appears, bring in the pots as desired to a dark place at about 50 degrees F. Let them stay in the dark until top growth is several inches high. Then expose gradually to light, ending up at a sunny window in a room which averages 60 degrees. Remove from direct sun during flowering.

A well-drained cold frame may be used in place of the trench, but leave off the glass while the bulbs are using it. Cover the pots with peat, leaves and branches, as in the trench.

The First Short Cut

Dogs and children have played havoc with my trenches, and several times they have been covered with a back-breaking drift of snow just when I wanted access, so I tried an easier way.

The outside wall of our unheated garage will accommodate all the hardy spring bulbs I am likely to raise in one season. In early fall the planted pots are set in single file on the garage floor along this cold wall. They are covered with inverted pots or balloons of aluminum foil loosely crimped around the top. This allows air to circulate and leaves room for the buds to emerge but keeps the plants dark. They remain there, conscientiously watered, until bitter weather arrives; then they are shifted to the inside wall of the garage, where it is a shade warmer, to keep them from hard freezing.

After the Christmas things are put away, the pots are moved to the coolest wall of the cellar. (It is about 50-60 degrees F. there.) Each is set in a saucer and the pots are watered only from the bottom, to encourage deep rooting. The covers are left on to keep them dark. Some bulbs will show shoots and no roots, but pay no attention to the tops. Keep the bulbs in the dark until a *mass* of roots shows in the drainage hole.

As I want them, pots with shoots showing and many roots protruding are then uncovered and placed in a slightly warmer part of the cellar to let the tops grow. The next stage is to accustom them to the light by easy stages, and then to place them in the sunny cool cellar windows. When buds show well, I bring them to a cool room upstairs and grow them on until the blooms are developed. Plants may be displayed in a heated room for short periods, but they spend the nights at least in a cool place. Space being at a premium, I return them to cellar windows for ripening the foliage until I feel it safe in spring to put them outside to finish the process.

The Shortest Cut of All

An unseasonably warm day in December or January finds me poking in the gardens for signs of bulb growth. This is re-assuring after a spell of dreadful weather, but I have more in mind. In certain sheltered places I know I will find crocus and daffodil shoots where long-established plantings are situated.

With my small potting shovel, I slice into the earth several inches away from the outside shoot. Gently I pry up the soil until I can see whether I have made the cut far enough away from the bulbs. Then I make three more cuts and lift out a square of soil in which are bulbs, roots and all. Earth from around the shoots is carefully removed until the tops of the bulbs show; then the whole clump is planted in a big clay pot in which I have put some potting mixture. Only enough soil is gently brushed away from the roots to fit them in the pot, and this is then brought into the cool basement.

Keeping these cool and shaded for a good two weeks in most cases, before they are brought to the sunny cool cellar windowsills and generous watering the first few days to assuage the disturbed roots are necessary precautions. They do not require darkness, only a shady corner. Plastic bags over the tops will help them get over the shock of transplanting.

Here is one year's record of some bulbs I grew in this way:

Bulb	Dug up outside	First bloom indoors	Same variety bloomed outside
Grape hyacinth			
(*Muscari armeniacum*)	1/13	2/26	4/14
	2/23	3/19	4/14
Lily-of-the-valley			
(*Convallaria majalis*)	1/13	2/28	5/8
Chives			
(*Allium schoenoprasum*)	1/2	*1/16	*4/1
Narcissus, small-cup	12/2	2/4	4/27
	2/22	3/21	4/27
February Gold	2/22	3/6	4/5
Laurens Koster	1/22	2/16	4/23
Crocus susianus	2/20	2/26	3/5
Tulipa clusiana	2/22	3/25	4/24
Star-of-Bethlehem			
(*Ornithogalum umbellatum*)	11/26	3/24	5/16
Puschkinia libanotica	2/22	3/3	3/18
Tritelia uniflora	2/23	3/22	4/17
Iris reticulata	2/23	3/4	3/24

    * Foliage ready for use.

I suspect I shall try more and more things by this method; it is so wonderfully simple. In a sheltered area of the garden, I contemplate special early September plantings just for this purpose with fresh bulbs set closely together for easy digging. Far northern gardeners probably will have to rely on the trench or garage method, but those of us who live where an occasional midwinter thaw is the rule can cut corners.

This method will not produce the *earliest* blooms for inside, and it is not recommended for tulips. Unless you make close plantings of bulbs just for this purpose, it works best for established plantings of bulbs which reproduce themselves well so a whole clump can be dug up with little root disturbance.

Grape hyacinths and tritelia respond well. Their foliage appears in fall here, but do not bring either in before late January since earlier digging does not hurry them much. Lily-of-the-valley can be traced by the old foliage on the ground. Knock off some of the original soil from the pips and roots so you can crowd as many as possible into a pot because only the biggest pips will blossom. I force all my daffodils and crocus this way; the later they are dug, the sooner they flower. Tulip species can be forced by the shortcut, but the stems are brittle in the cold and tend to snap.

DAFFODILS and HYACINTHS are the surest of the big three for indoor forcing, whatever method you choose. (More on hyacinths is found in Chapter 8). Daffodils by the first two methods should be potted as early in September as possible and given 10 to 12 weeks of cold growing before they are brought indoors to the cellar floor. Your catalogs will recommend numerous early trumpet and large-cupped varieties for forcing. Just as easy and even lovelier and more fragrant are some of the cluster-flowered types (Laurens Koster, Cheerfulness, Cragford and Geranium). Thalia, February Gold, Silver Chimes and Peeping Tom are dainty and wonderful for indoors. Plant as many bulbs as you can per pot for really dazzling color.

TULIPS for the indoor beginner should be chosen only from among the early singles and doubles or the less expensive and early species such as *T. kaufmanniana* and *T. fosteriana*. Pot them before the end of October, allow 12 to 14 weeks for rooting in the cold. The early doubles last longer in bloom and have proved easier for me than the singles. Do not try to force any tulip until a *mass* of roots shows in the bottom of the pot. Truthfully, tulips are the most frustrating hardy bulb to force; try something easier first. On your initial attempt do not begin forcing them at least until the middle of February. They will come quickly then if they are ready.

EASTER LILIES are not difficult but require patience. Choose the Croft, Ace, Estate or tetra types of *Lilium longiflorum*. Plant as early as you can each in a 6-inch pot with the tip of the bulb just below the soil. Keep them cool, but never freezing, and dark until they begin to show roots and a shoot. Then grow them cool, first at a shady window and then in full sun when the shoot begins to lengthen. Fertilize every two weeks from the time the shoot begins to spurt until leaves ripen.

It took 131 days from planting to the first open trumpet for my Croft lilies last year. That variety may be planted later in the garden and often blooms again in subsequent summers. Give it a protected spot if you live north of Philadelphia. Lilies grown on windowsills are taller than those given more sun in a greenhouse, but the satisfaction of doing it yourself is something else again. Slightly higher temperatures (70 degrees F. at the most) will hurry them the last week, but do not try this before the buds begin turning white. The Mid-Century Hybrids also respond well to forcing.

LITTLE SPRING BULBS must never be hurried, allowed to dry out or grown above 65 degrees F. Most welcome an even cooler site. Pot them early in September, store cold until good roots form and a shoot shows, then bring slowly to light and moderate warmth. *Iris reticulata* and *I. danfordiae*, puschkinia, eranthis, chionodoxa, the early scillas, species and Dutch crocus are fairly easy but require definite cool growing. *Scilla campanulata* is sweet but takes forever to bud as do hardy ornithogalum.

A good rule of thumb is to try first those which bloom earliest outside, since these naturally require the shortest rooting period. Grape hyacinths, tritelia and lily-of-the-valley are notable exceptions; although they bloom in late spring, they are among the easiest to force and will take the warmest temperatures of this group.

Bloom for Christmas

Iris reticulata and its hybrids if started cold in early September, can be forced for Christmas. Bring in during November, give the sunniest possible position and never more than 50 degrees F. Unfortunately, the blooms do not last long in the house. For hyacinths at Christmas, check Chapter 8; paperwhites and other half-hardy bulbs discussed in the first part of this chapter are also holiday possibilities.

Cold storage pips of lily-of-the-valley can be secured through most of the year. Pot them with the pips just at soil level and grow not warmer than 65 degrees F. Dim light is best until growth shows, then bring to sun. Allow a month for bloom to begin. In a pretty container these make a lovely gift for any occasion.

CAPSULE VIEW OF FORCING BULBS

Choose your bulbs for indoor growing according to the temperature possibilities of your house; try only the half-hardy sorts if you have no *cold* place for rooting; if your house is uniformly warm all winter, grow only the bulbs of Chapter 16.

Start with the easiest types, like daffodils or hyacinths, and do not grow too many at once.

Never try to hurry bulbs being forced; until you have had experience under your own conditions, do not chain yourself to a timetable but just be content to get them into flower.

Bring pots in from the rooting site at intervals of about two weeks to insure a long period of bloom; do not try to force until a bulb has made a real mass of roots—they should poke through the drainage hole.

Use flowers for cutting and keep plants growing cool; if you want to display the plants in living rooms, at least return them to a cooler place at night.

CHAPTER 18

How to Grow Bulbs from Seed

In a featured spot in my garden last year three bulbs of *Lilium formosanum philippense* produced a dozen gorgeous white trumpets. The satisfaction I felt each time I caught their fragrance went deeper than usual because I grew those lilies from seed.

Such a procedure may not appeal to the casual gardener, but those who really enjoy working with growing things have a treat in store. Starting bulbous, rhizomatous and tuberous plants from scratch does not differ materially from similar efforts with annuals and perennials, but it requires a little more patience and space. The gratification is something else again, and the budget-wise will exalt at such an inexpensive way to increase a garden's bounties.

Dahlias and Tigridias

Small dahlias and tigridias are two good subjects for beginners. Sow seed early, an inch apart and covered its own diameter deep with soil. Start the seed in flats in the house where it may develop undisturbed until warm weather. Use the regular potting mixture described in Chapter 16 and provide some coarse material at the bottom of the container to insure drainage (Figure 10).

After danger of frost is over, set these plantlets carefully outside where they are to bloom. Miniature tubers and bulbs will already show and must not be disturbed. Plant a little deeper than they are growing in the flat, and water and shade until they take. Both these plants will flower the first season if started indoors at least six weeks before your last frost. Harden them off for the last few weeks by putting the flats outside during the day; bring in while the nights are cool.

Dahlias do particularly well from seed and will produce several tubers per plant by fall. Grow the plants and tubers as described in Chapter 14. Catalogs list numerous varieties of seed, but best results come from the Coltness Singles and the Unwin's Dwarf Hybrids, many of which are double. Tigridia seed is available only in mixture, and the colors are vibrantly exciting; more on tigridias in Chapter 12.

Another very easy subject is liatris, a fine hardy tuberous perennial which has both white and purple varieties and blooms in late summer. It blossoms well the second season from seed, increasing the size and volume of its feathery spikes with the years. Sow seed outdoors as for any hardy perennial.

More Difficult Subjects

No matter what the catalogs predict, most other bulbous plants will not bloom the first season from seed. In my experience little is to be expected until the third season. Some bulbs like daffodils require six to seven years from seed and are seldom raised this way except in hybridizing. The first winter after sowing the seed of any hardy bulb or rhizome is crucial. The seedling plants must be mulched, preferably with coarse straw and evergreen branches.

I failed to do this one year with dierama, tritoma and asphodel. In each case the bulblets were heaved out and killed by the action of frost and drying wind. Even under a mulch there is some heaving. One winter I had a flat of lily bulblets that required constant watching. There was no snow on the ground, and each time I looked there were bulbs to be gently pressed back into the soil. Another year I poured a ½-inch layer of sand over such flats so the bulbs would winter deeper in the earth, and this worked. Good drainage is a must of course.

Tiny seed like that of begonias and gloxinias is never covered with soil but merely sprinkled on the soil surface. Spread a shallow layer of sand, fine peatmoss or vermiculite over the soil in containers where extremely fine seed is to be sown. The seedlings will have to be transplanted as soon as two pairs of leaves form. With larger seeds, plant far enough apart to avoid transplanting until the seedlings are ready to go outside.

For bulbs not hardy in your climate, some provision must be made to winter them over in the house. Because I am basically impatient, I try to keep them growing as long as possible so bloom will come sooner. If bulbs are still very small, I bring the whole container in from outside. With larger bulbs, I plant one or two in small pots which are placed in glass trays near a window. In some cases these will start to bloom when the light grows stronger in early spring. Or the foliage may ripen off in mid- or late winter. Keep them nearly dry until new shoots show. Then increase water as the leaves enlarge.

Japanese Iris and Ornithogalum

When dealing with both hardy and tender sorts, sow seeds very early, by February, in flats or pots in the house. In a few cases this may mean bloom by early fall in the garden; more likely it will insure blossoms the second year. Most important of all, it will grant those to be wintered over outside a much better chance of survival.

One of my most satisfactory adventures with seed gave me unbelievably beautiful Japanese iris. The seed was refrigerated first according to the directions on the packet, then planted in small cardboard containers and kept moist. Germination was sketchy, so after the plants had made some growth, I transplanted the whole soilblock into the garden in one piece in early summer, being careful to peel away the sides and bottom without disturbing roots. To my delight there was further germination the second spring, but no plants flowered until the third year. It was well worth waiting for to see those giant heads of color in June and July.

Just as satisfying were the flowers which finally came from *Ornithogalum thrysoides* seed. Since these are not hardy, some disposal of the plants in the house during the winter was necessary. The seed was sown in early spring. It germinated well, but made such slow foliage growth that the large container in which it had been planted originally seemed as good a place as any to keep the seedlings during the summer months in a shady spot in the garden. Came fall, and the bulbs were still hardly bigger than a pencil eraser. I wintered them over at a window in the house in the same container.

By spring they were crowded, and the foliage, though still green was ragged. I separated the bulblets and planted them a few inches apart in garden rows. The foliage died down completely, then reappeared in a few weeks as fine new shoots. I hoped for bloom that summer, but although by fall the shoots were full and thick, there was no sign of a bud.

Again I transplanted the bulbs, this time from garden row to small pots. The biggest shoots went in one to a pot, but to conserve space, the smaller ones went two and three to a 3-inch pot. They were placed in glass trays and put in sunny windows where they remained healthy looking but grew little until the days appreciably lengthened after Christmas. The shoot rosette thickened and began to grow upward. By February many had a bud hidden down in the foliage, and by March the first had begun to bloom spectacularly.

This treatment from beginning to end ought to work for any plant which is not hardy. If bulbs enlarge the first summer, they may be potted in hopes of bloom a year sooner than reported with my ornithogalum.

Lilies from Seed

Hardy lilies present a slightly different problem. At least they do not require space at a winter window! In all cases I have sown the seed in large pots or flats and wintered it over the first season outside in the same container with a mulch. With the *L. formosanum* I spread sand over the bulbs in the pot before sinking it for the winter in a raised bed in the open garden. I mulched it well with evergreen branches after the ground froze. Keep in mind that lilies must have good drainage at every step of the way.

One experienced gardener I know has raised all sorts of lilies and bulbous plants from seed. Those that are hardy she winters over in a cold frame in sandy soil, and she keeps them just as dry as she dares. Some are sunk in pots, others sown right in the frame.

Having survived their first winter without a cold frame, my three formosanum bulbs were ready to transplant. I turned the pot out and planted the whole thing undisturbed at the bottom of a hole a foot deep. The bulbs made good foliage that second summer but did not flower. When fall came, the hole was filled in to ground level to protect the bulbs and get them deep enough for normal growth. They have not been moved since. The third summer each had one gorgeous trumpet. This past summer one displayed five!

Lily seed is listed in many catalogs, and *L. formosanum* and *L. regale* are probably the two easiest. Remember that species lilies will come true to seed, but those of the new, named hybrids will not, and this is true of any hybrid plant.

Other Possibilities

Unless you have a greenhouse or lots of indoor window space, work on only a few kinds of tender bulbs at a time. Hardy bulbs do not present the same problems. It is little more effort to deal with several pots outside than with only a few. Since germination for many of them is uncertain and often occurs the second season after sowing, plan accordingly to leave pots undisturbed that long even if there is some growth showing; you are quite likely to get additional germination the second spring. Space seeds by hand rather than sowing broadcast, to avoid transplanting as long as possible. You will discover the price of a packet of such seeds brings only a few rather than the many in a package of common annuals.

I have gone into some detail here as an aid to the neophyte gardener. A second reading will show there is not nearly as much work involved as first appears, since it is spread over a period of several years. This is particularly true of hardy bulbs from seed. More than anything else they need to be left undisturbed for a year or so in a shady place where they will neither dry out too much nor rot from poor drainage. Seed of many hardy bulbs requires a cold period before germination will take place.

Seed is not difficult to find for such hardy bulbs as belamcanda, *Anthericum liliago,* calochortus, hardy cyclamen, eremurus and various iris, lilies and alliums.

Tender seed often listed includes calla lilies, tigridia, dahlia, zephyranthes, cyclamen, ornithogalum, gloriosa lily, gloxinia, freesias, begonias and various amaryllis relatives. Tritoma, dierama, asphodel and *Galtonia candicans* are hardy in many localities and often raised from seed.

Hybridizing

If some genus interests you enough for you to want to create your own hybrids, you will be growing them all this way, but you probably will gather seed from your own garden. Plant it as soon as it is ripe and allow the appropriate number of years before expecting bloom. The yearbooks of the various plant societies will be invaluable here with both advice and reports on what has already been tried. By all means join the society and get to know other members with similar problems if only by correspondence.

Raising the plants from seed will still be the same, but you must know the chromosome counts of varieties, how to protect your crosses from chance pollination by insects and how to select parents. Hybridizers tell me there are certain plants in each genus which are preferred for pollen (male) and others for producing seed (female). You will need to learn Mendel's laws of inheritance too.

Whatever path you take, you will be following in famous footsteps, and one of your crosses could well become a popular garden hybrid. It has happened to many other amateurs. Keep careful records of what you cross, and if something looks good, consult a specialist for an evaluation. Often the breeders will buy a fine new introduction, but the greatest dividend is in your own creative satisfaction.

CHAPTER 19

Other Methods of
Bulb Propagation

Most bulbs, corms and tubers are not commercially raised from seed except by hybridizers to produce new varieties. Instead they are propagated asexually (without male and female parent) either by natural or artificial methods. This means each bulb sold under a specific name like the daffodil, King Alfred, is a small piece of the original, and it will have exactly the same shape and color as its single ancestor. We met the term "clone" in the lily chapter. It can be used to identify any other specific variety of any other bulbous plant. A clone can be vegetatively reproduced forever as long as a healthy specimen exists from which to start.

You can take advantage of this biologic phenomenon to increase your own stocks. Indeed those types which naturally reproduce well will become too crowded if you do not separate them after a few years. With corms like gladiolus, the mature original you plant is often completely used up at the end of the growing season. In its place are several new corms, the biggest of which is already of flowering size. With others (like daffodils) the mother bulb does not disappear but divides to form additional bulbs of varying sizes.

The dahlia tuber you plant in spring becomes a cluster of tubers by fall, all attached to one stem. A rhizome or a tuberous root like a canna creeps along through the earth growing gradually longer and putting up additional fans or shoots of foliage.

You cannot stop these natural processes, and you have to take them into consideration when growing various bulbs; but you can also use them to your advantage if you want additional quantities of bulbs. (Figure 1). Often you can afford to buy only one of an expensive variety and yet soon you get all you need. I have classified these methods of propagation as those which occur naturally, requiring no more of you than to harvest the rewards, and those which are induced by some kind of cutting.

NATURAL INCREASE

Almost all of the true bulbs will increase by themselves at varying rates. You can speed up the process by shallower planting, by disbudding before the flower has time to mature and by separating the bulbs and their offsets every year or two instead of letting them go until they become crowded.

Offsets

Bulbs like daffodils actually split as the new bud within the mother increases in size. You need only dig them after the foliage matures and grade them by size. The largest are already of flowering stature and go back into the garden. The smallest may be raised in rows for a year; then planted where you want them to bloom. Deep planting slows this process, in case you are not interested in getting more bulbs and wish to leave them in one place as many years as possible.

New Progeny

With genera like tulips and gladiolus the old bulb actually dies each season if it has reached mature size. In its place are new bulbs or corms of varying dimensions. The largest again will flower, but some will be markedly smaller and require separate growing for one or more years, depending on size. Again deep planting retards this process. Crocuses seem to form many of the new bulbs on top of the old corms so after some years many will be at the surface and need transplanting. Sometimes these new bulbs wander, being produced at the tips of underground roots, which accounts for the way tulips spring up where you thought you had dug them all.

Bulblets and Cormels

Many genera also produce tiny new underground bulbs or corms in addition to the larger ones. These are stored cool and dry until spring, when they are soaked overnight and then planted in rows just like seed, about 2 to 3 inches deep. They must be treated like seedlings and grown on for several years. In severe climates gather and store every fall, even those which are hardy. Several lilies produce bulblets along the stem just above the main bulb. Winter these in a cold frame until they reach bloom size.

Bulbils

Some lilies, ornithogalums, hardy begonia and a few other bulbous plants also yield tiny bulbs aboveground—on the stems or where the stems meet the leaves. I had one clump of tulips produce such bulbils as big as pecans last spring, but this is unusual for tulips. When ripe, bulbils break off readily. With

lilies, plant bulbils immediately either in a cold frame outdoors or in the house for cool growing until spring transplanting time. Other bulbils may be stored cool until the proper
season for planting.

SURGICAL INCREASE

With a sharp knife and sturdy shears you can propagate
many other types of bulbous plants. The more important
techniques are briefly described.

Slicing

Dahlias form a cluster of starchy roots each season, but the
best flowers come from planting single roots. Every spring you
must divide your tubers, making sure each bears a sprouting
eye or bud at the stem end. Single roots like cannas may be
divided with a sharp cut; again each piece must contain at
least one eye. Creeping rhizomes and rootstocks such as various iris relatives, lily-of-the-valley or Solomon-seal are also increased this way, but each must contain at least one growing
fan or foliage or a "pip" where a shoot will come. Do this right
after flowering for spring species or in early spring for later-
blooming plants. Water well.

Have you noticed a crocus with several shoots showing?
These solid corms (true bulbs have concentric layers like an
onion) can also be surgically divided. Each piece must have
a growing bud at the top and a section of the basal plate.
Larger sizes of hardy cyclamen and tuberous begonias often
contain more than one new bud, and these too may be sliced
for increase with a bud on each section.

In every case, before storing or planting, air-dry the cut

surfaces a day or two until a thin layer of scar tissue forms, or treat with disinfectant.

Scooping

Hyacinths, which produce few offsets, are commercially increased by "scooping." A cone-shaped piece is cut out of the base of the bulb or a deep notch is made across the bottom in the summer. Some growers then prefer to keep the bulbs bottom up and warm and moist for about a month; others place them in sand bottoms down. When small bulbs form on the cuts, plant the whole thing, mother bulb with bulbils still attached, 3 to 5 inches deep and mulch for the winter. Notching will produce fewer but bigger bulbs in fewer years than scooping.

This process of injuring the bulb to stimulate reproduction works for other bulbs, but try it sparingly until you master the technique. This summer I inadvertently sliced through a tuberose bulb in bloom. Out of curiosity I replanted it in the garden and watered it several times. Two months later it had myriads of tiny bulblets on the cut portion!

Scaling

A lily bulb resembles an artichoke with many scales tightly packed in rows around the center. If some are removed from the outside, each with its base left carefully on, they will produce new bulblets. If you want only a few, dig down carefully around the lily stem while the plant is putting forth growth after flowering. Without disturbing either stem roots or basal roots, you can peel off a few scales.

The scales are then usually dusted with fungicide, planted in pots of sand or vermiculite, covered an inch or two and kept warm and moist but never wet for a month. After bulbs form, plant outside or in flats, depending on the weather. Late-blooming lilies usually must be wintered over with protection. It will take one to four years for them to reach bloom size. If too many scales are not removed, the original bulb will continue to grow and flower.

Tearing

Fleshy-rooted "bulbs" like *Dicentra eximia* or tritoma may be pried apart just as you would a big clump of perennials, but greater care must be exercised since these roots tend to be brittle. Dig up the clump, shake off excess soil or gently clean with a hose. You will want a sprout for each part and will have to tear them carefully away from the parent section with as many roots adhering as possible. I do this only in early spring, and such plants need faithful watering until they have established new root systems. Mulch the first winter to avoid heaving.

Cutting

Gloxinias are among the few bulbs propagated by leaf cuttings, and the new shoots of dahlias and tuberous begonias may also be rooted. In both cases dip the cut end in rooting hormone and insert in damp vermiculite and sand. Keep moist, warm and shaded until roots form well, after which they are transplanted.

When you remove a begonia sprout, leave several leaves below the cut for use by the old tuber. A dahlia cutting should contain two pairs of leaves, and two other pairs should be left on the tuber's sprout. Take these cuttings in the spring when you are getting the tubers ready for outside planting.

CHAPTER 20

Bulbs for Arrangements and Exhibits

This chapter is for those who enjoy exhibiting their garden treasures either in the horticultural divisions or the arrangement classes at flower shows. I suggest here some "different" bulbs for you to grow for your floral designs, leaving their use and alignment to your own creative imagination.

Many of these lesser-known species are also valuable for horticultural entries, but most schedules are made up with a goal of covering just about all the different types of a particular flower, so almost any well-grown variety has a chance. Certain varieties within a division do seem to take more prizes than others, but fashions change in flowers too. Close study of detailed, up-to-date catalogs plus visits to local shows will keep you in touch with this aspect of bulb growing.

Not long ago I heard a famous lecturer on floral design lament that gardeners are generally divided into two groups: horticulturists and arrangers. It would be a sad thing to have to add, "and never the twain shall meet," but a wide gulf often does exist between those who grow specimen flowers and those more interested in their arrangement, as the program chairman of any garden club will testify. This is not to the advantage or credit of either group.

I must confess I am a hybrid to be classified somewhere between; my main concern is a garden where groups of plants blend harmoniously. Actually there are three groups—horticulturists, landscapers and arrangers—and they have much to teach each other.

Growing for Arrangements

The horticulture enthusiast and the landscaper (perhaps we should substitute gardener for this last term) deprive themselves of certain pleasures when they fail to understand at least a little of the arranger's art. I do think, however, that the person who confines herself merely to manipulating the flowers she has bought loses out even more.

We who love to grow things may never learn to display them perfectly, but you whose artistic talents surpass ours may quite easily utilize our knowledge. This is particularly true for bulb flowers. They require so little skill, and space that in a small area you may raise a veritable sweepstake.

Since my bouquets are at best friendly bits of my garden brought inside for further enjoyment, I shall not hold forth here on how to arrange flowers. What I do give you are lists of bulb flowers so different that they may impress a jaded judicial appetite. Many have excited accomplished designers who have seen them growing in my garden. Flowers for specific color schemes are also tabulated.

Where no species has been added to the genetic name, you may assume there are several. The flowers included as brown, black or green will never be exactly or wholly those shades, but they are close. Where a species appears under two color headings, assume it bears both shades. Liatris was included among the miniatures because certain species tend to put out side branches which are appropriate as individual flowers. For large genera like tulips, narcissus, gladiolus and dahlias, check the individual chapters for descriptions. Additional facts about all blooms listed can be obtained through the general index.

My arranging friends tell me their hardest task is to find outstanding material. Florists do not take kindly to an order of a few of some strange species, since they must buy in quantity and so prefer to stock what is *sure* to sell. If you have condemned your florist for lack of imagination, remember his inventory becomes a liability if he does not move everything quickly.

Consider now the advantages on the side of the arranger who produces her own flowers: freedom of choice in color and form, opportunity to use new or unusual blossoms not obtainable through a florist, the widest possible range of expression due to the availability of favored flowers and lastly, inexpensive materials right at hand.

One arranger of my acquaintance who knows a great deal about horticulture owns a garden which is chaos if judged by the landscape artist's standards, but her show entries take prize after prize. While not underrating her proven creative ability, I know that some of her success is due to the wide range of material she has grown specifically for use in her original designs.

Serious study of current catalogs will suggest many bulbs that will help you build arrangements in your own style, using whatever containers you favor. My lists have been assembled as guides.

When growing bulbs for use in arrangements, schedule your plantings seasonally to give you material at the time you will need it. Most bulb flowers can be speeded up a little by bringing them inside after the buds show color. This is especially true of spring-flowering bulbs, which can also be held back slightly in a cool, shady place if your show is still a few days off.

Daffodils, lilies and gladiolus are not particularly responsive to changes in light, but some flowers like tulips will open or close their blossoms strictly according to the amount of light, and this may affect your design. Knowledge of these idiosyncrasies and of techniques for coping with them can be a great help. For example, by placing a drop of melted wax in the base of a tulip, you can force it to remain open no matter what the light exposure.

Bulbs for Horticultural Classes

Growing flowers for this type of showing is an art on which I do not pose as an authority. While the ordinary gardener delights in swathes of color outside or in bringing some recalcitrant immigrant through a bad winter, the show gardener must worry about straight stems, perfect foliage, storm damage, weather which refuses to cooperate with show dates, transporting blooms without damage, and a myriad of smaller details. Accurate records are important too, since proper labeling is a must and sometimes means the difference between a first and a second prize.

Members of your local garden club are often the best source of information about the problems of competition. Publications of the various state and national societies like the American Dahlia Society are helpful too, and the garden club will know how to join or to purchase booklets. A list of societies interested in bulbs is appended at the back of this book. Nothing is quite so helpful as attending the shows themselves. Here you will see what varieties consistently take ribbons, you will be able to talk with other exhibitors about common problems and you will learn from the judges' comments the perfections or defects which add and subtract from point scores.

When you decide to compete, study the show schedule carefully. If it calls for one bloom or three of a definite type, it means exactly that; failure to comply will meet only with failure to win. Always check to see whether foliage is expected with an entry. Several useful handbooks on show techniques are listed at the back of this book.

Common Problems

Both types of exhibitors share certain problems. Water and mud will ruin flowers, so heavy stalks such as those of gladiolus must be staked early to prevent injury, and a stake in time may save many another flower from ruin just before a show. A clean mulch like chopped corn cobs or buckwheat hulls will prevent splashing raindrops from soiling petals, and a plastic tent, made from a wire frame and clear pliofilm bags, can be easily erected around a variety you want to protect from rain. Unless the tent is well ventilated, it will be warmer inside than outside, so flowers may develop faster. This can be a boon for tardy daffodils in a cool spring but fatal for later flowers, which may cook in the sun.

To keep bright colors from fading in the sunlight or to slow down growth a little, a shade of some airy but opaque material like cheesecloth or lathing is helpful. Insect damage or evidence of disease on either foliage or flower does not win awards so the show gardener must follow a strict schedule of inspection and spraying. Cones made from a square of plastic screening and tied around the plant near the base of the stalk will protect show specimens from last minute depredations.

When you plan to exhibit, order at least four times as many

bulbs as you think you will need at show time. In the case of those planted in fall, give yourself insurance against spring weather by placing them in three different positions—one a protected southerly spot, one in the open and one facing east or even somewhat northerly—to stretch the bloom time of any one variety and give you the best chance of perfect flowers when you need them. Spring-planted bulbs like gladiolus should get staggered planting at intervals of a week or ten days, with the same end in mind. Dahlias for fall exhibition are better planted later than those for garden decoration. Details of such techniques are in the handbooks of the various societies.

For show purposes, new bulbs should be planted each season, especially of those which deteriorate with age (tulips) or which are likely to suffer from winter storage (gladiolus). Reset quick multipliers like daffodils every few years to keep the size of the blooms up to show standards. If you set aside a section of garden just for show entries, you can save yourself lots of trouble and still produce the finest blooms.

Conditioning cut blooms is a must for the exhibitor. Most authorities agree they should be cut with as long a stem as possible, placed immediately in warm water in a container large enough so the flowers will not be crushed and then put in a cool, dark place out of drafts for at least 12 hours before the show. A basement floor is usually the best available place. Dahlias and daffodils should be plunged into really hot water immediately after picking to discourage wilting. Some advise holding the cut stem in boiling water for a minute or in flame for half that time for any of these flowers which contain milky or drippy sap.

These are at best brief summaries of a few of the techniques necessary for successful showing. Experience and shop talk with experts at the shows will enable you to surmount the difficulties peculiar to this phase of gardening. There is a great deal of satisfaction in exhibiting; otherwise it would not be so popular, and you will meet many kindred souls if you become interested in it.

BULBS FOR ARRANGERS

BLUE

Allium azureum
Anemone blanda (and var.)
Camassia
Chionodoxa
Hyacinthus
    amethystinus
    azureus
orientalis (Dutch and
    Roman)
Iris Cantab
Iris (Dutch)
Ixiolirion
Muscari
Scilla

BLACK

Arum
    maculatum
    palaestinum
    pictum
Fritillaria camtschatcensis
Iris tuberosa (Hermodactylus)
Lilium papilliferum
Muscari paradoxum
Tulipa
    La Tulipe Noir
    Queen of the Night
    Black Parrot
    Uncle Tom
    Ace of Spades

WHITE

Acidanthera
Anemone
    blanda Bridesmaid
    coronaria
Bletilla hyacintha alba
Camassia
Chionodoxa
Convallaria
Crocus (spring and fall)
Cyclamen
Dahlia
Freesia
Fritillaria meleagris alba
Galanthus
Galtonia candicans
Gladiolus

Hedychium coronarium
Hyacinthus
Hymenocallis (Ismene)
Iris (Dutch)
Kniphofia
Leucojum
Liatris
Lilium

Muscari
Narcissus
Ornithogalum
Puschkinia libanotica alba
Scilla
Trillium
Tulipa
Zantedeschia

GREEN

Arisaema
  dracontium
  triphyllum
Gladiolus
Iris tuberosa (Hermodactylus)
Ixia viridiflora
Lilium
  Emerald Strain
  Green Dragon
  Green Knight Flares
  Moonlight Strain
  Nepalense
Narcissus

Ornithogalum nutans
Tulipa
  Artist
  Cherie
  Court Lady
  Emerald Knight
  Fantasy
  Farraday
  Formosa
  Greenland
  Hummingbird
  Pimpernel
  Viridiflora

BROWN

Fritillaria meleagris
Iris (Spanish, Dutch)
  Le Mogol
  Bronze Beauty
  Bronze Queen
Iris susiana
Lilium
  Black Dragon

Black Magic Strain
Bronzino Strain (Fiesta)
Muscari comosum
Tulipa
  Don Alma
  Don Eugo
  Don Pedro
  Indian Chief

Mahogany   The Skipper
Morocco Beauty

PURPLE, LAVENDER

Allium   Iris (Dutch)
Bletilla hyacintha   Iris reticulata and hybrids
Colchicum   Ixiolirion
Crocus (spring and fall)   Liatris
Dahlia   Muscari plumosum
Gladiolus   Tulipa

PINK, APRICOT, ROSE

Allium   Dahlia
  ostrowskianum   Eremurus
  unifolium   Gladiolus
Anemone blanda   Hyacinthus
Begonia evansiana   Lilium
Begonia (tuberous)   Lycoris squamigera
Canna   Narcissus
Chionodoxa   Scilla campanulata
Corydalis halleri   Tulipa
Cyclamen   Zantedeschia rehmanni

RED, ORANGE

Anemone   Gloriosa
  coronaria   Kniphofia
  fulgens   Lapeirousia
Begonia (tuberous)   Lilium
Belamcanda   Lycoris radiata
Canna   Montbretia
Dahlia   Narcissus
Eremurus   Tigridia
Gladiolus   Tulipa

YELLOW

Allium moly
Begonia (tuberous)
Canna
Corydalis lutea
Crocus (spring)
Dahlia
Eranthis
Eremurus
Freesia
Gladiolus
Hyacinthus

Iris danfordiae
Iris (Dutch)
Kniphofia
Lilium
Montbretia
Narcissus
Sternbergia lutea
Tigridia
Tulipa
Zantedeschia elliottiana

FOR MINIATURE EFFECTS

Allium
Anemone blanda
Belamcanda
Bessera elegans
Chionodoxa
Colchicum
Convallaria
Corydalis
Crocus
Cyclamen (hardy)
Dahlia (pompon and
    miniatures)
Gladiolus (hardy and
    miniatures)

Hyacinthus
    amythestinus
    azureus
    (French-Roman)
Iris (bulbous)
Liatris (branching species)
Muscari
Narcissus (species)
Ornithogalum
Puschkinia
Scilla
Sternbergia lutea
Tulipa (species)

INTERESTING FLOWERS FOR ARRANGERS

Botanical Name	Color	Season	Remarks
Allium	several	spring to summer	umbels of star flowers
Anemone blanda	several	early spring	daisy flowers unusual in spring
A. coronaria	several	spring to summer	resemble poppies
Caladium	several	summer, pots	striking foliage
Calochortus	many	late spring	strange flower shapes
Camassia	blue, white	late spring	airy spires of stars
Colchicum	white, lavender	fall	crocus-like flowers
Crocus (autumn)	several	fall	unusual at this season
Dahlia (cactus)	many	summer, fall	artistically-shaped
Dahlia (pompons)	many	summer, fall	dainty balls
Cyclamen (florists)	several	pots	leaves, flowers last well
Cyclamen (hardy)	several	spring, fall	tiny butterfly-flowers
Eremurus	several	early summer	bold spikes
Eucharis	white	pots	daffodil-like flowers
Galtonia candicans	white	summer	bold effects
Gladiolus (hardy)	several	late spring	unusual at this season
Gladiolus	many	summer	miniatures, ruffled, doubles, novel shapes and colors
Gloriosa	several	summer, pots	twisted, recurved petals, lily-like flower
Ixiolirion	blues	spring	arching stems resemble graceful hyacinths

Kniphofia	several	summer	spikes of firecracker flowers
Lachenalia	several	pots	flowers like tiny firecrackers
Muscari	blue, white	spring	tiny bunches of grapes
M. comosum	green, purple, brown	spring	simply weird
M. plumosum	lavender	spring	feathery flowers
Narcissus	several	spring	many novelties (Chapter 7)
Sternbergia lutea	yellow	fall	crocus-like
Tulipa			
Darwin hybrids	many	spring	immense flowers
Lily types	many	spring	graceful
Doubles	many	spring	resemble peonies
Bouquets	many	spring	branched flower stems
Parrots	many	spring	weird
Crystal or Fringed	many	spring	lacy petal edges
Green tulips	some green	spring	unusual color, many have waved petals
Picture	pink	spring	convoluted petals
Chinese Bandit	red	spring	huge flower
Treasure Island	yellow	spring	reflexed petals
T. acuminta	yellow, red	spring	long, wiry petals
T. chrysantha	yellow, red	spring	tiniest tulip
T. sylvestris	yellow	spring	nodding flowers
T. tarda	yellow, white	spring	star-shaped
Broken tulips	many	spring	old-Dutch atmosphere
Veltheimia	dusty rose	pots	like large kniphofia

CHAPTER 21

Colorful Companions for Bulbs

A garden where bulbs grow in lonely perfection leaves something to be desired. The more you work with plants the stronger becomes your conviction that the most beautiful gardens are those in which different kinds of plants mingle in friendly companionship. We have already acknowledged a debt to the annuals and perennials whose growth hides the browning foliage of our bulbs after they bloom, but that is far from the whole story.

Unconsciously or by design, most gardeners plant at least some of their favorites by two's and three's because some things just seem to go together naturally. How many of us remember a magic spot where white lilies, pink roses and blue delphiniums wove their fragrant spell! Generally we strive to combine plants which blossom harmoniously at the same time, but foliage can be equally important. Often the leaves of one plant are the perfect foil for the flowers of another. Many amaryllis like hymenocallis and lycoris, for example, produce fine clean foilage which helps hold the garden picture together. The autumn crocus and colchicums, on the other hand, must have the leaves of groundcovers or low-growing annuals to hide their nakedness since those bulbs bloom before producing foliage.

Growth habits are important too. *Vinca minor* and many

ivies spread by rooting their branches and are not suitable
where there is not enough room to wander. A groundcover can
spread in low mats, trail downward or have considerable height
when flowering. Some bulbs like *Ornithogalum umbellatum*
and many perennials (common ajugas are a good example)
have weedy habits and must not be allowed where very choice
plants are being encouraged. All these points must be taken
into account when planning a garden.

Groundcovers with Bulbs

Groundcovers like the creeping members of the dianthus
tribe, the thymes, forget-me-nots or the various alyssums are
made-to-order as companions for all the little bulbs of Chapters
3 and 4 as well as the species tulips and daffodils. Their dainty
flowers look more at home if given some evergreen planting
instead of bursting alone from the barren earth, and their low-
growing flowers thus remain fresher through the muddy spring
rains.

For a gardener whose memory needs jogging and whose
markers are always being moved by small children, the groundcovers are also a good way to tag bulb patches. Seedling plants
of such perennials (or annual seed) may be planted either
when the bulbs go in or after they have begun to emerge in
early spring. A big, clumped perennial needs too large a hole
for this technique, but once it is in place, new bulbs can be
planted around it.

Common sense is as good a yardstick as any in determining
which groundcover goes with what bulbs. A plant which bears
single blossoms like tritelia looks fine popping its stars through
a thick mat of the emerald-green *Dianthus arenarius*. The
looser foliage of *Vinca minor* or perennial iberis is quite enough
for the sturdier species tulips. A tiny gem like winter aconite

22. The green foliage of *Dianthus arenarius* provides a ground-cover for the bluish-white stars of tritelia (*Ipheion uniflora*). With the perennial candytuft in the background, this is a fine rock garden combination. Author's garden.

holds its blooms scarcely 2 inches above the ground; mine are planted to the south of an abelia bush whose small dropped leaves are sufficient "groundcover" for the dainty aconite. You do not ever want to hide or smother your bulbs with their covering plant. Arabis and certain thymes are good low-grow-ing groundcovers, for example, while many dianthus make a mound of considerable height.

If the groundcover will be in flower at the same time as your bulbs, you must consider that. Lungwort (*Pulmonaria angustifolia*) has electric blue flowers in early spring with the crocus, and its dark green leaves make a sparse cover much of the year. White and yellow crocus combine much better with it than do purple or lavender crocus. At the other end of the year leadwort (plumbago) again provides bright blue flowers while the gold of the sternbergia is splashing the fall garden. Some autumn crocus and many of the colchicums will not look at all well with plumbago.

A few groundcovers have foliage whose color must be reckoned with. White flowers may lose something when rising from the light gray leaves of snow-in-summer (*Cerastium tomentosum*), but the blue-gray blanket of dwarf dianthus in my garden looks just right for the pure white snowdrops which have seeded themselves there. It is always harder for me to integrate plants which have reddish or yellow tones in their leaves than those which are green or gray.

Planning for Contrast

Contrast in height, color and foliage of plants brings interest and beauty to the garden, but too many abrupt changes produce a spotty effect. I try to protect myself from this by planting almost everything in groups. (It takes a dozen tiny bulbs to make a patch of any dimension at all.) And when planting a part of the garden, I try to think in terms of two or three different genera at a time. If there is space, I will repeat the same planting in another section of the same garden.

For example, in my tiny rock garden I put in a sprawling mature plant of perennial candytuft (*Iberis sempervirens*), then placed White Emperor tulips around it so the big tulip cups would show to their greatest advantage above the leathery green candytuft leaves. On the slope below the iberis is early *Iris reticulata*. Later the iberis bursts into pure white bloom to blend with pink dianthus on either side. Behind the iberis rise the sharp swords of bearded iris, and its low mound helps bridge the distance between the ground and the tall iris. In September the upfacing sternbergia flowers and their daffodil-like foliage make another contrast with the graceful iberis. None of these flowers looks as well by itself as it does with friends.

Taller-growing bulbs are best planted toward the middle or back of the flower border, especially the summer-blooming kinds and most hybrid tulips and daffodils. With such an arrangement, it is easier to curtain their maturing with another plant.

There is no reason why you cannot make an exception, however. In my garden a clump of tall tulips appear here and there in the foreground just because I wanted some bright exclamatory splashes there. With these are companionable small azaleas, a clump of big-leaved *Brunnera macrophylla* (*Anchusa myosotidiflora*) or a quick-leafing amsonia to take the curse from the drying tulips and also to help tie their height down to the rest of the garden.

In drawing up your garden plans, try to have a plant which grows in a pointed fashion next to one with a bushy habit. Tritomas with dwarf dahlias, for instance. Those with sharp foliage are more graceful with those having feathery leaves as daffodils with *Dicentra eximia* (Illustration 11).

Ideas on Color

Where color is concerned, the choice is up to you. Do you like sharp contrasts of primary colors like vivid red dahlias and yellow marigolds or blends of soft pastels, such as pale blue *Phlox divaricata* with pink tulips? If you plant a section with different tints of the same hue, try out a few plants first. A catalog "pink" can mean many things. A pink-hued garden could be ruined by a poor combination of salmon or yellow-pink with bluish pinks going into magenta.

Green and gray foliages and white and pale yellow flowers make good transitions. Try to use them in large swathes to guide the eye from one part of your garden to the next. Among the early tall bulbs there are good whites in tulips of all kinds, in daffodils and hyacinths. Good lower-growing spring whites include snowdrops, snowflakes, the grape hyacinths, wood hyacinths and crocus, all fairly inexpensive so you can use them generously. For the later garden there are whites among the lilies, tritomas, dahlias, gladiolus, hymenocallis, *Milla biflora*, tuberous begonias, caladiums, autumn crocus, colchicums, zephyranthes, tuberoses and liatris. Pale yellow is found in *Allium moly,* begonias, tritoma, dahlias, gladiolus, hymenocallis, lilies, tulips and a host of daffodils. There are creamy tints too in spring crocus and tigridias.

Pictures with Perennials and Bulbs

My garden contains many more perennials than annuals for easiest up-keep. Several are such perfect companions for bulbs I have never planted them without first deciding what bulb would go with them. For the sunny garden the best perennials for this purpose are those with evergreen foliage. My oft-mentioned darling, iberis, is the star. There are several good ones in commerce, some of them quite dwarf and others nearly a foot high. Those with white flowers are my favorites. Shear iberis lightly after flowering to keep it neater and healthier, and it will continue to grace your garden with its undemanding greenness indefinitely. Occasionally it even produces a few bonus blossoms in December! Iberis is easily layered for progeny. Press a side branch into the earth and hold in place one season with a bobby pin. After a year, cut your rooted plantlet loose from its parent with a sharp shears, transplant, and the next season you will have another thrifty bush. There is no bulb with which one of the iberis is not lovely. (Color Plate VII.) It will grow in light shade although it prefers sun and protection from sharp winter winds. Its idea of paradise is a sunny bank facing south.

Daphne, aethionema, saponaria, dianthus in variety, doronicum, alyssum, *Arenaria montana, Phlox stolonifera, P. stellaria, P. subulata,* tall garden phlox, dwarf chrysanthemums, amsonia, heucheras and many veronicas are among the most dependable perennials for use with bulbs in the sunny garden.

In shadier spots no plant can compare with the plumy bleedingheart (*Dicentra eximia*) which is native to American woodlands and is semi-bulbous. It blooms early and late, the first rose flowers appearing with the early daffodils. If seed heads are kept removed, it then blooms intermittently all summer and covers itself with color again in the fall. It seeds itself rapidly. Mature plants may be broken apart so each crown has a good root system and transplanted with plenty of water in either spring or fall. Bountiful is a pink hybrid, and Sweetheart is a good white form. There are other woodland dicentras which flower only in the spring. All are hardy cousins of the Japanese bleedingheart. They do best with some humus.

You will also find these good with spring bulbs for partially shaded places: the violas, primroses, *Phlox divaricata,* mertensia, pulmonaria, forget-me-nots, trollius, barrenworts and brunnera. The violas and forget-me-nots bloom intermittently most of the year, the foliage of *P. divaricata* and primroses is evergreen and the brunnera sometimes flowers again in the fall. Later in the season in light shade use Japanese anemone, thalictrums, lythrum and hostas.

In the darker depths of woodland (where only a few bulbs

23. In this wall garden tulips provide dramatic contrast to the lower-growing perennials (Roche).

will grow) ferns, bishop's cap (*Mitella diphylla*) and black snakeroot (*Cimicifuga racemosa*) are rewarding.

For sunny spots where bulbs are a major planting my favorite annuals include alyssums, pansies, petunias, dwarf marigolds, California poppies and lantanas. In partially shaded spots use annuals like linaria, myosotis, nemophila, lobelia and impatiens.

Transplanting in Bloom

Where you notice that two different small bulbs bloom at the same time, you can make a companion planting by transplanting one kind to the other's site while in bloom. Take as much earth with each bulb or clump as you can, choose a cloudy day and water well several times afterward. This trick is harder with larger bulbs, which are usually planted deeper. To achieve a desired effect, it is better to do the moving of larger bulbs when the foliage is beginning to yellow with maturity but before either plant has lost its leaves. It is difficult to add new things in the fall without injuring established bulbs unless everything has been very well marked.

Discover Your Own Good Companions

As you begin to appreciate just how much easier it is to perfect your garden pictures by planting various groupings, you will begin to collect favorite combinations. I have searched industriously for a plant to complement one I already had or contemplated adding to my garden. Just as often, my garden itself suggests useful juxtapositions. When I noticed, for example, my white arabis bloomed at the same time as my early red tulips, it was natural to think of planting them together.

24. Lilies and phlox are admirable companions for the summer garden. Pink and red phlox are perfect for the many white lilies. White phlox combines well with the brilliant orange and red lilies (Genereux).

During the coming year jot down those plants which flower at the same time in your climate. Then as you transplant and revamp, you will have the best guide for making truly memorable garden pictures. Some of the easiest and prettiest groupings I know are listed here as a start for your own collection of treasured floral alliances.

SPRING PICTURES

Early red tulips, white hyacinths and any iberis
Blue *Pulmonaria angustifolia* with yellow or white crocus
Yellow daffodils with blue *Mertensia virginica*
Bright-eyed narcissus with blue *Brunnera macrophylla;* red primroses added in light shade
Yellow doronicum with almost any color tulip
Yellow jonquils, blue grape hyacinths and iberis in bloom
White *Anemone blanda* and blue *Hyacinthus azureus*
Creamy cluster-flowered narcissi with rose *Dicentra eximia* in light shade
Purple *Iris reticulata* and yellow *I. danfordiae* with arabis
Any daffodil with primroses
Light blue *Phlox divaricata* with yellow, white or pink tulips
Species tulips *kaufmanniana* and *biflora alta* or *turkestanica*
Blue chionodoxa and white or creamy yellow crocus
Early daffodils with early bulbous iris
Daffodils and early tulips
Daffodils with blue scillas
Deep-toned tulips behind clumps of white Dicentra, Sweetheart, in light shade
Orange *Fritillaria imperialis* and white trumpet daffodils
Blue *Polemonium reptans* with May-flowering tulips
Fritillaria meleagris with primroses
White lily-flowered tulips with pink *Daphne cneorum*

Milky puschkinia or white or blue chionodoxa or squill with yellow crocus

Large species tulips with iberis

Blue *Amsonia tabernaemontana* as a screen for any big tulip

Dutch iris and blue flax

Blue *Anemone blanda* and snowdrops or *Leucojum vernum*

Hardy gladiolus and *Dianthus arenarius*

Blue ixiolirion with late tulips

SUMMER ASSOCIATES

Caladiums in contrasting colors

Caladiums and tuberous begonias in shade

Golden asphodel and foxgloves in lightest shade

Hymenocallis with red or pink phlox and/or blue veronica

Low yellow *Allium moly* for contrast with all the pinks and blues of early June

Blue *Allium azureum* toward the middle of the June-July border

Acidanthera for white accents in July-August border

Pink, white or yellow tritomas with floribunda roses or with phlox

Red and orange tritomas with white phlox and blue veronica

Lighter shades of Aurelian lilies with orange asclepias

Tritomas with Shasta daisies

White lilies with pink roses and blue delphinium or with pink phlox and blue veronica

White phlox and blue veronica with any of the yellow, red and orange lilies

Ferns with lilies that take light shade

Cannas with bedding dahlias or as accent in annual plantings

Cannas or lilies as accents in shrubbery border or against evergreens
Tritomas with petunias
White galtonia with early purple liatris
Belamcanda with white or blue veronica
Eremurus as accent in summer border
Tuberoses with late purple liatris
Tuberoses with belamcanda
Mid-Century lilies with blue flax or Shasta daisies
Belamcanda with tall blue ageratum and white petunias
Any brilliant lily with silvery artemisia
Lilies with thalictrums

LATE SUMMER AND FALL COMPANIONS

White caladiums with pink *Begonia evansiana*; add achimenes
Achimenes with *Dicentra eximia*
Late lilies with blue monkshood
Tigridias and montbretias with white liatris
Montbretias with yellow marigolds, calendulas; add white alyssum
Pink *Lycoris squamigera* with ferns or black snakeroot
Tuberoses with chrysanthemums
Late lilies with early chrysanthemums
Dahlias with marigolds and zinnias
Yellow sternbergia with thyme or blue plumbago or annual alyssum
Colchicums with thyme or alyssum; add grape hyacinths for foliage
White colchicum with blue plumbago or *Brunnera macrophylla* foliage
Dahlias with chrysanthemums

Zephyranthes with dwarf artemesia
Autumn crocus with dianthus foliage
Autumn crocus with alyssum
Sternbergia with ageratum
Late white liatris with gaillardias and calendulas
Hardy cyclamen in front of ferns or epimedium foliage
Montbretias with early chrysanthemums
Cannas with chrysanthemums
Late lilies with perennial asters

CHAPTER 22

To Keep Bulbs Healthy

No group of plants is less likely to fall prey to insects and disease than those classified loosely as bulbs. Given the site they require and infrequent applications of bonemeal and dried cow manure, they may survive for generations. Even without feeding, many bulbs go on flowering well season after season.

There are, however, a few precautions which will insure the health of your bulbs, the most important being the planting of sound stock; plant nothing that appears rotten or diseased. Bulbs that are light in weight, spongy or decayed are suspect. Throw them out! Do likewise with those showing spots or lesions or sticky seepage. Then report to your supplier. A reputable bulb house will always replace such stock since their existence depends on satisfied customers. Cheap bulbs are likely to be leftovers or infected stock, often from dubious sources. Stay away from bargain offers from unknown growers, and you may well never see a diseased bulb, since our Department of Agriculture has stringent rules about the importation of healthy stock, while the Dutch and American growers themselves have equally good programs of control and inspection.

Sanitation

Having planted healthy stock, you can keep it that way best by garden sanitation. This means eliminating weed colonies which harbor pests as well as rob the soil of nutrients, keeping unplanted areas mowed to discourage high grass and weeds which also provide breeding grounds for insects, cultivating the soil to keep it in good tilth and placing your plants so they have room between for air circulation and sunshine. A crowded garden asks for trouble.

Pick up garden trash, since many diseases are spread through this medium, which also encourages the survival of insect eggs and larvae. Bugs not only wreak their own havoc but carry disease. Faded blossoms are best snipped off (this also prevents formation of seed with consequent draining of the bulb's vitality). When foliage has matured, leaves and stalks are possible sources of infection; gather and burn them.

Strange mottled streaks on petals or leaves are possible symptoms of disease. Where you suspect a virus, throw out the plants involved, since these diseases are systemic and there is no cure. Foliage that yellows, browns or wilts *prematurely* is a bad sign, too. There are commercial sprays and fumigants available for treatment of certain infections, but the average home gardener is better advised to weed out diseased plants (often called roguing) than to embark on complicated programs better adapted to commercial growing.

Diversification for Health

Just in case—there are several other good rules to follow, all having to do with diversification. Do not plant all your lilies, tulips, daffodils or anything else in one spot. At the same time, plan your garden so it has a variety of bulbs from different families. Then if disaster strikes one planting, it will be less likely to lay the whole garden low. When replacing bulbs which have deteriorated for any reason, plant the fresh stock in soil which has not supported the same genus. Do the same when transplanting.

Not long ago I read a description of peasant garden plots in Central America and Mexico. Intensive cultivation has been carried on for generations, but the soil continues to yield good, healthy crops, and the author suggested this might be the result of the way the gardens are cut up, rotated and diversified. All the beans do not grow in one section, there is a fruit tree here, another there. Organic gardening, to return nutrients to the soil, is probably a factor too. It is only common sense to advocate such planting and practices for our own gardens too, both to conserve the soil and to prevent concentrations of insects and disease.

When to Water

It may be convenient to water your garden after dinner when there are no other pressing jobs, but *it is the worst possible time* since this late wetting encourages mildew, wilt, and the spread of Botrytis which are always more prevalent in cool, damp weather. Dusting sulphur aids the fight against mildew, and bordeaux mixture has fought Botrytis for years since it was first used in the French vineyards; but it is much easier to limit your watering to the sunny part of the day so leaves dry before sunset. In hot weather such daytime watering also cuts transpiration (evaporation of moisture) through the leaves, so plants need less water. Hairy-leaved bulbous plants like achimenes, however, are harmed by direct sunshine when wet.

Is Spraying Necessary?

I do not spray much in my garden. Partly this is laziness, but there is another side to the coin. We encourage lady bugs and praying mantises to make our garden their home. They eat huge quantities of noxious insects, as do the many birds which call at feeders and bird baths. The sprays which kill the Japanese beetles will also harm our friends, and then we will have no help at all in combatting the villains. In any one season we have had less trouble from insects which have plagued our neighbors, so we feel our stand has justification.

We do hand-pick insect invaders on occasion and spread poison bait for the slugs which infest our section and damage young plants of summer and fall-flowering bulbs. Bait for wireworms is also effective if they are bad. So far I feel the birds and I, with an assist from the beneficial bugs, are winning the battle. At least be selective about how, where and what you spray.

Forestalling Disease

Bulbs can fall ill just as people do, but here again we have not had serious trouble, nor should you if you heed the warning about using only healthy stock plus diversified planting and sanitation. Should some plague strike your garden, I think the best advice is to either burn or throw out the sickly things in the trash. (Not in the compost where they may spread infection everywhere.) Then start with fresh bulbs planted in a different part of your garden.

Like humans, healthy plants are less apt to develop disease, which is why it is important to feed your bulbs and see that they have enough sun or shade, water or aridity, sweet or acid soil and summer or winter mulching, as the case may be. When a planting has increased to the crowding point, it should be dug up and the biggest bulbs reset in a new site. And for almost any hardy bulb that is really all you ought to have to do.

For Summer-Blooming Bulbs

Dahlias, gladiolus and other tender bulbs are more subject to disease and insects, partly because bugs are more prevalent in hot weather and partly because these bulbs are seldom stored under the best conditions. Bulbs like gladiolus and its relatives should be dusted with DDT after harvesting. It may be necessary to dust the plants themselves during the summer if thrips, aphids or leafhoppers are serious. Silvered leaves and streaked deformed flowers are danger signs of thrips. Aphids suck vital plant juices and with leafhoppers, carry various diseases.

When choosing a site for summer bulbs, avoid spots near uncultivated land where high grass and weeds encourage insects and the diseases they carry. Do not plant or harvest a bulb or tuber which contains eaten or rotten spots, and keep the rows well weeded. If yellows are a problem (the plants turn yellow and wilt), plant only resistant varieties and rotate your plantings so the same species or genus does not grow consecutive summers in the same spot. Certain bulbs are more liable to disease or insects, and these are summarized in the chart at the end of this chapter.

All-purpose sprays for summer gardens are now packaged in aerosol cans which are handy for the home gardener, since they keep well and do not require complicated mixing for a relatively small amount of use. Follow the manufacturer's directions carefully because there is danger of killing your plant or injuring yourself if adequate precautions are not taken. Your bulb plantings will never require complex spray schedules except perhaps where you are trying for special exhibition blooms. Incidentally, aerosol sprays to combat household insects must never be used on plants.

Four-Footed Invaders

There is no way to guarantee your bulbs against the depredations of mice, rabbits, chipmunks and squirrels, but good garden practices make it harder for such animals to work undetected. Crocus, tulips and lilies are their favorite foods. This is one reason daffodils are so popular for naturalizing: their bulbs and leaves are toxic and not eaten.

The emerging shoots are the tenderest morsels on a rabbit's menu. By covering them with loose piles of evergreen boughs from old Christmas trees (easily collected for nothing), you can guard them effectively. Rabbits seldom bother tulips in bloom (deer love them though), but they will eat crocus flowers to the soil, so I often keep a few stray branches on long after the crocus are in full color. This makes for less-than-perfect garden pictures, but does insure blossoms. Later in spring when more natural food is handy, rabbits are less bother. I do not know what you can do about deer.

Guard your choicest bulbs by planting them close to the house since animals tend to raid the outlying beds most. Some gardeners swear by a good sprinkling of red pepper around their bulb shoots. Our rabbits seem immune to this, and there is always the chance a child or pet will get a dose by mistake. If you garden where marauding animals are a real menace, steel yourself to a good fence, evergreen boughs and a cat or dog. At worst you may have to plant only bulbs which are inedible or have unsavory foliage.

There is no real substitute for a gun to discourage some of these small pests, but in crowded cities and suburbs the police are understandably opposed. A slingshot or even a decent throwing arm and some small stones are partially effective. We had a squirrel constantly digging in the garden when not raiding our bird feeder until I hit him square with a rock while he sat gorging himself in the middle of the sunflower seed in the feeder. He comes back every fall, and we go through it all over until I either score a hit or come very close. Then he leaves us alone. I am no pitching whizz, but even when you miss, it upsets them some!

Mice and rats eat bulbs too, and here you need have no scruples about cleaning them out. They are a serious threat when snow lies on the ground for long periods. The rodents tunnel beneath the snow undetected and completely undermine a garden. Where this is a serious problem, it will help to incorporate small stone chips liberally in soil when planting choice bulbs. This is easier than making wire baskets for each. Good housekeeping practices make your place less inviting to such guests: keep garbage securely covered, turn compost heaps often, do not leave piles of brush around and don't scatter bird food on the ground. Make periodic inspections to keep aware of conditions, particularly in winter. Mice and rat poison pellets are easy to drop into cracks in stone walls or into the rodent runs themselves and work very well. I consider poison baits spread on bread too dangerous to children, pets and birds unless put in inaccessible places.

Moles apparently do no real damage themselves, but their runs disturb roots and allow mice egress. The old-fashioned spring trap placed along a main mole run is the best defense against these pests, but carry such a program on over a whole season to be effective. Cyanide gas pellets are probably thorough, but this is too deadly a poison for the average gardener to fool with.

Some gardeners insist a few bulbs of crown imperials

(*Fritillaria imperialis*) will hold off all manner of animal pests. I can only say the bulbs do smell strongly of skunk. If your garden can accommodate them, give it a try!

Health for Bulbs Indoors

The dry heat of modern houses encourages certain diseases and insects. Prompt action is the one cardinal rule, since in the limited confines of a windowsill, any infestation spreads rapidly. Isolate or even throw away immediately any plant which bears telltale signs. Leave space between plants for air circulation. Feed and water them adequately but not too much. Do not plant them in soil from a possibly infected part of your garden. Sterilize pots which have contained sick plants. Mites, aphids and white flies are the common pests. Malathion hits the last two; dimite or kelthane combats mites.

FIRST AID FOR AILING PLANTS

Dr. Cynthia Westcott, the famous Plant Doctor, concurs that it is better to start with healthy stock than to try and clean it up afterwards. However, things do happen in any garden. With her permission I have adapted pertinent parts of a recent pamphlet she wrote for *Flower and Garden* magazine to aid you in combating pests and disease among your bulbs.[1]

Host, Pest	Damage	Control
AMARYLLIS		
Convict caterpillar (*Xanthopastis timais*)	Dark larvae with creamy bands, 2 inches long, devour leaves	Dust with DDT or lead arsenate

[1] Reprinted by permission from *Flower and Garden's Pest Control Book*, by Dr. Cynthia Westcott, copyright by the Mid-America Publishing Corp.

Bulb mites (*Rhizoglyphus spp.*)	Minute (less than 1/25 inch) white mites in rotting bulbs; growth stunted or lacking	Discard soft bulbs
Narcissus bulb fly (*Lampetia equestris*)	Fly resembling bumblebee, lays eggs on leaves near ground in early summer. Fat yellow maggot (larva) tunnels in rotting bulbs	Sprinkle napthalene flakes on ground around plants to prevent egg-laying. Dust trench and bulbs with 5 percent chlordane before planting.
Leaf scorch, red blotch (*Stagonospora curtisii*)	Reddish spots on flowers, leaves, bulb scales; stalks deformed	Discard bulbs or remove diseased leaves and scales; avoid heavy watering; spray with zineb or ferbam

TUBEROUS BEGONIA

Black vine weevil (*Brachyrhinus sulcatus*)	Grubs eat roots	Spray in June when adults emerge with dieldrin, chlordane, DDT or lindane
Powdery mildew (*Erysiphe cichoracearum* and *oidium sp.*)	Foliage white, deformed	Spray with Actidione PM or Phaltan
Botrytis blight (*Botrytis cinerea*)	Dark blighted areas with gray mold	Spray with zineb or captan

CANNA

Japanese beetle (*Popillia japonica*)	Metallic green and copper beetle feeds on flowers, foliage	Spray or dust with DDT or lead arsenate

Larger canna leaf roller (*Calpodes ethlius*)	Large green caterpillar rolls leaves; serious in South	Spray or dust early with DDT or lead arsenate
Lesser canna leaf roller (*Geshna cannalis*)	Small yellow-white caterpillar ties leaves together	"
Bacterial bud rot (*Xanthomonas cannae*)	Yellow to brown leaf spots; gummy stalks; decayed flowers	Discard diseased plants

CYCLAMEN

Cyclamen mite (*Steneotarsonemus pallidus*)	Plants deformed, stunted; buds turn black; microscopic mites	Spray with endrin, kelthane or dimite; discard badly infected plants

DAHLIA

European corn borer (*Pyrausta nubilalis*)	Flesh-colored caterpillars, 1 inch long, tunnel in stems which break over	Destroy old stalks and weeds in fall; dust or spray stems with DDT
Stalk borer (*Papaipema nebris*)	Brown, white-striped caterpillars, to 2 inches, in stalk	"
Spotted cucumber beetles (*Diabrotica unde-cimpunctata*)	Small, greenish beetle with twelve black spots eats flowers	Malathion, DDT or methoxychlor
Japanese beetles	See canna	
Potato leafhopper (*Empoasca fabae*)	Leaf margins are brown, curled; plants stunted	Spray or dust with DDT

Tarnished plant bug (*Lygus lineolaris*)	Tips wilt, turn black, buds are punctured and deformed by small, mottled brown bugs	DDT or pyrethrum
Powdery mildew (*Erysiphe cichoracearum*)	White coating on foliage in late summer	Control unnecessary except for appearance; spray with sulphur
Dahlia mosaic, stunt (a virus disease)	Yellow-green areas in leaves, with margins often uprolled; plants short, bushy; transmission by aphids	Rogue infected plants; control aphids
Dahlia ring spot	Concentric rings or zig-zag markings in leaves due to strain of tomato or spotted wilt virus; spread by thrips	Rogue plants; use DDT to reduce thrips

GLADIOLUS

Gladiolus thrips (*Taeniothrips simplex*)	Leaves silvered, flowers deformed, streaked	Spray or dust with DDT, dieldrin or malathion starting when plants are 6 inches high; dust corms with 5 percent DDT after harvest
Flower blights (*Botrytis gladiolorum, Curvularia sp.*)	Flowers, leaves, stalks, spotted, then blighted; corms rot	Spray with zineb every three days
Scab (*Pseudomonas marginata*)	Yellow to brown sunken lesions on corms, horny margins, exuding gum; reddish spots on foliage followed by rotting	Soak corms, unhusked, two hours in mercuric chloride, 1-1000, just before planting

Dry rot (*Stromatinia gladioli*)	Brown spots on corms, husks, with very small black sclerotia; plants are yellow, die early	Dust corms with Arasan before planting; select unblemished stock
Hard rot (*Septoria gladioli*)	Resembles dry rot	Discard infected corms
Yellows, Basal rot (*Fusarium oxysporum f. gladioli*)	Plants infected through roots by soil fungus; turn yellow, wilt, die	Use resistant varieties; try a new location

HYACINTH

Bulb mites	See amaryllis	Discard infested bulbs
Bulb nematode (*Ditylenchus dipsaci*)	Dark rings in bulb; growth abnormal with lumps in leaves	Discard infested bulbs
Soft rot (*Erwinia carotovora*)	Vile-smelling bacterial rot, often after mites	Discard bulbs

BULBOUS IRIS

Bulb nematode	See hyacinth
Tulip bulb aphid	See tulip

LILY

Crescent-marked and purple-spotted lily aphids (*Myzus circumflexus, Macrosiphum lilii*)	Yellow and black lice infest buds, leaves and transmit mosaic; leaves may curl down with many aphids on underside	Spray with malathion or lindane
Bean, melon, green peach and other aphids	Black or green lice; melon aphid carries virus	"

Botrytis blight (*Botrytis elliptica*)	General but more serious on madonna lilies; oval, red-orange spots grow together, leaves turn black, droop in wet weather	Spray with Bordeaux mixture at seven- to ten-day intervals, starting early, or spray with micronized copper.
Mosaic and other virus diseases	Leaves mottled light and dark green, plants stunted; virus carried in bulbs not seed	Buy virus-free bulbs or grow from seed in isolated part of garden; rogue diseased plants; control aphids

LILY-OF-THE VALLEY

Lily-of-the-valley weevil (*Hormorus undulatus*)	Leaves notched in from margins in crenulated effect	Control is impractical

NARCISSUS

Narcissus bulb fly	See amaryllis	
Lesser bulb fly (*Eumurus strigatus*)	Bulbs soft and light in weight, many small maggots, gray to yellow-white, ½-inch long and wrinkled, in rotting bulbs; adult resembles small wasp	Same as for above
Bulb nematode	See hyacinth	
Basal rot (*Fusarium oxysporum f. narcissi*)	Chocolate brown rot at base of bulb scales	Discard bulbs with rot

Smoulder (*Sclerotinia narcissicola*)	Plants stunted or missing; masses of black sclerotia on rotting leaves or bulbs	Remove diseased plants; inspect bulbs before planting; put new bulbs in different location
Leaf scorch (*Stagonospora curtisii*)	Red, yellow or brown spots blight tips of leaves	Spray or dust with zineb, maneb or copper
Narcissus mosaic, streak (virus)	Mottling, streaking, deformation	Rogue diseased plants

SPIDER LILY (Hymenocallis)

Convict caterpillar	See amaryllis

TULIP

Tulip bulb aphid (*Anuraphis tulipae*)	Powdery white or grayish aphids common on stored bulbs	Dust with 1 percent lindane before storing
Green peach and other aphids	Transmit virus	Spray with malathion or lindane
Botrytis blight, fire (*Botrytis tulipae*)	Plants stunted, buds blasted, white patches on leaves; dark spots on white petals, white spots on colored petals, then gray mold, general blighting; small, shiny black sclerotia formed as petals and leaves rot into soil, and on bulbs	Discard all bulbs with dark specks of sclerotia; plant new bulbs in different location; spray with ferbam or zineb, starting in early spring; remove flowers as they fade, remove all tops as leaves turn yellow
Cucumber mosaic	Yellow streaking or flecking of foliage	Do not grow tulips near cucurbits or gladiolus

Lily mottle viruses	Cause broken flower colors, mottled foliage	Do not plant near lilies; keep variegated tulips away from plain colors; control aphids

CHAPTER 23

The Commercial Story

Only rarely will the bulb you plant have been collected in the wild. Usually it is the result of unique cooperation between retailer, wholesaler, importer and commercial grower with an assist from state and federal departments of agriculture as well as from scientists in various foreign countries. The work of all these members of the team combines to assure you healthy, flowering bulbs in your garden.

Where to Buy

Given a choice, you get the best bulbs from established, reliable dealers, many of whom publish advance catalogs of what will be available at what prices for the coming season. Purchases over the counter at retail outlets other than those of firms specializing in nursery stock are never as dependable. Such stores do not have facilities for cool, ventilated storage which is of paramount importance with hardy bulbs for fall planting. The bulbs they handle may have been top quality on arrival, but they can well deteriorate before you buy them. Such sources also handle only the most popular varieties of bulbs.

To give my garden that original or unusual touch so easily obtained from many different genera and species, I look to the catalogs of the mail-order bulb dealers. Write in early sum-

314

mer for those detailing hardy selections so your fall order can go in long before planting time. Catalogs for spring planting are ready right after Christmas. Garden magazines list dozens of sources. Many catalogs are free, others cost only a nominal sum. They have the best up-to-date information on current bulb selections. Local nurserymen and garden centers also handle bulbs, and most will be happy to accept special orders for unusual bulbs they may not ordinarily stock. Ask yours how long in advance he needs to secure your selection for each season.

The know-how of a good dealer will get you the best bulbs at the fairest prices at the best time for planting in your climate, if your order goes in early enough. And the dealers are jealous enough of their reputations to guarantee you good stock. Of the many hundreds of bulbs I have ordered since I started to garden, only one order contained "bad" bulbs, and my money was unquestionably refunded with an apology. A firm which consistently mislabels bulbs, sends poor or under-sized stock, or which misrepresents its offerings is rare; if you deal with such, try a better one.

A dealer may be stung too, but he is not likely to let this happen twice. If you get poor bulbs, complain so your dealer can go to the source or change his suppliers. Huge though it is, this industry is founded on trust. Yours for the dealer, his for the supplier, and in almost all cases everyone is working for the same end—the best possible bulbs for you, the ultimate consumer. Even the bulb auctions in Holland are founded on this theory; few of the dealers ever see the bulbs they bid on, depending rather on the reputation of the seller.

Holland Leads

The Netherlands leads all the rest of the world in production of bulbs for gardening. Indeed bulbs are the second most important agricultural export of that tiny nation, being exceeded only by their hams. In 1960 they exported to the United States more than 158 million tulip bulbs, nearly 43 million crocus, 22 million daffodils and 26 million hyacinths. And we are not their most important customer either in total bulbs or in per capita consumption!

This means Holland has a very great stake in keeping her bulb industry healthy. Her climate and her land with its perfect water table are big factors in her success, but so is the experience gained through years of growing and of handing down knowledge from father to son. Training programs for apprentices, research programs to combat disease and pests and intensive hybridizing add continuing excellence to the Dutch product.

Harvesting of bulbs in Holland begins in July with the lifting of daffodils by hand and machine. Tulips and hyacinths come next, with the "little bulbs," which must be out of the ground as short a time as possible, taken last. The bulbs are then washed for the American market, graded by machine for size and packaged for use in aerated containers which are then crated. Bulbs below flowering-size are replanted in Holland, and those for export are graded into top-size and slightly smaller bulbs before packaging.

Even on the ocean the bulbs are carefully watched. The lines which carry shipments take pains to insure adequate ventilation in the holds during loading and in transit as well as optimum temperature and moisture controls. A Dutch bulb committee checks constantly to see the requirements are met. One crew member is responsible just for the safe passage of the bulbs. His job includes opening and shutting vents to prevent high seas from wetting the bulbs and to maintain proper temperature and humidity.

Unloading on this side of the Atlantic is rapid, to prevent

deterioration; the crates move out by surface carriers as fast as possible. The big American bulb dealers maintain storage rooms where the bulbs are kept under the best conditions. Here crates are opened and bulbs carefully placed in labelled bins to be repacked when your order is filled. I find such a storage room an unnerving place. Choosing from a catalog is bad enough, but here are hundreds and hundreds of embryo flowers, and the temptation to say, "Pack a few of those too," cannot be stifled!

Other Bulb Producers

Our own country has its share of the world bulb market. Although our growers cannot always compete with lower foreign production costs, they have been particularly active in the creation of fine new hybrids adaptable to our climate, especially among the lilies and the daffodils. Such new narcissus as Azalea, High Sierra, Bithynia, Aircastle, Towhee and Moonlight Sonata are American introductions. I do not think you can buy better lilies than those produced in this country. Much of the lily and daffodil growing is done in Washington, Oregon and northern California.

Most of the world's supply of caladiums is grown in Florida, while many of the states have extensive plantings of dahlias and gladiolus. Bulbous iris from the state of Washington are in demand even in Europe, and this state also produces tulip bulbs, most of which are marketed in the West or used for greenhouse forcing. California is famous for its begonias as well as for other miscellaneous bulbs, especially those in the tender categories.

Belgium, Italy, France and Japan also produce bulbs for export. The Japanese have been sending increasing amounts of tulip bulbs to this country. Since I have not grown any of them, I cannot in all fairness report first hand, but West Coast sources tell me the Japanese tulips have fine skins and are considerably cheaper than other tulips. Since the Japanese record before the war, particularly for lily bulbs, left much to be desired on the score of healthiness, I prefer to adopt a wait-and-see attitude. The Japanese industry undoubtedly recognizes the dangers inherent in exporting diseased stock, but the small farm setup for growing bulbs in that country makes organized inspection and control difficult.

In the final analysis your best course is to buy from a reputable dealer who will have tested the bulbs he carries from various sources. No good dealer will continue to handle unsatisfactory bulbs. (A limited list of retail suppliers who publish catalogs is given at the end of this book.)

Safeguards

Dedicated scientists and inspectors from our state and federal departments of agriculture are our greatest protection against importation of diseased and pest-laden bulbs. Since the 1950's the main European sources of bulbous stock have cooperated with our plant quarantine division to the mutual advantage of all in a program of pre-shipment clearance inspection both in the growing fields and the packinghouses. No longer are bulbs held up for certification on piers in this country since they have been indorsed before they leave the country of origin. This program is now in effect for bulbs from Holland, Belgium, France, Italy and Western Germany.

Bulbs grown in this country are not subject to such thorough appraisal, but in the case of larger growers, the various states perform somewhat similar duties. The growers must obtain a certificate in order to make out-of-state shipments, and stocks are examined through the growing season and again after harvesting by inspectors from the state of origin. My Pennsylvania Department of Agriculture points out that the various states thus protect each other. Spoilsport that I am, I must add that the bulb you smuggle through customs in your purse or the box of soil around plants brought from grandmother's garden could introduce a pest as bad as the Japanese beetle to your locality.

Non-Commercial Helpers

Our USDA does more than merely inspect foreign bulbs. In such research centers as that at Beltsville, Maryland, problems are solved for both commercial and amateur growers. These range from how to safeguard crops against disease to treating lilies with colchicine to change their chromosome count. Lily crosses at Beltsville have produced particularly hardy stock, a valuable addition for the severe climates of much of this country. States with a big stake in bulbs like Washington maintain their own experiment stations, performing valuable work for the commercial growers and ultimately the consumers. All these governmental sources have information available in pamphlet form free or for a small fee.

Private interests help too. Hardiness tests and exhibition gardens are only two of the contributions made by botanical gardens and foundations. No better place exists for you to see bulbs growing. At the same time commercial growers watch performance reports and may base their orders on what they learn from the arboretums and their botanists.

Lastly, a good word for the various national societies like the American Daffodil Society, the American Dahlia Society and the North American Lily Society. Their yearbooks and judging information, the many shows they and their affiliates sponsor and the rigid standards of excellence they encourage have been an inspiration to both commercial and non-professional growers.

Hybridizers—Here and Abroad

The tulips, daffodils and lilies we grow are not the same as those our parents knew. There have been new kinds discovered in the intervening years, but the big difference is in the multitude of hybrids, most of them man-made by crosses between different parents within a genus.

What are these men like who create new flowers? They must have patience: as long as seven years may elapse before even the first flower appears from a narcissus cross. They must be gifted with imagination to visualize what might happen, and they must have a working knowledge of genetics, the science of heredity. If luck plays an auxiliary part in their success, they have wooed her first.

Jan de Graaff of Oregon is an outstanding example of a hybridizer working in America. Although born in the Netherlands to a family traditionally deep in the bulb business, he himself mentions the fresh, new land, ideas and methods used here as contributing to his success with lily and daffodil breeding. At least a dozen Americans and Canadians share his laurels for the development of the new hybrid lilies, but it was Mr. de Graaff who had the imagination and foresight to see the fantastic possibilities inherent in the crossing of lily species. More recently he has refined the techniques of hybridizing by his system of selecting strains and then of reselecting and recrossing toward a desired end.

More efficient ways to spray, fertilize, harvest and pack bulbs are also being developed by American hybridizers. Names like Grant Mitsch (daffodils) and Edgar Kline (lilies) are only two of many who are working toward finer bulb flowers for American gardens.

In Holland the modern bulb trend is personified by the career of Dirk Lefeber of Lisse, the man who gave our gardens the Red Emperor tulip, a hybrid with fosteriana blood whose official name is Madame Lefeber. More recently he has been doing other wonderful things with species tulip crosses. The recently introduced Greigi Hybrids are his—brilliant, early bloomers, as are his early Darwin Hybrids like General Eisenhower and Gudoshnik. Many of the new "green" tulips come from the same talented hands. Anyone who thinks he has seen everything in tulips has only to view these introductions to know the genus is far from static, and that men like Mr. Lefeber are providing us with fine new examples of an old favorite.

After the patient crossing and selecting and testing, the commercial growers begin to propagate the new varieties so we may buy them at reasonable prices. Naturally, they are more expensive the first few years, but the modern breeder aims at a mass market and consciously favors hybrids which reproduce well, so it is seldom long before many of them are possibilities for the average gardener. "I sometimes wonder what the vintners buy one half so precious as the stuff they sell," is as true of the bulb growers as of Omar Khayyam's winemakers.

Bulbs for Special Uses

FOR FRAGRANCE

Acidanthera
Chlidanthus fragrans
Claytonia
Convallaria
Cyclamen europaeum
Freesia
Gladiolus tristis
Hedychium
Hyacinthus
Hymenocallis

Ixiolirion
Lilium
Lycoris squamigera
Muscari
Narcissus (selected)
Polianthes tuberosa
Puschkinia
Tritelia (Ipheion)
Tulipa sylvestris

EARLIEST BLOOM

Anemone blanda (and var.)
Bulbocodium vernum
Crocus
  ancyrensis
  imperati
  sieberi
  susianus

  tomasinianus
  vernus
Eranthis
Galanthus
Iris
    danfordiae
    reticulata (and var.)

Hyacinthus azureus
Narcissus
   asturiensis (minimus)
   lobularia (Lent lily)
   telamonius plenus (Van
      Sion)

Tulipa
   biflora alta
   kaufmanniana
   turkestanica

LATEST BLOOM

Canna
Colchicum
Crocus (fall flowering)
Cyclamen neapolitanum

Dahlia
Sternbergia lutea
Zephyranthes candida

FOR CARPETING

Anemone blanda (and var.)
Eranthis
Galanthus
Chionodoxa
Convallaria

Crocus
Muscari
Ornithogalum umbellatum
Scilla

MOIST AREAS (BUT NOT WET)

Arisaema
Camassia
Claytonia
Convallaria
Erythronium

Hedychium
Muscari armeniacum
Ornithogalum umbellatum
Trillium

DRY PLACES

Allium
Calochortus

Crocus
Eremurus

Iris reticulata (and var.)
Liatris
Narcissus (species)
Ornithogalum umbellatum

Oxalis
Sternbergia
Tritelia (Ipheion)
Tulipa (species)

FOR PARTIAL SHADE

Achimenes
Allium moly
Anemone
Anemonella thalictroides
Arisaema
Begonia
   evansiana
   tuberous
Caladium
Camassia
Chionodoxa
Claytonia
Colchicum
Convallaria
Corydalis
Crocus
Cyclamen

Eranthis
Erythronium
Fritillaria
Galanthus
Hyacinthus amethystinus
Lilium (selected)
Muscari armeniacum
Narcissus (selected)
Ornithogalum
   nutans
   umbellatum
Polygonatum
Scilla
Smilacina racemosa
Trillium
Tulipa sylvestris

FOR ACCENTS (HARDY)

Belamcanda
Eremurus
Fritillaria imperialis
Gladiolus
Hyacinthus orientalis (Dutch)
Hymenocallis occidentalis

Kniphofia
Liatris
Lilium
Lycoris squamigera
Narcissus
Tulipa

FOR ACCENTS (TENDER)

Acidanthera   Gladiolus
Canna   Hymenocallis
Dahlia   Montbretia
Galtonia candicans   Polianthes tuberosa

FOR ROCK GARDENS (HARDY)

Allium   Iris
Anthericum   danfordiae
Brodiaea   reticulata
Bulbocodium vernum   Leucojum
Calochortus   Lilium
Chionodoxa   Liriope
Crocus   Muscari
Eranthis   Narcissus (species)
Fritillaria   Ornithogalum umbellatum
Galanthus   Oxalis adenophylla
Hyacinthus   Paradisea liliastrum
   amethystinus   Puschkinia
   azureus   Scilla
Hypoxis   Sternbergia
                           Tritelia (Ipheion)
                           Tulipa (species)

Planting Chart
for Tender Bulbs Outside

(North of Washington, D.C.)

Name	Distance apart in inches	Planting depth in inches [1]	Remarks
Achimenes	3–10	1	Start indoors; grow in shade outdoors
Acidanthera	4–5	3	Sun; fragrant and long-lasting
Anomatheca: see Lapeirousia			
Bessera elegans	2–6	2–3	Start indoors; grow in sun outdoors
Begonia (tuberous)	6–12	1–2	Start indoors; grow in light, open shade
Butterfly lily: see Hedychium			
Caladium	6	2	Start indoors; grow in shade, moisture
Calla lily: see Zantedeschia			
Canna	18–24	3–4	Start indoors in coldest sections; sun

[1] Inches of soil above shoulder of bulb; deepest planting for light soil or largest bulbs.

Cooperia	2–6	2	Sunny rock garden; rare
Dahlia	18–48	5	Cover tuber with 2 to 3 inches of soil at first planting, fill up hole after growth starts; sun

Fairy lilies: see Zephyranthes

Galtonia candicans	6–12	3–4	For accents; sun, bug-resistant; may be hardy
Gladiolus	4–6	3–5	Sun; accents and cutting
Gloriosa	6–12	2–3	Give support, sun; feed and water well
Hedychium	12–18	3–4	Needs moisture, sun, long growing season
Hymenocallis	5–12	3	Wait to plant until weather is warm and settled; fragrant

Ismene: see Hymenocallis

Lady's eardrops: see Bessera

Lapeirousia	4	2–3	Start indoors; sun, bright color

Mexican star: see Milla

Milla biflora	4–6	2–3	Start indoors; sun; long bloom period
Montbretia	2–3	3–4	Sun; for late summer color
Oxalis	2–4	2–3	Sun; quick to bloom

Peruvian daffodil: see Hymenocallis

Polianthes tuberosa	6	3	Never expose to cold; plant only after nights warm up; sun

Rain lilies: see Cooperia

Shell flower: see Tigridia

Summer hyacinth: see Galtonia

Tigridia	3–4	2–3	Sun; bright color; easy from seed
Tuberose: see Polianthes			
Zantedeschia	12–36	2–3	Moisture; lightest shade
Zephyranthes	2–6	2–3	Start indoors in pots; evergreen but rest periodically

Planting Chart for Hardy Bulbs

Name	Distance apart in inches	Planting depth in inches [1]	Remarks
Allium	2–4	2–3	Undemanding; varied; sun
Alstroemeria	6–12	2–6	Unreliable in North; showy
Amaryllis halli: see Lycoris			
Anemone			
blanda	4–5	2–3	Needs humus; hardy; plant early
coronaria	7–8	2–3	Needs humus; not reliable North
fulgens	4–6	2–3	Needs humus; fairly hardy
Anemonella			
thalictroides	1–2	1	Needs humus; partial shade
Anthericum liliago	4	1	Alpine; cool summer mulch
Arisaema	8–12	5–6	Moist, shaded woodland; interesting fall berries
Asphodeline	5–6	3	Raise from seed; fragrant
Autumn crocus: see crocus			
Begonia evansiana	6	1–2	Shade, humus; winter mulch
Belamcanda	6	1	Rhizomes creep; late summer color

[1] Inches of soil over shoulder of bulb; deepest planting for north or light soil or largest bulbs.

Blackberry lily: see Belamcanda

Blazing star: see Liatris

Bletilla	4–6	4	Moist, part shade; fairly hardy
Brodiaea	2–4	3–4	Difficult in East; give dry spot
Bulbocodium vernum	2–3	3	Rock gardens in patches for spring

Butterfly tulip: see Calochortus

California hyacinth: see Brodiaea

Calochortus Mariposa group	2–3	3	Difficult in East; dry, full sun; easiest of genus
Camassia	10	4–5	Moist, half shade; ethereal
Chionodoxa	2	2–3	Sun in patches; good for foreground
Claytonia	2–3	2–3	Moist, shady, humus in patches
Colchicum	6	3–4	Part shade; fall bloom but spring foliage; give ground-cover
Convallaria	4–6	1	Part shade; spreads
Corydalis	4	3	Part shade; diminutive
Crocus (spring and fall types)	2–6	2–3	Plant by color in patches; fall types need groundcover

Crown imperial: see Fritillaria imperialis

Cyclamen	3–6	1–2	Shade, humus; may need lime

Daffodil: see Narcissus

Dierama	3–5	3	Raise from seed; fairly hardy

Dogtooth violet: see Erythronium

Eranthis	2–4	2–3	Humus; light shade; plant early
Eremurus	12–36	3–5	Mulch first winter; for accents
Erythronium	4	2–3	Moist, woodsy soil; plant early; Western species best for gardens and need less moisture

False Solomon-seal: see Smilacina

Fawn lily: see Erythronium

Foxtail lily: see Eremurus

Fritillaria imperialis	8	5–6	Sun; pungent odor; for accents
Fritillaria (other species)	3–6	3–4	Part shade for many; varied
Galanthus	2–4	3	Plant in patches; undemanding

Giant bellflower: see Ostrowskia

Gladiolus, hardy	4	3–4	Mulch above Philadelphia

Glory-of-the-Snow: see Chionodoxa

Grape hyacinth: see Muscari

Grecian windflower: see Anemone blanda

Guinea hen flower: see Fritillaria (other species)

Hyacinthus amethystinus	4–5	3	Part shade; delicate looking
azureus	4–5	3	Plant early; sun; long-lasting color
orientalis (Dutch)	5–8	5–6	Stake large trusses; sun; buy smaller-sized bulbs for garden

Hypoxis	5–6	2	Rock gardens; long bloom period
Indian lily: see Camassia			
Ipheion uniflorum	4	3	Rock gardens especially
Iris, Dutch	4–6	3–4	Mulch north of Philadelphia
I. reticulata, danfordiae	3–4	3–4	Dry summer site; very early
Ixiolirion	3–4	3	Tends to fall over; delicate looking
Jack-in-the-pulpit: see Arisaema			
Kniphofia	12	1	Not hardy far north; sparse bloom first year; plant in spring; for accents
Lebanon squill: see Puschkinia			
Leucojum	3–4	3	Not for foreground
Liatris	6	1	For back of garden; very hardy
Lilium Small bulbs	6–8	2–3	Many varied species and
Large bulbs	8–15	5–6	hybrids
Candidum and Chalcedonicum	4–6	1–2	
Lily-of-the-valley: see Convallaria			
Lily turf: see Liriope			
Liriope	4–6	1	Spreads; interesting berries
Lycoris squamigera	5–8	4–6	Light shade; quite hardy
Magic lily: see Lycoris			
Mariposa: see Calochortus			
Meadow saffron: see Bulbocodium and Colchicum			
Muscari	4	2–3	Undemanding; varied

Narcissus
Hybrids	3–8	5–6	Great variation
Species	2–4	2–4	Dry summer site; species hybrids less demanding

Ophiopogon: see Liriope

Orchid, hardy Chinese: see Bletilla

Ornithogalum
nutans	3–4	3–6	Woodlands
umbellatum	2–4	2–4	Spreads; undemanding
Ostrowskia	4–6	2–3	Not reliable north
Oxalis adenophylla	3	2–3	Sunny rock garden

Paradisea
liliastrum	4	1	Alpine; cool summer mulch
Polygonatum	4–6	2	Creeps; leafmold, partial shade

Poppy anemone: see Anemone coronaria

Puschkinia	4–5	2–3	Plant in patches; delicate looking
Ranunculus	4–8	2	Humus; not reliable north

Red-hot-poker: see Kniphofia

Resurrection lily: see Lycoris

Rue anemone: see Anemonella thalictroides

St. Bernard's lily: see Anthericum liliago

St. Bruno's lily: see Paradisea liliastrum

Scilla (early)	3–4	2–3	Plant early in patches; varied

Scilla campanulata,
nonscripta	4–6	3–5	Does well in part shade; delicate looking
Smilacina	4–6	2	Creeps; leafmold, partial shade; fall berries

Snowdrop: see Galanthus

Snowflake: see Leucojum

Solomon-seal: see Polygonatum

Spring Beauty: see Claytonia

Star-of-Bethlehem: see Ornithogalum umbellatum

Sternbergia	4–5	4	Warm, sunny spot; plant early

Torch lily: see Kniphofia

Trillium	4–6	2–4	Moist, half shade

Tritelia: see Ipheion

Tritoma: see Kniphofia

Trout lily: see Erythronium

Tulipa			
for exhibition	3–6	6–7	Where bulbs must be lifted annually
Hybrids	4–8	7–12	Depth depends on soil
Species	3–4	4–6	Plant early, dry summer site

Wake Robin: see Trillium

Wood hyacinth: see Scilla campanulata

Wand bell: see Dierama

Winter aconite: see Eranthis

Plant Societies

If you are particularly interested in certain types of bulb flowers, you will benefit from meetings and publications of the society in question. Many of those listed also have regional affiliates. Your horticultural society or garden club will be able to provide current addresses.

American Begonia Society
American Daffodil Society
American Dahlia Society
American Gesneria Society
American Gloxinia Society
American Iris Society
American Plant Life Society
National Tulip Society
North American Gladiolus Council
North American Lily Society

Suppliers of Bulbs (Retail Only)

Space permits only a limited listing of bulb suppliers here, and I have attempted to choose firms from different geographical areas. All these furnish detailed catalogs, free or for a nominal fee. If possible, order from the nearest spot since postal delays can be considerable. Plant societies are helpful in finding sources of rare bulbs. Many local garden centers and small retailers do not publish catalogs but offer a limited variety of good quality bulbs. Given enough prior notice such outlets can supply you with any bulb you want through special orders from their wholesaler.

GENERAL

Breck's, 240 Breck Bldg., Boston 10, Mass.
Burnett Bros., 92 Chambers St., New York 7, N.Y.
Burgess Seed & Plant Co., Galesburg, Mich.
W. Atlee Burpee Co., Hunting Park Ave. at 18th, Philadelphia 32, Pa.
*P. de Jager & Sons, 188 Asbury St., S. Hamilton, Mass.
*J. Howard French, Baltimore Pike, Lima, Pa.
*Growers Exchange, Farmington, Mich.

* Particularly varied and inclusive listings

Joseph Harris Co., Moreton Farm, Rochester 11, N.Y.
Inter-State Nurseries, Hamburg, Iowa
Kelly Bros. Nurseries, Dansville, N.Y.
*Walter Marx Gardens, Boring, Ore.
*Charles E. Mueller, River Road, New Hope, Pa.
Nellis Nurseries, Holland, Mich.
Oakhurst Gardens, P.O. Box 444, Arcadia, Calif.
*George W. Park Seed Co., Greenwood, S.C.
*Pearce Seed Co., Moorestown, N.J.
Spring Hill Nurseries, Tipp City, Ohio
*Vaughan's Seed Co., 10 W. Randolph St., Chicago 6, Ill.; 24
 Vesey St., New York 7, N.Y.
*Wayside Gardens, Mentor, Ohio

AMARYLLIS

Wyndham Hayward, Lakemont Gardens, 915 S. Lakemont
 Ave., Winter Park, Fla.
Cecil M. Houdyshel, 1412 Third St., La Verne, Calif.

DAFFODILS

Little England Daffodil Farm, Bena, Va.
The Daffodil Mart, Nuttall, Gloucester Co., Va.
Grant E. Mitsch, Daffodil Haven, Canby, Ore.
Gerald D. Waltz, Rt. 1, Box 150, Salem, Va.

DAHLIAS

Dahliadel, Vineland, N.J.
Swan Island Dahlias, Canby, Ore.
Rocky River Dahlia Gardens, 13089 E. River Rd., Columbia
 Station, Ohio

GLADIOLUS

Champlain View Gardens, Burlington, Vt.
Kundred Gladiolus Farms, Goshen, Ind.
Noweta Gardens, St. Charles, Minn.
Redwood Nurseries, Box 587, Salem, Ore.

LILIES

Sandy Best, Greenock Farm, Georgetown, Ontario, Canada
Gardenside Nurseries, Shelburne, Vt.
Walter Marx Gardens, Boring, Ore.
Romaine B. Ware, Canby, Ore.

Extra Reading

Bacon, Edward. *Digging for History.* New York: John Day, 1961.

Blunt, Wilfrid. *Tulipomania.* Harmondsworth, England: Penguin Books, 1950.

Camp, Wendell H., Boswell, Victor R. and Magness, John R. *The World in Your Garden.* Washington, D.C.: National Geographic Society, 1957.

Ceram, C. W. *The March of Archaeology.* New York: Alfred A. Knopf, 1958.

de Graaff, Jan, Rockwell, F. F. and Grayson, Esther C. *The Complete Book of Lilies.* Garden City, N.Y.: Doubleday, 1961.

Favretti, Rudy J. *Growing for Showing.* Garden City, N.Y.: Doubleday, 1961.

Hollingsworth, Buckner. *Flower Chronicles.* New Brunswick, N.J.: Rutgers University Press, 1958.

Lawrence, Elizabeth. *The Little Bulbs, a Tale of Two Gardens.* New York: Criterion Books, 1957.

Layard, Austen H. *Discoveries Among the Ruins of Nineveh and Babylon.* New York: Harper & Bros., 1853.

Marinatos, Spyridon. *Crete and Mycenae.* New York: Harry N. Abrams, 1960.

Peters, Ruth Marie. *Bulb Magic in Your Window.* New York: Barrows, 1954.

Rickett, Harold W. *Botany for Gardeners*. New York: Macmillan, 1957.

Speiser, E. A., Hayes, William C., Stillwell, Richard and Carpenter, Rhys. *Everyday Life in Ancient Times*. Washington, D.C.: National Geographic Society, 1951.

Westcott, Cynthia. *Are You Your Garden's Worst Pest?* Garden City, L.I.: Doubleday, 1961.

————*Plant Disease Handbook*. Princeton, N.J.: Van Nostrand, 1960.

Wood, Anne Wertsner. *Flower Show Guide*. New York: Barrows, 1954.

Index

Achimenes, 194–95, 326
Acidanthera, 183–85, 326
Aconites, winter: *see* Eranthis
Adder's tongue: *see* Erythronium
Allium, 68–70, 329
Allium schoenoprasum, 239, 329
Allium stellatum, 225
Alocasia, 189
Alstroemeria, 177, 329
Amarcrinum, 172
Amaryllis: *see also* Hippaestrum
Amaryllis,
    insects, diseases of, 306–07
Amaryllis formosissima, 238
Amaryllis halli: *see* Lycoris
Amazon lily: *see* Eucharis
American Begonia Society, 335
American Daffodil Society, 112, 319, 335
American Dahlia Society, 208, 335
American Gesneria Society, 335
American Gloxinia Society, 335
American Iris Society, 335
American Plant Life Society, 335
Anemone canadensis, 75
Anemone coaronaria, 74, 329
Anemone fulgens, 74, 329
Anemone pulsatilla, 75
Anemone, rue: *see* Anemonella
    thalictroides
Anemone sylvestris, 75
Anemonella thalictroides, 50, 329
Anomatheca: *see* Lapeirousia
Anthericum liliago, 70, 329
Arisaema, 65, 329

Arum pictum, 242
Asphodeline, 177, 329
Atamasco lily: *see* Zephyranthes
Autumn wild onion: *see* Allium
    stellatum

Babiana, 194, 249
Basketflower: *see* Hymenocallis
"Bargain bulbs," 33
Begonia, hardy, 222, 329
Begonia, tuberous, 185–88, 240–41, 326
    insects, diseases on, 307
    seed, from, 262
Belamcanda, 172, 329
Beltsville, Md., 319
Bessera, 193, 326
Bibliography, 339–40
Binomial nomenclature, ix
Blackberry lily: *see* Belamcanda
Blazing star: *see* Liatris
Bletilla, 63, 330
Botanical gardens, 319
Bluebells, English, Spanish: *see*
    Scilla, late
Brodiaea, 62, 330
Bulbils, 269
Bulblets, 269
Bulbocodium vernum, 59, 330
Bulb,
    dealers, 314–15, 336–38
    hybridizers, 320–21
    societies, 319, 335
    supplies, 10

Bulbs,
  advantages in garden, 2–4, 5
  animal pests, 304–06
  as house plants, 228–42
    capsule view, 242
    environment for, 228–31
    fertilizing, 232–33
    health of, 306
    potting, 231–32
  asexual propagation, 267–72
  color in, 44, 279–81, 289–90
  commercial growing of, 314–21
  companions for, 8, 285–98
    autumn, 297
    late summer, 297
    spring, 295
    summer, 296
  contrast with, 288–90
  cover plants for, 15, 285–98
  culture, 14–41
  disease in, 299–313
  diversification, 300
  dividing, 270–72
  drainage for, 18–19
  Dutch, 315–17
  early ordering, 36
  early planting, 36
  exhibiting, 273–84
  exposures for, 41
  fertilizing, 26
  fleshy-rooted, 272
  foliage, 14–17
  for
    accents, 324–25
    arranging, 273–84
    carpeting, 323
    Christmas, 245, 258
    dry areas, 323–24
    early flowering, 42–44, 57, 322–23
    fall flowering, 219–27
    forcing, 243–59

  fragrance, 322
  house plants, 228–42
  indoors, 228–42, 243–59
  late bloom, 323
  miniatures, 282
  moist areas, 323
  partial shade, 324
  pots, patios, 182–83
  rock gardens, 325
  special purposes, 322–25
  spring, 42, 135
  summer, hardy, 136–67, 168–78
  summer, tender, 179–218
  forcing,
    half-hardy, 244–51
    hardy, 251–59
  from cuttings, 272
  geographical range, 2
  government aid for, 319
  groundcovers for, 286–88
  grouping, 30–33
  growers of, 315–18
  health in, 299–306
  history of, 12–13, 47, 78–82, 104–05, 129–30, 137–40, 207
  horticultural showing, 276–78
  hybridizing, 266
  inspection of, 318
  natural increase, 268–69
  need for sun, 27
  offsets, 268
  perennials with, 290–93
  planting depths for, 28–30, 326–34
  planting markers for, 26
  preparation for planting, 21
  preventing seed in, 16
  sanitation, 300
  seed, from, 260–66
  sizes, 34
  soil for, 19–23

spraying, 302
storage, 37–38
surgical increase, 270–72
transplanting, 38–9, 293
types, 4–5, 6–7
watering, 301
Bulbs, hardy,
    planting chart, 329–34
Bulbs, tender,
    planting chart, 326–28
Busbecq, 80
Butterfly tulip: see Calochortus

Caladium, 188–89, 239, 326
California hyacinth: see Brodiaea
Calla lily: see Zantedeschia
Calochortus, 73, 330
Camassia, 65–7, 330
Canna, 189–90, 326
    insects, diseases on, 307
Canna, black: see Arum pictum
Cape cowslip: see Lachenalia
Cat's ears: see Calochortus
Chincherinchee: see Ornithogallum
    thrysoides
Chionodoxa, 51, 329
Chives: see Allium schoenoprasum
Chlidanthus, 238
Claytonia, 64, 330
Clivia, 239
Clone, 5, 142, 267
Clusius, 80
Colchicum, 223–24, 330
Colchicum, spring: see Bulboco-
    dium vernum
Colocasia, 189
Convallaria, 54, 256, 258, 329
    insects on, 311
Cooperia, 193, 327
Corm, 4–7, 267
Cormel, 203, 269
Corn lily: see Ixia

Corydalis, 60, 330
Crinum, 172
Crocosmia: see Montbretia
Crocus,
    fall-flowering, 225–26, 330
    forcing, 256
    spring-flowering, 46–9, 330
    winter-flowering, 48, 330
Crown imperial: see Fritillaria im-
    perialis
Cyclamen,
    fall-flowering, 222–23
    insects on, 308
    spring-flowering, 63, 330
    tender, 249–51

Daffodils: see Narcissus
Dahlias, 207–18, 327
    capsule view, 218
    classification, 208–12
    culture, 212–17
    cutting, 212
    disbudding, 212–13
    dividing, 214–15
    harvesting, 216
    history, 207
    insects, diseases on, 308
    planting, 214
    pinching back, 213
    seed, from, 217, 260
    staking, 213
    storing, 216
    watering, 213
Dames, Nicholaas, 85, 130
de Graaff, Jan, 138, 146–48, 159,
    320
Dierama, 178, 333
Dogtooth violet: see Erythronium

Elephant ear: see Colocasia
Elisena, 192
Endymion: see Scilla, late
Eranthis, 45, 331

Eremurus, 173, 331
Erythronium, 64, 331
Eucharis, 238

Fairy lantern: see Calochortus
Flame flower: see Tigridia
Forcing, 244–59
Foxtail lily: see Eremurus
Freesia, 194, 247–48
Fritillaria imperialis, 60, 331
Fritillaria, small types, 61, 331

Galanthus, 46, 331
Galtonia, 190, 327
Gardens,
    color in, 289–90
    contrast in, 288–90
    diversification in, 300
    groundcovers, 286
    sanitation in, 300
Gayfeather: see Liatris
Giant bellflower: see Ostrowskia
Ginger lily: see Hedychium
Gladiolus, 200–06, 327
    capsule view, 206
    classification, 201–02
    culture, 202–05
    harvesting, 205
    insects, diseases on, 309–10
    miniature, 200–01
    planting, 204
    sizes, 202–03
    storing, 205
    thrips on, 204
    where to buy, 205
    wintering, 203
Gladiolus, hardy, 72–3, 331
Globe tulip: see Calochortus
Gloriosa, 235–36, 327
Glory lily: see Gloriosa
Glory-of-the-snow: see Chionodoxa
Gloxinia: see Sinningia

Gold star grass: see Hypoxis
Grape hyacinth: see Muscari
Groundcovers, 286–88
Guinea hen flower: see Fritillaria
    meleagris

Habranthus, 193
Hardy amaryllis: see Lycoris
Hedychium, 198–99, 327
Hippaestrum, 236–38
    insects, diseases on, 306–07
House plants, bulbs as, 228–42
    health in, 306
Humus, 19
Hyacinth, California: see Brodiaea
Hyacinth, feathered: see Muscari
Hyacinth, grape: see Muscari
Hyacinth, starch: see Muscari
Hyacinth, summer: see Galtonia
Hyacinths, 129–35
    capsule view, 134–35
    color in, 130
    culture, 132, 331
    French-Roman, 134
    grouping, 129, 132
    history, 129–30
    indoors, 132–34, 256
    insects, diseases on, 310
    miniatures, 133–34
    scooping, 271
Hyacinthus amethystinus, 51, 331
Hyacinthus azureus, 50, 331
Hyacinthus candicans: see Galtonia
Hyacinthus orientalis, 129
Hymenocallis, 191, 327
    insects on, 312
Hypoxis, 170, 332

Indian lily: see Camassia
Indian turnip: see Arisaema
Ipheion, 62, 256, 332

Iris, bulbous, 58–9, 71–2, 258, 262, 332
  insects on, 310
Iris, danfordiae, 59, 332
Iris, Dutch, 71–2, 332
Iris, Japanese, from seed, 262
Iris, reticulata, 58–9, 258, 332
Iris, rock garden: see Iris reticulata
Ismene: see Hymenocallis
Ixia, 249
Ixiolirion, 68, 332

Jack-in-the-pulpit: see Arisaema
Jacobean lily: see Amaryllis formosissima
Jacob's rod: see Asphodeline

Keukenhof gardens, 2, 3
Kline, Edgar, 320
Kniphofia, 176, 332

Lady's eardrops: see Bessera
Lachenalia, 249
Lapeirousia, 194, 248, 327
Lebanon squill: see Puschkinia
Lefeber, Dirk, 321
Leucojum, 54, 332
Liatris, 169, 222, 261, 332
Lilies, 136–67, 332
  aphids on, 159
  capsule view, 166–67
  classification, 150–53
  clones, 142
  diseases of, 158–60
  drainage, 154
  fertilizing, 157
  for forcing, 257
  from seed, 264–65
  history, 139–40
  hybridizing, 143
  insects, diseases on, 310–11
  modern hybrids, 140, 148–49
  need for light, 157
  planting depths, 156–57, 162–66, 332
  revolution in, 136–39
  scaling, 271
  soil preparation, 155
  species, American, 165–66
  species, foreign, 161–64
  strains, 142–44
  tetraploids, 138
  transplanting, 158
  variation, 144
  ventilation, 154
  when to plant, 155–56
  where to buy, 141
Lily, fawn: see Erythronium
Lily of Peru: see Alstroemeria
Lily of the Altai: see Ixiolirion
Lily-of-the-valley: see Convallaria
Lily, trout: see Erythronium
Lily turf: see Liriope
Liriope, 175, 332
Little bulbs, major, 42–56
Little bulbs, second wave, 57–76
Littonia, 236
Lycoris, 170–72, 332

Magic lily: see Lycoris
Mariposa: see Calochortus
McWhorter, Frank P., 159
Meadow saffron: see Colchicum, Bulbocodium
Mendel, 143
Mexican star: see Milla biflora
Milla biflora, 192, 327
Milla uniflora: see Ipheion
Mitsch, Grant, 320
Montbretia, 196, 327
Mulching, 23–4
Muscari, 52, 256, 332

Narcissus, 103–28, 333
  aftercare, 107

Narcissus (cont.)
  capsule view, 128
  classification, 114–15
  cyclamineus hybrids, 115, 119
  doubles, 115, 118
  early planting, 106
  forcing, 256
  Greeks, and, 104
  grouping, 110
  habits, 106
  hardiness, 109
  history, 104–05
  insects, diseases on, 311–12
  jonquilla hybrids, 115, 119
  large-cupped, 114, 116
  naturalizing, 110
  planting depths, 107, 333
  poeticus, 115, 120
  polyanthus, 245–47
  small-cupped, 114, 118
  special effects with,
    color, 123
    different, 126
    fragrance, 125
    height, 124
    lengthen season, 122
    semi-shade, 123
  species, 115, 120–21
  species hybrids, 121
  tazetta, 115, 119
  transplanting, 111
  triandrus hybrids, 115, 118
  trumpet, 114, 116
National Tulip Society, 335
Naturalizing, 16, 110
Nerine, 172
North American Gladiolus Council,
  202, 335
North American Lily Society, 138,
  142, 335

Offsets, 268
Ophiopogon, 175, 333

Orchid, hardy Chinese: see Bletilla
Ornithogallum, hardy, 55, 333
  nutans, 55, 333
  umbellatum, 55, 333
Ornithogallum, tender, 233–35
  seed, from, 263
  thrysoides, 233–35
Ostrowskia, 178, 333
Oxalis, 194, 327
Oxalis adenophylla, 177, 333

Pancratium, 192
Paper-whites: see Narcissus poly-
  anthus
Paradisea liliastrum, 70, 333
Pardanthus: see Belamcanda
Parkman, Francis, 137
Pasqueflower: see Anemone pulsa-
  tilla
Peruvian daffodil: see Hymenocal-
  lis
Plant societies, 335
Planting chart (hardy bulbs),
  329–34
Planting chart (tender bulbs),
  326–28
Polianthes, 197–98, 327
Polygonatum, 65, 333
Poppy anemone: see Anemone co-
  ronaria
Puschkinia, 51, 333

Rain lily: see Cooperia
Ranunculus, 76, 333
Red Spider lily: see Lycoris
Red-hot-poker: see Kniphofia
Resurrection lily: see Lycoris
Rhizome, 4–7, 268
Rose, Don, 2
Rue anemone: see Anemonella tha-
  lictroides

Saffron, spring meadow: *see* Bulbocodium vernum
St. Bernard's lily: *see* Anthericum liliago
St. Bruno's lily: *see* Paradisea liliastrum
Scaling, 271
Scarborough lily: *see* Vallota
Scilla, early, 52, 333
Scilla, late, 55, 333
Scooping, 271
Shell flower: *see* Tigridia
Sinningia, 198, 240–41
  seed, from, 262
Smilacina, 65, 333
Snowdrops: *see* Galanthus
Snowflakes: *see* Leucojum
Snow glories: *see* Chionodoxa
Solomonseal: *see* Polygonatum
Solomonseal, false: *see* Smilacina
Sophocles, 1
Sparaxis, 194, 249
Spider lily: *see* Hymenocallis
Sprekelia: *see* Amaryllis formosissima
Spring beauty: *see* Claytonia
Spring star-flower: *see* Ipheion
Squill, blue: *see* Scilla
Squill, Lebanon: *see* Puschkinia
Star-of-Bethlehem: *see* Ornithogallum umbellatum
Star tulip: *see* Calochortus
Sternbergia, 224–25, 334

Tiger flower: *see* Tigridia
Tigridia, 195–96, 328
  seed, from, 260
Tools, 39–41
Torch lily: *see* Kniphofia
Trenching, 252
Trillium, 65, 334
Tritelia: *see* Ipheion

Tritoma: *see* Kniphofia
Tritonia: *see* Montbretia
Trout lily: *see* Erythronium
Tuberose: *see* Polianthes
Tuber, 4–7, 268
Tulip, Mariposa: *see* Calochortus
Tulipomania, 81
Tulips, 77–102, 334
  aphids on, 88
  bouquet, 84, 92
  "breaking" in, 81, 88
  capsule view, 93
  colors, 78
  concealing foliage of, 89
  cutting, 89
  Darwin, 82, 91
  Darwin hybrids, 82, 97
  double, 83, 91, 93
  fertilizing, 87
  forcing, 256
  fringed, 83, 92
  "green," 83, 280
  grouping, 87
  history, 78–82
  insects, diseases on, 312–13
  late planting, 87
  lily, 83, 92
  Mendel, 82, 91
  parrot, 83, 92
  planting depth, 86, 334
  species hybrids, 82, 97
  triumph, 82, 91
  Turks, and, 78–80
  types, 82–5, 91–3
  watering, 87
Tulips, species, 94–102
  biflora, 99
  capsule view, 102
  characteristics, 95–6
  chrysantha, 100
  clusiana, 100
  culture, 94

Tulips, species (*cont.*)
  dasystemon, 100
  fosteriana, 98
  greigi, 99
  habits, 95–6
  hybrids, 97
  kaufmanniana, 98
  rare types, 101
  sylvestris, 99
  tarda, 100
  turkestanica, 99
  types, 97–101
  viridiflora, 100

United States Dept. of Agriculture,
  319

Vallota, 238
Veltheimia, 241

Wake robin: *see* Trillium
Wallace, Roy M., 137
Wand bell: *see* Dierama
Wand flower: *see* Sparaxis
Westcott, Dr. Cynthia, 159, 306
Widow's tears: *see* Achimenes
Wilson, Ernest, 138
Windflower: *see* Anemone
Windflower, Grecian: *see* Anemone
  blanda
Windflower, scarlet of Pyrenees:
  see Anemone fulgens
Winter aconite: *see* Eranthis

Xanthosoma, 189

Zantedeschia, 241–42, 328
Zephyr lily: *see* Zephyranthes
Zephyranthes, 193, 238, 328